29 DEC 2009

658.84 S631
Slaunwhite, Steve.- The complete idiot's

Grass Lake Branch
Jackson District Library

W9-CGQ-874

THE COMPLETE IDIOT'S GUIDE® TO

Starting a Web-Based Business

by Steve Slaunwhite

ALPHA

A member of Penguin Group (USA) Inc.

For Tom Stoyan. Thanks for the inspiration!

ALPHA BOOKS

Published by the Penguin Group

Penguin Group (USA) Inc., 375 Hudson Street, New York, New York 10014, USA

Penguin Group (Canada), 90 Eglinton Avenue East, Suite 700, Toronto, Ontario M4P 2Y3, Canada (a division of Pearson Penguin Canada Inc.)

Penguin Books Ltd., 80 Strand, London WC2R 0RL, England

Penguin Ireland, 25 St. Stephen's Green, Dublin 2, Ireland (a division of Penguin Books Ltd.)

Penguin Group (Australia), 250 Camberwell Road, Camberwell, Victoria 3124, Australia (a division of Pearson Australia Group Pty. Ltd.)

Penguin Books India Pvt. Ltd., 11 Community Centre, Panchsheel Park, New Delhi—110 017, India

Penguin Group (NZ), 67 Apollo Drive, Rosedale, North Shore, Auckland 1311, New Zealand (a division of Pearson New Zealand Ltd.)

Penguin Books (South Africa) (Pty.) Ltd., 24 Sturdee Avenue, Rosebank, Johannesburg 2196, South Africa

Penguin Books Ltd., Registered Offices: 80 Strand, London WC2R 0RL, England

Copyright © 2009 by Steve Slaunwhite

All rights reserved. No part of this book shall be reproduced, stored in a retrieval system, or transmitted by any means, electronic, mechanical, photocopying, recording, or otherwise, without written permission from the publisher. No patent liability is assumed with respect to the use of the information contained herein. Although every precaution has been taken in the preparation of this book, the publisher and author assume no responsibility for errors or omissions. Neither is any liability assumed for damages resulting from the use of information contained herein. For information, address Alpha Books, 800 East 96th Street, Indianapolis, IN 46240.

THE COMPLETE IDIOT'S GUIDE TO and Design are registered trademarks of Penguin Group (USA) Inc.

International Standard Book Number: 978-1-59257-889-4
Library of Congress Catalog Card Number: 2009923289

11   10   09   8   7   6   5   4   3   2   1

Interpretation of the printing code: The rightmost number of the first series of numbers is the year of the book's printing; the rightmost number of the second series of numbers is the number of the book's printing. For example, a printing code of 09-1 shows that the first printing occurred in 2009.

Printed in the United States of America

Note: This publication contains the opinions and ideas of its author. It is intended to provide helpful and informative material on the subject matter covered. It is sold with the understanding that the author and publisher are not engaged in rendering professional services in the book. If the reader requires personal assistance or advice, a competent professional should be consulted.

The author and publisher specifically disclaim any responsibility for any liability, loss, or risk, personal or otherwise, which is incurred as a consequence, directly or indirectly, of the use and application of any of the contents of this book.

Most Alpha books are available at special quantity discounts for bulk purchases for sales promotions, premiums, fund-raising, or educational use. Special books, or book excerpts, can also be created to fit specific needs.

For details, write: Special Markets, Alpha Books, 375 Hudson Street, New York, NY 10014.

Publisher: *Marie Butler-Knight*
Editorial Director/Acquiring Editor: *Mike Sanders*
Senior Managing Editor: *Billy Fields*
Development Editor: *Nancy D. Lewis*
Production Editor: *Kayla Dugger*
Copy Editor: *Emily Garner*

Cartoonist: *Steve Barr*
Cover Designer: *Kurt Owens*
Book Designer: *Trina Wurst*
Indexer: *Celia McCoy*
Layout: *Chad Dressler*
Proofreader: *John Etchison*

658.84 S631
Slaunwhite, Steve.- The complete idiot's

Grass Lake Branch
Jackson District Library

Contents at a Glance

Contents

Introduction

I remember the first sale I made on my website, ForCopywritersOnly.com. It was for a $29 how-to guide I had self-published. Although the profit from that first order was barely enough to buy lunch, it was a spectacularly exciting moment for me. It proved that I could, indeed, make money with my web-based business.

You can do the same.

In fact, I know many people with little or no business background who have, in just a few months, launched profitable web-based businesses. Sure, there's some work involved—at times, hard work. But compared to other types of entrepreneurial pursuits, it doesn't take long to figure out how to create a website, promote and manage it effectively, and generate revenues. Everyday people are doing it all the time.

What do you need to get started?

You've picked up this book, so you already have one thing going for you: a desire to learn. You'll need to find out how doing business online works, what types of products and services you will sell, whether or not you'll use advertising programs to make money, how to create a persuasive website, and of course, how to persuade lots and lots of potential customers to drop by for a visit.

This book will show you how.

In these pages you'll find hundreds of tips, clear explanations, step-by-step instructions, and suggested strategies—all of which have been well tested in real web-based businesses. I've also included hundreds of recommended websites, online tools, products, services, and other resources.

The information is all here. The next move is yours. Ready to get started? Let's go ....

How to Use This Book

This book is organized into parts to help you quickly find the information you need.

Part 1, "Getting Started," gives you the skinny on how online commerce works and explores the types of web-based businesses you can start. It also explains how to identify a viable niche market and create a practical business plan. (Don't fail to plan, or you'll plan to fail!)

Part 2, "Casting Your Line Into the Hot Revenue Streams," deals with how your website will actually make money. You have a few choices. You can tap the booming information products market, provide services, sell physical goods online, or support your website with ad revenues.

Part 3, "Creating a Website That Sells," explains everything you need to know to get your website up and running. You'll learn how to develop a great domain name, get your site designed and written, and go live.

Part 4, "Managing Your Web-Based Business," helps you deal with all the nitty-gritty administrative and technical details of your business, from accepting payments online, to doing the books, to delivering products.

Part 5, "Marketing Your Site," gives you a "Marketing 101" lesson in attracting lots of potential customers to your website, and explains more than a dozen top traffic-generating tactics in detail.

Part 6, "Turning Clicks Into Customers," provides you with tips and strategies on converting website visitors into paying customers. You also learn how to build customer relationships so people buy from you again and again and tell others about your wonderful website.

I've also created two useful appendixes for you.

Appendix A helps you decipher all those strange online business terms and acronyms you may not be familiar with. If you've ever wondered what the heck a spider is, you'll find the answer here!

Appendix B contains a list of free (and almost free) tools and resources that are available online. These can really help to build and manage your business, as well as save you a lot of money.

Extras

As you work through these pages, you won't be alone. I've added a few helpers to define terms used in the main text and to provide you with additional tips and warnings. You'll find these guys located in little boxes throughout this book.

def•i•ni•tion

These will help you understand Internet business buzzwords or acronyms used in the text.

Sales Builder

These are extra tips and tricks for boosting sales and revenues on your site. A sales builder is a money maker!

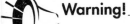 **Warning!** ___

These are like caution signs. They warn you of potential dangers on the road ahead and how to avoid them.

 Success Tip ___

These are tips that help you save time, save money, or do something better.

Acknowledgments

No one ever writes a book like this without the support of many people.

I owe a big thank you to Bob Diforio, the agent who helped me get this project. Bob, you're the best. Let's work together again someday soon!

I really appreciate the terrific research and editorial assistance that Lisa May Huby and Karen Braschuk provided for key sections of this book. Both of you saved me a lot of time.

A special hello to the clients of my copywriting and marketing coaching programs. I have a confession to make. I often learn more from you guys than you do from me! Thanks for all your support.

And thank you to Mike Sanders and the entire team at Penguin for working so hard to make this book a winner.

And finally, I owe undying gratitude to my "home team"—my wife Sue and daughter Erin. Thanks for putting up with all the long hours. I promised you a ski trip. Let's get packing!

Trademarks

All terms mentioned in this book that are known to be or are suspected of being trademarks or service marks have been appropriately capitalized. Alpha Books and Penguin Group (USA) Inc. cannot attest to the accuracy of this information. Use of a term in this book should not be regarded as affecting the validity of any trademark or service mark.

Part 1

Getting Started

So you want to start a web-based business. Where do you begin? What will you sell on your site? Do you need to attract advertisers? If so, how? How much start-up cash do you need? How do you get a website created? How much money can you expect to make in your first year? Second year? Third?

Questions, questions! The first part of this book will help you find the answers. You'll learn the fundamentals of doing business online, including how to create a business plan that works.

The Basics of Doing Business Online

In This Chapter

- ◆ Discovering the booming world of online business
- ◆ Learning how a web-based business works
- ◆ Finding a niche

Ready to get started building your *web-based business?* Read this chapter first. It will give you an "in a nutshell" overview of the entire process, while the rest of this book goes into everything else in a lot more detail.

This chapter is a lot like sitting down at a café together for an hour while I give you an introduction to creating a web-based business that is fun and profitable. I've anticipated many of your questions. So sit back, relax, and let me give you the scoop on websites that sell.

Why a Small Business Can Do Big Business on the Web

Eight hundred and seventy-five million. That's how many consumers have purchased something online, according to statistics by the renowned research firm Nielsen—a growth of 40 percent in just two years (2006 to 2008).

Here's another interesting number: $204 billion. According to Forrester Research, that's the estimated U.S. dollar value of purchases made online in 2008, a volume that continues to grow by double digits year after year. And that number doesn't include the billions of dollars in sales that originated on a website but were ultimately transacted offline.

No doubt about it. Online business is booming. As more and more people learn how to use a computer and surf the net—and as shopping online becomes easier, safer, and more commonplace—an increasing number of people are going to be buying their iPods, purchasing deck plans, or hiring a life coach online.

def•i•ni•tion

A **web-based business** is any business that is conducted primarily on a website, rather than a traditional physical location. Many websites sell products and services, such as knitting patterns or bookkeeping advice. However, as you'll discover in this book, a web-based business can also make money through affiliate programs and advertising.

You can sell just about anything from a website these days:

- All kinds of products, such as e-books, snowboards, and even industrial pumps.

- All types of subscriptions and registrations, such as club memberships, newsletters, seminars, and online software.

- All types of services, such as virtual assistants, life coaching, and human resource consulting.

I even know of a website that sells airplanes online!

And you don't even have to sell anything to make money. You can build a website around an interest, passion, or expertise and earn revenues through affiliate products and advertising. A friend of mine, a coffee lover, reviews his favorite coffee beans on his site, CoffeeDetective.com. He earns an impressive income from affiliate commissions when visitors click on links and ads for products sold on other sites.

Another reason why a small business can do big business on the web is the growth in the ease and use of Internet transactions. A growing number of people are comfortable paying for things online. And it's never been easier for web-based business owners to accept credit cards, PayPal, and other popular forms of payment right off the website!

Overall, a web-based business is cheaper and easier to start and run than its brick-and-mortar cousin. Unlike an office or retail store, you don't have to maintain a physical location for your customers to access. Indeed, the overwhelming majority of web-based business owners run their operations out of their homes. As a web-based business owner myself, I often work in my pajamas until noon! (Much to the chagrin of my wife.)

There's no doubt about it. Starting a web-based business can be alluring. But don't get fooled into thinking the road to success is always going to be smooth. It takes plenty of work to get this type of business off the ground and operating profitably. But once you do, a successful web-based business is a beautiful thing!

How a Web-Based Business Works

How does a website make money? There are basically three ways. A website can sell physical products like running shoes, intangible services like blog consulting, or not directly sell anything at all, earning income instead through affiliate programs and advertising.

You'll have to decide which approach to generating revenues works best for you. This book explains all the options in detail.

If your website is selling a product or service, the process of making money goes something like this:

- A customer finds out about your website in some way, perhaps through your promotional efforts or through word-of-mouth.

- They visit your website.

- Your website holds their interest and motivates them to explore the information and products you offer.

- Some will leave without taking any action.

- Some will sign up for your e-mail newsletter or other free compelling offer. (A free compelling offer is a must, as explained in Chapter 16.)

- Some will become interested in your product and read the web page that describes it.

- That product page contains a Buy Now button of some kind. (It doesn't necessarily have to be called "Buy Now.")

- The customer decides to place an order for the product and clicks that button.

- The customer is taken to a checkout page where he or she fills out an online form to pay for the order.

- Once the online transaction is complete, the customer is provided with information—usually by e-mail—confirming the order and providing product delivery information.

- The money gets deposited into your bank account or other payment account (such as PayPal).

When you compare that process to buying something from a traditional store, where all you have to do is bring the merchandise to the checkout counter and get your credit card swiped, that's a lot of work that the customer has to do to order something online.

So the main challenge in your web-based business is to make the process of learning about your product or service and placing an order as easy and hassle-free as possible. You'll want to make sure your website is easy to navigate, the information is easy to find, the web copy is written clearly, and the checkout process is intuitive and not intimidating in any way.

All these things you'll learn throughout this book.

If your website is going to be supported primarily through affiliate programs and advertising, then the money-making process works a little differently. The first two steps listed previously are the same. Then:

- The visitor becomes interested in your website articles, resources, and other content.

- They sign up for your e-mail newsletter, which provides them with additional information they want.

- Because they keep returning to your website for the excellent content and reading your e-mail newsletter, they notice the advertisements and other blurbs for related products and services.

◆ They decide to click on one of these advertisements and are taken to another website.

◆ On that other website, they place an order for the product or service advertised.

◆ You get paid an affiliate commission from that company.

Many businesses use a combination of methods for generating revenue: selling products, offering services, and earning commission from affiliate programs.

Turning Your Idea Into a Profitable Business

I started my own web-based business almost by accident several years ago. At the time, I had a popular book out on how to be a successful freelance copywriter, and I was increasingly getting e-mails from people asking me questions about that subject. *How do I learn copywriting? How do I get clients? How much do I charge for my services?*

I did my best to answer these e-mails, which were coming in on almost a daily basis.

What I was painfully slow to realize at the time was that the most powerful opportunity in business was tapping me on the shoulder: demand. There were obviously thousands of people out there who were interested in copywriting as a career, and perhaps hundreds or even thousands more who were established freelancers that needed ongoing information and support on how to build their businesses.

Within the next few weeks I created a simple website called ForCopywritersOnly.com. Originally, the site featured just an e-mail newsletter and was supported by affiliate programs and advertising. Eventually, I expanded my business by offering my own how-to guides, home-study courses, and coaching services.

Warning!

There must be a demand for the products, services, or information your website will provide. If there is a real demand, then you can overcome just about any obstacle to creating a successful web-based business. But if there is little or no demand, then your website has little or no chance of success because few people will be motivated to visit it.

Within two years that site went from zero revenues to generating a steady six-figure annual income. And it all started by me simply identifying a demand and then creating a website that addressed it.

That's the key to success in this business. You need to identify a group of people who are looking for something online—a solution to a problem, an answer to a question, a particular type of product or service—and then create your web-based business around helping them find it.

Chapter 3 features simple strategies for identifying target markets and gauging how much demand there may be for the products or services you intend to sell, or the information you intend to provide.

The Basic Steps to Launching a Web-Based Business

Okay, say you have a great idea for a web-based business. You're going to create a website that sells knitting patterns! You've checked (using the strategies in Chapter 3) and you're confident that there are thousands of knitting enthusiasts out there just waiting for a website like yours to pop up.

What steps do you need to take to get started? Here is a basic overview:

- Set up your basic business structure. Make it legal. Get a business bank account. Find a place in your home to run your business (see Chapter 3).

- Dream up a terrific domain name and register it (see Chapter 7).

- Find products to sell or services to offer. Or sign up with a few good affiliate programs (see Chapters 4, 5, and 6).

- Plan your website and get it designed and written (see Chapters 8, 9, and 10).

- Figure out how you're going to accept payments on your website (see Chapter 12).

- Sign up with a web hosting service and upload your site (see Chapter 11).

- Decide how you're going to promote your website to attract lots of website visitors (see Part 5).

- Plan how you're going to turn website visitors into customers (see Part 6).

Finally, after you get your website launched, you have to take steps to get your business running smoothly and profitably. You learn that in Chapter 15.

Each of these steps is important to starting a web-based business that is fun and profitable. There are no shortcuts. You have to do them all and do them well.

Finding Your Niche or Specialty

A few blocks from my home is a small model train shop. It's a fascinating place. Rumor has it that rocker Rod Stewart, a model train enthusiast, once visited. All this store sells is model trains and accessories. Yet it's always packed with shoppers and, I'm guessing, very profitable. To my knowledge the shop owner has rarely, if ever, advertised. He doesn't have to. The very fact that the store specializes in this niche attracts every model train aficionado in town!

To succeed on the Internet, your business has to be like that little train shop. It has to focus on a specific *niche market* so it attracts customers to your site rather than you having to spend a fortune promoting it. Trying to be a Wal-Mart on the web is a recipe for failure. Online shoppers are looking for specialty shops, not general stores.

Regardless of whether your website will sell products and services or be supported by affiliate programs and advertising, find a niche. That could be major league baseball bats for sports fans, Ford Mustang parts for classic automobile enthusiasts, or adventure travel tips and information for thrill-seeking wanderers.

My web-based business became successful so rapidly because I focused on a narrow niche market: freelance copywriters. Word of my website spread throughout this community rapidly. And I was able to quickly learn what types of products, services, and information this group was looking for, and then cater to that need.

def•i•ni•tion

A **niche market** is a group of potential customers that share the same characteristics. They could be work-at-home moms, snowboarding enthusiasts, self-employed accountants, dog owners, or first-time job hunters. Establishing your web-based business with a specific niche market that wants the type of products, services, or information you provide is a key to business success online.

Just about every successful small web-based business I know focuses on a specific niche market. That's strong empirical evidence that you should do the same.

How do you select a niche? Think about your own interests, experience, and knowledge. Are you a cat lover? Then perhaps a website that features products and information on natural health for cats would be popular. Do you have a background in industrial pumps and valves? Then create a website that helps business buyers select the right pump or valve for their needs. Are you an accountant? Then create a website that helps self-employed accountants build their businesses.

To make it big on the web, you have to think small!

The Least You Need to Know

- ◆ Online sales are growing by leaps and bounds.

- ◆ A web-based business makes money by selling products or services, or through affiliate programs and advertising.

- ◆ You'll have a better chance of success if you focus on a specific niche market.

Types of Web-Based Businesses to Start

In This Chapter

- ◆ Proven models for creating a profitable web-based business
- ◆ The basics of how each model works and makes money
- ◆ How to select the business model that's right for you

In the early days of the Internet, most websites were merely online brochures for offline "brick-and-mortar" businesses. Then Amazon, eBay, and other websites came along and taught the world that you can, indeed, make money online. Since that time, Internet entrepreneurs have experimented with dozens of different approaches to creating a profitable web-based business. Some of these approaches have worked like gangbusters. Others, well, not so much. (Remember the dot-com bust of the '90s?)

This short history lesson is good news for you. These early pioneers have flushed out and refined a set of proven business models for selling products and services, or generating advertising revenues, on the Internet. This chapter will help you select which type—or combination of types—will work best for you.

The Online Store

You can buy just about every conceivable item imaginable from online stores or *e-tailers* these days, from books and music to industrial pumps and even airplanes! According to InternetRetailer.com, online purchases account for more than $200 billion in the United States alone. And that number is predicted to increase by billions annually over the next decade. Talk about a booming sector!

There's no doubt about it. More and more people are buying things online. And this makes the *online store* business model a viable type of web-based business to start.

def•i•ni•tion

There are many terms used to describe a website that sells products: **e-tailer,** e-commerce site, **online store,** online catalog, e-shop. Although there can be minor differences between each of these categories, they all refer to selling stuff to website visitors, much like a traditional retail store does in the offline world.

By online store, I mean a website that sells multiple products directly from the website. Amazon.com is the granddaddy of them all. Originally an online bookstore—an image that the company is having a difficult time shaking—Amazon today is more like a department store where you can purchase a wide range of merchandise online and have it delivered to your doorstep.

An online store website typically showcases the range of products it sells, provides a detailed description of each, and provides instructions on how to place an order online. If it's a physical product, such as a home study course or custom engraved boogie board, then further instructions will be provided as to how the order will be shipped. If it's a downloadable product, such as an e-book or software program, then the buyer will be advised as to how to access his or her purchase.

Some website businesses are pure e-tailers—that is, their primary focus is to get orders for their range of products and deliver them to their customers, very much like a print catalog company would do. In fact, there are many similarities between an online store and a print catalog.

However, many websites are hybrids. They focus on promoting a service or providing information—and, in fact, are primarily a different type of web-based business entirely—while having an online store contained somewhere within the site where visitors can buy related products.

Example of an online store.
(Courtesy of Charlie Cook)

For example, marketing coach Charlie Cook provides small business coaching services at MarketingforSuccess.com. So it's essentially a service site. (That model is explained in the last section of this chapter.) However, Charlie also has a section within his site that sells a wide range of how-to marketing guides. So he is also an e-tailer.

Single Product Microsite

While an online store is similar to visiting a brick-and-mortar retailer, a single product microsite is more like a direct mail letter that attempts to persuade you to purchase just one product. As the owner of such a site, you don't want your visitors to shop around—even if you have other ancillary products to offer. Instead, you want them to be singularly focused on learning about your main product, impressed by all its features and benefits, and, ideally, persuaded to place an order then and there.

It's for this reason that single product microsites often have just a few basic pages—and sometimes just one. The idea is to have no extraneous links or other information that may distract the prospect in any way. The sole purpose of the site is making the sale.

Example of a single product microsite.
(Courtesy of Dean Jackson)

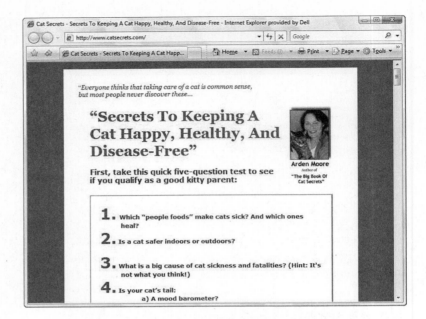

Sales Builder

Despite your best efforts, the majority of visitors to your microsite will not make a purchase. But that doesn't mean they won't buy at some future date. They just need to get to know you a little better first. That's why it's important to include a free offer of some kind—such as an e-newsletter, special report, or series of tips sent by e-mail—so you can continue to communicate with them.

A single product microsite is ideal if you have only one product to sell, such as a puppy training video or fold-flat binoculars for hikers. Even if you're planning to expand your product line later on, starting with this model is a great way to build sales initially. When the time is right, you can easily convert your microsite to a more traditional online store.

How Micro Should You Make It?

As I said earlier, a single product microsite has very few pages. The typical structure is a persuasive *sales page* that contains the entire sales pitch, product details, and other information necessary to motivate the visitor to place the order. Other pages are created to support the main sales page and may include customer testimonials, frequently asked questions, terms and conditions of sale, an online demo, how to get help, company information, an order form, and so forth.

So it's no surprise that the most crucial element of a single product microsite is the sales page. In fact, sometimes the sales page *is* the site! It has to be designed and written in such a way that it persuades the maximum amount of visitors to purchase the product. (In Internet marketing lingo, this is often referred to as "conversion.") Single product microsites don't get as many return visitors as, say, an online store. So the sales page is often your only chance to convince the prospect to buy or at least sign up for a free offer of some kind, so you can continue to communicate with that person via e-mail.

def•i•ni•tion

A **sales page** is any page on a website that is primarily designed to make a sales presentation of the product or service being offered. In the Internet marketing world, this type of page can also be referred to as a landing page or online sales letter.

Membership and Subscription Sites

Imagine if you only had to convince your website visitor to make just one purchasing decision, and then you received income from that customer every month from that point on. Wouldn't that be nice?

That's the idea behind a membership or subscription site. It's a special type of site where you sign up to use a product or service and pay a regular fee for doing so—usually monthly, quarterly, or yearly.

Does that sound a lot like a newspaper subscription or a health club membership? Yes, both of those are comparable offline cousins of this online business model. In fact, many newspapers, magazines, and other publications also offer subscriptions—some even call them memberships—to their website content.

A membership or subscription website works best if you sell a product or service that needs to be accessed frequently. You can't sell "membership" to an iPod. That's a product that is best sold as a one-time purchase. However, you could sell memberships to an iPod Cartoon-of-the-Week club, which would automatically download a five-minute cartoon into your customer's device each week. (I just made up that business idea. Steal it if you like!)

Example of a membership site.
(Courtesy of Marcia Yudkin)

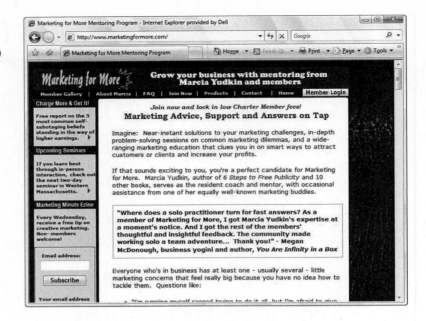

You can have a membership site for a wide variety of products and services, including:

- ◆ Information and other content, such as online magazines, articles, how-to information, special reports, databases, online tutorials and courses, etc.

- ◆ Entertainment, such as audiobooks, videos, games, etc.

- ◆ Software-as-a-service, such as contact management tools, financial calculators, e-commerce shopping carts, project management tools, etc.

- ◆ Professional services, such as coaching, business advising, financial counseling, etc.

- ◆ Professional and special interest communities, such as forums, clubs, virtual meetings, etc.

- ◆ Databases and directories, such as matchmaking services, business information, investment reports, etc.

Notice I've used the word "etc." a lot. There are hundreds, perhaps even thousands, of viable products and services that can work well within a membership or subscription model.

A colleague of mine, Marcia Yudkin, created a successful membership site for small business owners that offers monthly group meetings (conducted via teleconference), marketing coaching, and exclusive content. So she has successfully combined a service, information, and a community into a profitable membership model.

Sales Builder

The most successful membership and subscription sites offer a free trial of some kind, or have free "basic" and paid "premium" pricing levels. This technique can be an effective sales builder for your site. Prospects who aren't convinced to buy right away can try the service and, ideally, get so enamored by all the great benefits that they'll upgrade or sign up when the free trial is over.

The key to a successful membership site is to offer content and services that are not easily available anywhere else for free. This isn't easy. The Internet is packed with information and online services that can be accessed at no charge—or purchased for just a one-time fee. So you have to make sure the content or services you're providing are so valuable, it's worth it to the customer to keep on paying.

Setting Up a Membership Site

It is possible to set up and run a membership site manually. You can hire a web designer to upload the appropriate files to the server where your website is hosted. Then you can manually assign usernames and passwords as sales roll in, deal with such issues as customers losing passwords or having difficulty logging in, handle refund or cancellation requests, and so forth. However, once you have more than a couple dozen members, the preceding tasks become a serious administrative nightmare. You just won't be able to keep up.

That's why most website business owners use some type of membership software, or similar online service, to handle those pesky administrative details automatically. Here are the most popular options:

◆ MemberClicks (www.memberclicks.com)

◆ Interlogy (www.interlogy.com/products/pmpre)

◆ MemberGate (www.membergate.com)

◆ VisionGatePortal.com (www.visiongateportal.com)

◆ MemberStar (www.memberstar.com)

◆ MemberSpeed (www.memberspeed.com)

◆ SyncNet.com (www.syncnet.com)

Review these software packages and online services carefully to make sure you get all the features and benefits you need. You want to choose one that makes your membership site run smoothly, with as little administrative intervention required by you as possible.

The Service Site

There are many businesses that, while they may deliver most of their services offline, generate the majority of their sales through their websites. In many cases, they even handle customer payments, support, and administration online. Take away their website and you take away their business.

Say, for example, you're a work-life balance coach. You work with clients throughout North America doing coaching sessions by phone, as well as group sessions via a teleconference line.

How is this a web-based business? It is because your website is set up strategically to attract potential clients, provide them with detailed information about your coaching services, and motivate them to sign up for your newsletter or download your special report packed with work-life balance tips. Your website is the marketing engine of your business, helping you attract clients and fill your schedule. Clients even book sessions and make payments through your site.

This is a typical example of a service site. The website is not merely an online presentation of what is, essentially, an offline business. In just about every way that matters—location, marketing, transactions, customer support—the website *is* the business.

Here are some examples of web-based businesses that use the service site model:

◆ A printer of business cards, brochures, flyers, and other materials where you can place orders and arrange for shipping online.

◆ A consulting service where you book appointments on their website and ask follow-up questions via e-mail.

◆ A website where you can register for professional development courses, seminars, and other types of education and training.

◆ An overnight delivery service where you can schedule a pick-up, track the shipment, and pay your bill online.

◆ A travel company where you can shop for a vacation package, view pictures and descriptions of destinations, book your trip, and pay for it, without leaving the website.

Just about any service can be sold, managed, and in some cases even delivered online. (I often teach classes in webinar format.) It's easy to set things up so you can have customers purchase a service, book appointments, initiate requests for support, and even make payments—all online. In this case, your website becomes very similar to an online store in its functionality. The only difference is that instead of delivering a product, you are providing a service.

Here is an example of such a service site.

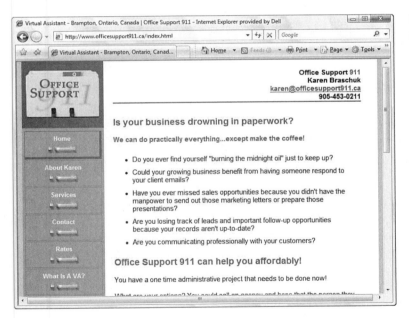

Example of a service site.
(Courtesy of Karen Braschuk)

Many service sites, especially those that provide a professional service such as bookkeeping or consulting, also sell related products, such as e-books and home study courses. So they are both a service site and an online store. If there are products you can source or create that relate to your services, make them available for sale on your website. Doing so can increase your income dramatically.

The Information Source

The majority of people who access the Internet are doing so to find information. That's why search engines such as Google and Yahoo! are so popular. People are hungry for answers—*How do I install a toilet? Where can I buy gourmet coffee online? How do I prepare for a job interview? Why does my dog bark at the moon?*—and they scour the Internet in hopes of finding them.

That's why being an information source is so important. If your website contains the answers your target audience is looking for, they will stay on your site longer, return again and again, and tell others about it—all activities that lead to more clicks and sales.

It's a smart idea to pack your website with great information regardless of whether it's primarily a service site, membership site, or online store. However, many web-based business owners have created profitable websites by focusing primarily on providing content and either selling that information in a variety of formats (e-books, audio classes, how-to guides) or generating revenues through advertising.

Success Tip

The more niche your information source website is, the more likely it is to be successful. For example, you'd have a tough time competing with the thousands of rose-growing websites on the Internet. You'd be lost in the crowd! But a site dedicated to growing roses in tough climates would be more likely to stand out and get noticed. Especially by rose lovers in Alaska!

Say, for example, you love magic tricks. You could create a website filled with information about this topic, everything from techniques and magic craftsmanship to learning established tricks and creating your own. Your e-newsletter could feature a "Trick of the Week" and a review of a magic book or other product. You could attract hundreds, perhaps thousands, of people just like you who love magic and can't get enough information about it.

How would you make money? There are basically two options.

You could display advertising on your site. Magic product companies and show producers would be eager to promote to such a keen and targeted audience. Advertising space can be sold, or ads can be displayed on your site on a pay-per-click basis, where you get paid each time someone clicks on it. (See Chapter 6 for more information on how this works.)

You could also sell products on your website. You could create your own—such as an e-book or a beginner's magic course taught through a series of e-mails—or sign up as an affiliate of products from other companies. (Affiliate programs are explained in Chapter 6.)

Example of an information source site.
(Courtesy of Nick Usborne)

One of the best ways to create a successful information source site is to focus on a topic you already have some knowledge and interest in.

My friend and coffee lover, Nick Usborne, did just that. He created an information source for his fellow caffeine addicts that features articles, reviews, how-to tips, and more. This website generates revenue primarily through affiliate links to coffee-related products he reviews and features on his site, plus advertising from Google and other advertisers.

Got a passion, such as surfboarding or antique shopping? Or special expertise on a particular topic, such as hydroponic gardening or parenting twins? Then you might have the makings of a compelling information source site that would attract a large audience of visitors looking for that kind of information.

The Least You Need to Know

- ◆ There are five basic business models that are proven to be successful for web-based businesses.

- ◆ The model you select depends on the product or service you're selling, or the information you're providing.

- ◆ You can combine different models into the same web-based business. For example, you can be both an information source and an online store.

Creating Your Game Plan

In This Chapter

- ◆ Creating a business plan that really works
- ◆ Calculating start-up costs and projected revenues
- ◆ Registering your business and making it legal

There's an old saying: if you fail to plan, you plan to fail. I agree with that philosophy. However, I admit that there have been many times when I, to use another popular expression, shot first and aimed later. Which approach works better? I have a lot of experience with failure, and fortunately with success, too, and I can confidently report that you'll have a much better chance of getting from A to B if you have good plan.

Your plan should provide you with a basic road map for what you want to achieve: the successful launch of a profitable web-based business. And like any trip, you'll need to make some initial preparations for the journey.

Creating a Practical Business Plan

Say you want to go on a weekend skiing vacation to Mount Treblaunt, Quebec. (A trip I'm actually planning with my family as I write this.) I suppose you could just jump in your car and start driving in that direction. That would certainly be adventurous. But you would probably make a lot of wrong turns along the way, get lost a few times, run out of gas in more ways than one, spend too much on meals and lodging, and take a lot longer to finally get your butt onto a ski lift than you thought!

Success Tip

A well thought out business plan can help convince partners, lenders, or investors to get on side with your web-based business idea. It gives them an opportunity to see if your business is viable and what resources are required to get it off the ground and profitable. If you are courting investors, or applying for a business loan or government grant, you must have a business plan.

However, if you planned ahead by mapping out your route in advance, booking a nice lodge room at a discount, making sure you packed all the gear you need, and identifying a couple of nice rest stops along the way, your chances of arriving on time and having a great family skiing experience would increase dramatically.

Now think of that analogy in terms of your web-based business. Do you really want to stumble around, get lost, waste cash and resources, and risk not getting your business up and running profitably? Of course not. So although you may have an entrepreneurial spirit—and if you do I applaud you for it—don't rush into building a business online without a plan. A solid action plan for your business really does make the difference between success and failure.

A Simple Yet Effective Business Plan System

Want to create an effective business plan quickly? Here is a technique I use to help me accomplish just about anything in my business, whether it's creating a new course or launching a completely new web-based venture. It quickly helps you identify what you need and how you're going to accomplish it.

You'll need a few sheets of paper or a notepad. You can also do this on your computer using a spreadsheet program like Microsoft Excel or Google Docs.

Take a sheet of paper and turn it sideways. Draw two lines from top to bottom so that there are three columns. Ideally, the first two columns on the left should be the widest. At the very top of the page write down your goal. For example:

Goal: Start a profitable web-based business that sells knitting patterns online.

Now title each column as follows:

◆ What needs to get done?

◆ How will I get it done?

◆ When?

On the left column, brainstorm all the things you suspect you need to get done in order to launch your web-based business. That may include such things as finding a good affordable web designer, learning how to accept payments online, researching the costs of getting your knitting patterns professionally drawn, coming up with a name for your business, determining how many hours per week you're able to devote to your business, and so forth.

You will probably have a long list of things that need to get done, some that will be more of a priority than the rest.

Using your best judgment, put a star next to the 10 most important items on the list. Then, in the middle column, write down how you are going to get those items done.

Warning!

It's okay to be ambitious. But don't make the mistake of biting off more than you can chew in terms of accomplishing tasks on your business plan. That will only lead to frustration. Strive for the right balance between being ambitious in getting your business off the ground and being realistic in what you can achieve and when. You want to be the turtle that wins the race, not the hare that conks out from exhaustion before the finish line. By the way, turtles are much faster than most people think!

For example, if you have "Learn how to accept payments online" in your left column, then you might write "Study Chapter 12 in *The Complete Idiot's Guide to Starting a Web-Based Business*" in the middle column.

Finally, in the right column, under *When?*, make a commitment. Decide right now when you can realistically complete that action step. Be careful here. If your schedule is packed to the rafters over the next three days, then you might not have time to read the chapter until this weekend. That's fine. Simply write down "Saturday by 3 P.M." in the column. That's realistic, but still ambitious.

Then move on to the other nine items you have identified as priorities.

There are two main benefits to this type of business plan. First, it's very easy to create. Unlike a formal document that you might have to show your banker, this type of business plan can be changed and updated on the fly. In fact, I always have one on the go. Secondly, it moves you forward by describing exactly what you need to do to get to the next step in your business and when. That clarity alone is motivating.

Try this system for planning your web-based business. It works.

When You Need to Get Formal

Okay. You can't wear comfy slacks and a sweater to every party. Sometimes the occasion calls for a fancy suit.

The same holds true for business plans. The system I described previously is for your own use. It tells you what you need to do, how you're going to do it, and when. However, there may be circumstances when you need to create a more traditional business plan to show to a potential partner, investor, or lender.

The topic of formal business plans is covered in detail in *The Complete Idiot's Guide to Business Plans* (Alpha, 2005), a terrific book.

However, let me give you a quick overview here.

Success Tip

The content of a business plan is often influenced by the loan, investment, or grant you're applying for. For example, a bank may require you to address a long list of very specific questions before okaying a small business loan. So, when creating a business plan that will be presented to others, make sure it contains all the answers and other information they expect to find in it.

A formal business plan is often used by others to make decisions about your business. You'll have a tough time convincing an investor to back you without one! Here are the basic elements:

◆ An overview description of your web-based business.

◆ An identification of how your web-based business is going to earn revenues. (Product sales? Services? Affiliate income?)

◆ The start-up costs.

◆ The cost of products or the costs of completing services.

◆ Estimated monthly costs of doing business. (Keeping the lights on!)

◆ How much you plan to pay yourself and other staff, including temporary employees, contractors, and freelancers.

◆ How you intend to promote your business to attract customers, including your marketing budget.

◆ A schedule for starting up your web-based business. (When do the doors open?)

◆ A forecast, monthly or quarterly, of expected revenues.

◆ How much money you need up front, in addition to start-up costs, until your business becomes profitable and can pay for itself.

◆ Where is the money going to come from? (Your own savings, a loan, a grant?)

A typical business plan is divided into sections for each of the above categories and can be dozens of pages in length. If it will be shown to others, make sure it is written clearly and that all the information is easy to find. You might want to hire a freelance editor to polish it for you. Presentation counts, too. Take it over to Kinko's or some other quick print shop to get it printed and bound. If you're asking an individual or organization for money, it's worth a few bucks to make your business plan look good.

Calculating Start-Up and Ongoing Costs

One of the toughest tasks in planning your web-based business is figuring out what you need and how much everything is going to cost.

Doing business online is certainly a lot less expensive than opening a retail store or other type of brick-and-mortar business. However, don't buy into the hype about getting a website up for just a few dollars and making your first million before the end of the month. Like any business, there are start-up and ongoing costs that you need to plan for. And if you don't, you might be in for an unpleasant surprise when the bills come in!

Most business owners watch sales and revenues carefully and celebrate when they have a good month. And so they should! But I can't emphasize enough how important is it to pay at least as much attention, if not more so, to your costs. Expenses like transaction fees, monthly services, subscriptions, freelance fees, virtual assistant hourly fees, and so forth can creep up on you. If you don't plan your costs carefully, you might find that although your website is generating healthy sales, your profits—sales minus expenses—are low.

Things You Need to Get Started

If you're starting from scratch, you're going to have to go shopping! There are many things you'll need to buy to get your web-based business off the launching pad. Here is a list of the basics:

- **A computer.** You need a good computer, ideally one that is dedicated just to your business. Mixing family and business use on the same computer can cause problems. You don't want your teenager to accidentally instant message one of your customers! Ask your computer dealer for a computer with enough processor speed and memory to run serious business applications such as Microsoft Office and Adobe Dreamweaver. Estimated cost: $1,000 to $2,500.

- **Internet connection.** I strongly advise you to get a high-speed connection, either through your cable company or via a satellite service. Dial up is just too slow to run your business effectively. And you don't want to rely on wireless Internet "hot spots" in your area just to check your e-mail. Estimated cost: $25 to $75 per month.

- **E-mail account.** You need an e-mail account to communicate with prospects, customers, suppliers, and other contacts. I suggest getting an account that enables you to use your own domain name—*yourname@yourdomain.com*—as an e-mail address. Also make sure your account has the capability to set up multiple e-mail addresses for employees and for other purposes, such as *support@yourdomain.com*. Estimated cost: $0 to $25 per month.

- **E-mail marketing service.** You'll want to be able to broadcast your newsletter and other e-mails to customers and those who visit your website. You'll need a special e-mail marketing service for that. See Chapter 22 for more details. Estimated cost: $25 to $75 per month.

◆ **A web designer.** Unless you're a talented designer yourself, you'll need to find a good web designer to create your website for you. You'll have to budget for the initial costs of developing the website, and then for ongoing changes and tweaks as your business moves along. Find out more about this in Chapter 9. Estimated cost: $500 to $2,500 for an initial website template.

◆ **Payment processing system.** If you intend to accept credit cards and other forms of payment from your website, then you need to think about things like merchant accounts, payment gateways, application and set-up fees, transaction fees—oh my! All that is described in detail in Chapter 12. Estimated cost: $0 to $75 per month plus transaction fees.

◆ **Web management software.** Even if you hire a freelance designer to help you, you may still want good website management software, like Expressions Web, on your computer to makes changes and updates on your own. Do you really want to have to call your web guy just to change an "a" to a "the"? Some web hosts offer online web builder programs for free. Estimated cost for traditional software: $200 to $500.

◆ **Telephone.** I suggest you have a separate line for your business. Don't use your personal phone. When a customer calls your voice mail, you don't want them to be greeted with, "You've reached the Slaunwhite Family!" Estimated cost: $50 per month.

◆ **Business registration fees.** In most jurisdictions, businesses need to be registered. You can't open a business bank account without such registration. Estimated cost for basic registration: $50 to $150.

Keep in mind that these are just the basic expenses of getting your business registered, your website up and running, and other things and services you need in place. There may be other expenses, too, depending on the kind of business you're starting. For example, if you intend to sell your own products you'll need to budget for an initial inventory.

And don't forget what may be the biggest start-up expense of them all: you. How will you support yourself until your web-based business starts earning a decent income? Will you rely on your "day job" and work on your business in your spare time? Will you live off your savings or spouse's income? You need to give this some thought because, as I mentioned earlier, it may be weeks or even months before you start seeing your business bank account growing. Experts say that, at a minimum, you should have enough savings, or the equivalent from other sources, to meet your personal income needs for at least six months.

Warning!

When calculating start-up costs, multiply any monthly fees by at least three. For example, if your telephone business line is going to cost you $50 per month, plan for three times that amount, or $150, in your start-up estimates. Why? It can take up to three months to start earning revenues from your web-based business. And you want to be able to cover those monthly expenses during that start-up period.

Does everything sound expensive? I've tried to be as realistic as possible with the start-up estimates. The good news is, there are many low-cost, and even free, versions of almost everything on the previous list. GoDaddy has free web building software and pre-designed website templates. You can make low-cost long-distance calls using Skype. PayPal offers a free shopping cart that you can use on your website. Don't you love the Internet?! (Appendix B features a long list of free, and almost free, online tools and resources. Check them out.)

So shop around. Take advantage of the free stuff. And when that's not possible, get the best deals you can.

Some final advice when estimating start-up costs. In the popular wilderness survival TV series *Survivorman*, the host suggests that you gather as much firewood as you think you need to get you through the night. Then double it. That's what I suggest you do when getting your start-up cash together. Add up the amount of money you think you'll need to get your web-based business off the ground. Then double it.

Business owners—myself included—almost always underestimate expenses.

Don't Forget to Budget for Your Time

So far we've talked about the things you need to buy and pay for to get your web-based business off the ground. But aside from money, there is something else you'll be spending a lot of: your time.

For example, if you intend to generate revenues for your website through advertising, then you're going to have to explore affiliate programs (see Chapter 6). You'll have to create a shortlist of programs you want to get involved in, study how each one works and how much commission they pay, sign up, learn how to use the banner ads and affiliate links provided, and much more. That takes time—time that you need to budget for.

Like start-up costs, the many things you need to do in your business during this phase are probably going to take you a lot longer than you expected. So budget your time accordingly. And be realistic. I can understand the bravado of saying, "I'm going to work on my business every weekday evening for three hours and all day Saturday." But be honest. Can you really?

You'll create a much better plan for your business if you're realistic about the time you can spend on it.

Forecasting Sales and Revenue

How much income can your web-based business generate in the first quarter after start-up? The second quarter? The first year? You'll have to have at least some estimation of revenues in order to stay financially healthy. And if you intend on getting a business loan, investment, or grant, then forecasting sales and revenue is a must.

How do you do that?

First understand that there's a huge difference between forecasting and goals. Is your goal to earn $100,000 in income in your first year of business? Go for it! If you fall short by even 20 percent, you'll still be doing great. But a forecast has to be realistic. You, and perhaps others, will be making important decisions around what your forecasted revenues are, so you'll need to be as conservative as possible.

When creating a forecast, think of the most pessimistic person you know—and then pretend you're that guy or gal! Question every assumption you make. Be ruthlessly realistic. Then, when you come up with how much money you expect to bring in once your web-based business gets going, lower that estimate by 25 percent.

It's far better to underestimate sales and revenues. That way, when you look at your figures each month, you'll have far more happy surprises than disappointments.

Warning!

Don't forecast a lot of sales and revenues for the first three months of your business. It takes time for customers to learn about your website, become familiar with its offerings, and then start placing orders or clicking on your affiliate program ads and links. Expect your website revenue activity to be very low at the beginning.

Calculating Market Potential

The logical place to start when determining how much revenue you can expect to generate is to take a closer look at your target market: your potential customers. How much of a demand is there for the types of products, services, and information your website will feature? Obviously, the more potential customers there are actively looking for what your website offers, the more clicks and sales you can expect to get.

Unfortunately, calculating market potential does take some guesswork. However, here is a simple strategy that will get you started:

◆ Go to the Google Keyword Tool. (Adwords.Google.com/select/ KeywordToolExternal)

◆ In the keyword search field, type in the type of product, service, or information your website will provide.

◆ Click **Get keyword ideas.**

◆ A keyword results field will display showing you how many searches per month are made using terms related to your website offerings on Google.

◆ If there is more than one relevant keyword, add up the results.

◆ About half the searches done on the Internet are done with Google. So double the number.

The result will give you an idea of how many people are actively searching for what your website offers and are therefore potential customers.

Now this isn't an exact science by any means. But this technique does give you a fairly good idea of the market size. For example, if your site is going to sell knitting supplies, then you'll be happy to know there are more than 54,000 searches for that keyword phrase—knitting supplies—done on search engines each month. That's a lot of people looking for what you sell!

However, if you discover that few people are searching for what you sell, or the kind of information that your site will feature, then you might need to rethink your business idea.

Putting the Numbers Together

Once you have an idea of the size of your market, and the number of competing websites there are, you can begin the process of estimating how much in sales and other revenues you can realistically generate.

At this point, you have to make a number of educated guesses. Be realistic. There may be 54,000 searches per month done on search engines for knitting supplies. But you can't expect them all to find out about your website. At best, you might be able to reach 10 percent.

Then there's the competition. Other websites that sell knitting supplies, perhaps some that are very established and well known to the target audience, will get their share of the sales.

And how many visitors to your new site can you reasonably expect to convert into paying customers? Before you make an optimistic estimate, keep in mind that Amazon.com reportedly turns about 12 percent of visitors into buyers.

If I'm sounding a little pessimistic, it's only because I want you to be as realistic as possible with your revenue projections. It's far better to make more money than you thought you would than less.

Making It Legal

Requirements vary from state to state and in other jurisdictions around the globe but, in most cases, you are required to register your business. This typically involves filling out a registration form that provides such details as the business name, type of business, owner (that's you), address, and other information. Once your business is registered, you are given a registration number and can operate legally.

Success Tip

Although you usually have the option of registering your business in person or through the mail, many jurisdictions give you the alternative of doing it all online. This can save you a lot of time and you will typically get your registration document right away. Check the website of your local government for "business services" for information, costs, and options regarding registering your business.

A business registration fee is typically $50 to $100. My business registration costs $79 and is good for five years.

Don't skip this step. It's very difficult to run an unregistered business, and in many cases it may be illegal to do so. You may not even be able to open a business account at your bank without your business registration number.

Once your business is registered, you need to decide which legal form your business will take. There are basically three types:

- A sole proprietorship

- A partnership

- An incorporated entity

A sole proprietorship is, by far, the most common legal form for small web-based business owners. It's simple to set up. You don't need an accountant or a lawyer to help you. In fact, in most cases, all that's required is for you to register your business.

When you are a sole proprietor, you're essentially a self-employed individual. In other words, you are the business. The income from the business belongs to you, as well as the debt.

A partnership is a more complex legal form for a business because it involves at least one other person who has a say in how the business is run. Legally, you can still set up your business as a sole proprietorship, with both you and your partner listed as the proprietors. But you may also need to draw up a *partnership agreement.*

def•i•ni•tion

A **partnership agreement** describes the rights and responsibilities of each partner in a business. It spells out the duration of the partnership, what happens if one partner leaves the business for some reason, how the business assets are divided up should the partnership dissolve, how the salary of each partner will be determined, and more. It's advisable to get the help of a lawyer when drawing up a partnership agreement.

Say you and an illustrator plan to launch a web-based knitting patterns business. The plan is that you will take care of business operations and marketing while the illustrator will design and produce the knitting patterns. You both agree to hold off from drawing a salary for six months to give the business time to become profitable. Then, you'll each receive 25 percent of the monthly net income.

Sounds like a reasonable partnership plan. Get it in writing. I suggest you get a lawyer to help you work through such contingencies as: *What happens if one partner wants to quit? What happens if the business is sold? What happens if one partner doesn't fulfill his or her responsibilities to the business? Can one partner buy the other partner out?* Having these questions answered in advance in a partnership agreement will make your business run more smoothly by avoiding unpleasant disagreements.

The third type of business is an incorporated entity, sometimes also referred to as a statutory business entity. This type of legal form turns your business into a corporation, which, under law, is considered a separate entity from you.

The main advantage of your business being a corporation, rather than a sole proprietorship, is that your personal assets—such as your house and savings—are protected, to a degree, from any liabilities your business might incur. For example, if your business were successfully sued, you might lose your business assets but not your house.

But there are disadvantages, too. You'll need a lawyer to set up a corporation, and the total costs can run as high as $2,500. Then there's the paperwork. A corporation is usually required to maintain more records than a sole proprietorship, and submit separate tax returns. The fees are higher, too. In my jurisdiction, in addition to business registration, a corporation must pay a $50-per-month fee.

Depending on where you're located, there may be several options for incorporating your business. In the United States, for example, business owners can take advantage of a simpler type of business structure called a limited liability company (LLC), which, as the term implies, provides some protection against personal liability to the business owner or partners.

For more information on this topic, I suggest *The Complete Idiot's Guide to Starting Your Own Business, Fifth Edition* (Alpha, 2007).

The Least You Need to Know

- You'll have a much better chance of success if you create an actionable business plan.
- When calculating start-up costs and projected revenues, be extra conservative.
- You must make your business legal by registering it and deciding on a legal form.

Part 2

Casting Your Line Into the Hot Revenue Streams

There are many ways to make money with a web-based business. Which approach will work best for you? That's what this part of the book is all about. You'll learn how to take advantage of the growing demand for information products, deal with the intricacies of selling physical goods online, and generate revenues without having to sell anything at all via affiliate programs and advertising.

Chapter 4

Join the Information Products Revolution

In This Chapter

- ◆ The basics of creating and selling information products
- ◆ How to select a topic that sells well on the Internet
- ◆ Creating information products in a variety of popular formats

With so much free information available online, it may be surprising to you that anyone at all, let alone a decent-sized market, would be willing to pay for it. Yet information products—e-books, courses, audio programs, webinars, teleclasses, special reports—are the hottest-selling items on the Internet.

The reason is that people who are looking for answers don't want to spend hours sifting through search engine results and websites. They crave the information they need in the format they want, and are willing to pull out their credit cards to get it quickly. This chapter will show you all the basics of creating and selling profitable information products on your website.

The Basics of Info-Marketing

An information product is any product that is designed primarily to convey information to the customer. The book you're reading right now is, in fact, an information product.

My first info-product was a short handbook on writing case studies for companies. There wasn't much on this topic available within the freelance writing community, which I found surprising. After all, as a freelancer myself for many years, I had written hundreds of case studies—also known as product success stories—for several clients. They were fun to create and paid very well. So I suspected that other writers would be interested in a how-to guide to this potentially lucrative niche market.

The handbook ended up being about 50 pages. A designer friend of mine created a nice-looking cover for it and I published my new information product as a *Portable Document Format* (*PDF*) file so it could be sold as a download. The title: *Cracking the Case Study Market.*

def•i•ni•tion

The standard in publishing documents for selling or sharing on the Internet is **Portable Document Format (PDF)**, a format created by Adobe. Just about everyone with a computer can easily open and view these types of files. In fact, most web browsers have the Adobe Reader plug-in already installed. For more information on how to create PDF files, visit www.adobe.com.

Although there were already some good articles available online for free on the topic—some written by me!—I was banking that many writers would be willing to pay $29 for a soup-to-nuts guide on the topic. I had no idea if I would sell even a single copy.

Within a few hours of announcing the availability of my handbook in my e-newsletter, it sold over 35 copies. I was grinning like a Cheshire cat most of the day! Over the years, that product has gone on to sell more than 2,000 copies.

My experience with creating and selling my first information product is fairly typical of even the most experienced web-based info-preneur.

◆ You select a topic that you suspect your target audience would be interested in and willing to pay for.

◆ You decide on the best format to convey that information: e-book, teleclass, audio CDs, special report.

◆ You create the information product.

◆ You set a price that earns you a profit—one that you suspect your target audience would be willing to pay. (And that price may be higher than you suspect.)

- You promote the product effectively to your target audience.

- You deliver the product, either by making the download instructions available to your buyer or by packaging and shipping the published material.

Of course, not all information products sell as well as my first one did. (I've had a few flops, too!) A lot depends on how hungry your target audience is for the information and the availability of that information from other sources. For example, if there were several other e-books and audio programs on case studies, the stiff competition would have made my book much more difficult to sell. (However, it still could have been profitable.)

Then, of course, there's the ultimate competition: free information. You have to create a product that people are willing to pull out their credit cards and purchase. If, for some reason, they feel the information just isn't worth paying their hard-earned cash to acquire, then your info-product is going to flop.

Types of Information Products

Information products can be published in an astonishingly wide variety of formats, from e-books to CD sets to podcasts to online video. However, when you break all these down to their basic components, there are essentially three types: document, audio, and audio-visual.

Let's take a look at each type in more detail.

Selling the Written Word with Document-Type Products

A document-type information product is any product that is primarily meant to be read.

The format that has taken the Internet by storm in recent years is the e-book. This is simply a book published in electronic format, usually as a PDF file, although other formats such as Amazon Kindle are becoming increasingly popular. Although it's called a "book," it's rarely as long as its print cousin. The typical length is 25 to 90 pages. Why not longer? Hey, no one wants to print off 300 pages or read them online!

Sales Builder
Typically, an information product is perceived to be more valuable—and therefore potentially more profitable for you—if it contains multiple components. For example, a best-selling home study course includes a course manual that students download, a series of audio classes that can be listened to on a special web page, and an online video of the instructor providing additional instruction. It sells more, and for a higher price, than if it was just a manual.

E-books are popular among web-based business owners that sell information products because they are relatively easy to produce. And, of course, if they're published in electronic format, there are no printing and shipping costs to worry about.

But e-books aren't the only format for information products of this type. Others include:

◆ Special reports

◆ Handbooks

◆ How-to guides

◆ Plans and instructions

◆ White papers (short "how-to" reports popular with business people)

◆ Manuals

◆ Home study courses

◆ Traditional books

◆ Newsletters

All of these formats can be published electronically and in print form. Many web-based business owners prefer to stick exclusively to the electronic downloadable format. They cite "fewer hassles" as the main reason. And that's true. There are fewer issues to worry about. However, a significant portion of the population still prefers to receive something tangible rather than downloading electronics. So you'll increase sales by offering a print version, usually by at least 20 percent.

Getting the Ear of Your Customers with Audio-Type Products

If you're as ancient as me, you'll remember the days when audio programs came in just one format: a set of cassette tapes. These days, however, there are a variety of ways that customers can listen to audio: on a CD, on their iPods or *MP3* players, on a web page that plays the sound automatically as a *streaming audio*, or as an MP3 that can be downloaded and played using the many free audio players that are available on the Internet.

def•i•ni•tion

MP3 is the most popular computer sound file used for audio products. An MP3 file can be played using Windows Media Player, RealPlayer, or QuickTime—the basic versions of which are available free on the Internet. You can also listen to these files on MP3 players, iPods, and other sound devices, or burn them onto a CD to play in your car. A **streaming audio** is a sound file with a built-in player. Your customers don't have to download anything; the recording plays right from the web page it's on.

Audio-type information products can come in many forms. Here are the ones that sell best on the Internet:

◆ Teleclass or teleseminar recordings

◆ Podcast or iTunes audio products

◆ Audio classes, courses, or seminars

◆ How-to instructions

◆ Audio newsletters or magazines

◆ Motivational or inspirational programs

As people become more familiar with downloading and playing computer sound files, audio programs are becoming increasingly popular among web-based business owners. You can sell the audio on your website and then "deliver" it as a download. That makes it potentially very profitable. (However, you'll sell even more if you also offer customers the option of receiving a CD.)

Putting on a Show with Audio-Visual Products

Ever dream of making a movie or TV show? Or starring in one? Then creating an audio-visual type of information product may be your best opportunity!

An audio-visual product can be created in a variety of forms. The most popular sellers on the Internet are:

◆ Webinar recordings

◆ Online videos

◆ Web-based classes, courses, and seminars

◆ DVDs

Audio-visual products give you the chance to put on quite a show. However, they can be expensive to produce because they involve either the creation of narration and slides, as in the case of a webinar or web-based course, or the production of a video.

Yet, despite the production time and expense involved, audio-visual types of information products are becoming increasingly popular.

Selecting a Marketable Topic

The most important decision you'll make when creating and selling info-products is the topic. After all, if the topic of your e-book or audio program doesn't interest your website visitors, few, if any, will purchase it. So you need to spend some time thinking about the topic and content of your information product and determine, as best you can, whether your target market will be willing to pull out their wallets and buy it.

Here are some questions to ask yourself when assessing whether an info-product topic is worth pursuing:

◆ Does the information help solve a problem or fulfill an aspiration? Ultimately, those are the only reasons why people will purchase an information product. They either have a problem, such as wanting to prevent a divorce, or they have an aspiration, such as a desire to make money buying and flipping houses. If your info-product doesn't address at least one of those two "master motivators," then you should seriously question whether it will sell.

◆ Is your target market hungry for this information? Is your information product going to be a "nice to have" or a "must have"? The more your target audience feels that your topic is something that is absolutely crucial for them to know, the more likely it is that it will be a profitable info-product.

◆ Has your target audience asked for it? If you know your target audience well enough, you'll discover they keep complaining about the same problems or dreaming about the same aspirations. In a way, they are telling *you* what information products they want you to create for them. Listen!

◆ Does the information duplicate what's already available for free? People will pay for information because it's hard to find, it comes from a trusted source, or it's packaged in such a way that it saves them time and is convenient for them to access (such as listening to an audio program on their iPod). For example, there is a lot of information on the Internet about starting a business. But how much free information is available on starting a carpet-cleaning business?

Here's an example of how to use these questions to select an info-product topic.

Say your website caters to the information needs of snowboarding enthusiasts. You consider publishing a directory of ski clubs that have sick snowboarding runs. (By the way, *sick* means *great* in snowboarder lingo!) Would such a directory sell? Well, if you discovered that lists of snowboarding runs can easily be found in magazines and on websites, then your product would be destined to flop. On the other hand, if you found that good information on snowboarding runs is tough for the eager snowboarder to find, then your guide could potentially sell like a John Grisham thriller.

As with any product development project, there are no guarantees of success. Ultimately, you have to make the best decision you can and, should you decide to create the information product, jump in with both feet and make it the best you can.

> **Sales Builder**
>
> Often one type of format can sell well while another does not. For example, written instructions on how to install a toilet may not sell well because that information is readily available for free on the Internet. However, a video showing how to do this malodorous job step-by-step would certainly motivate the weekend do-it-yourselfer to pull out his wallet.

What If Your Information Product Flops?

Okay. So you spend countless late nights developing your e-book or audio program, and even more hours promoting the heck out of it, only to discover that it doesn't sell well.

That's disappointing. But all is not lost. Unlike a physical product, where you might get stuck with a garage full of engraved bowling balls, there are two ways you can leverage your low-selling information product to get some, if not all, of your investment returned to you.

One way to salvage it is to create other more sellable products. Often, rethinking how you're packaging and presenting the information can transform an unprofitable product into a winner. A friend of mine once wrote a how-to book that didn't sell well. So she divided it into a series of smaller special reports and made them available on her website for $10 each. Within just a few months, she was generating $5,000 per month in sales!

Another option is to give it away for free. (Sounds crazy, I know, but stay with me!) You can use parts of your information product as articles for your website and e-newsletter. Videos can be placed on YouTube.com and other similar sites. Audios can be made available as a free download on iTunes.com. You're not making any money through direct sales, but by distributing free information you are, at least, generating interest in your website … interest that could very well turn into more visitors and sales of other products.

That's the great thing about creating information products. Rarely, if ever, do you have to throw your hard work into the trash bin. It's the most recyclable type of product there is!

Getting Your Info-Product Created

Intimidated by the thought of publishing your own e-book or audio program? I know I was. In the days before the Internet, I dabbled with the idea of creating a set of CDs that I could sell at seminars. However, when I looked into what was involved in recording and production, I recoiled. I was facing thousands of dollars in costs and untold hours and stress dealing with recording studios, duplication services, printers, packaging, and storage. Ouch! It was more than enough to turn me off the project.

These days, however, producing an e-book, audio program, or even video to sell on your website is a lot easier. There are a myriad of services available that make the entire process relatively quick and cost-effective.

Let's take a look at the basic steps of creating the three main product types: print, audio, and audio-visual.

Getting It Printed or PDF-ed

Perhaps the easiest information product to create yourself is a document type, such as an e-book, handbook, or special report. You could probably create something that looks pretty good on your computer using your word processing program and some decent clip art. However, if you need a more professional-looking piece, you can hire a freelance designer to do the cover design and text layout for you.

The simplest format in which to publish your e-book or other document is PDF (Portable Document Format). The cost is near zero. All you have to invest in is software or an online service for creating PDF documents—and some of these services are free. Check out the following options:

Success Tip

Most word processing programs, such as Microsoft Word, come with a range of pre-formatted templates for a variety of document types, including books and reports. This can save you a lot of time in formatting your information product and ensuring that your layout looks professional. You simply type your information into the layout template.

- ◆ Create PDF (http://createpdf.adobe.com)

- ◆ Primo PDF (www.primopdf.com)

- ◆ PDF995 (http://pdf995.com)

- ◆ Cute PDF Writer (http://cutepdf.com/products/cutepdf/writer.asp)

- ◆ PDF Online (www.pdfonline.com)

You can also buy Adobe Acrobat software and get the full range of PDF creation features.

Selling just PDF documents on your website is tantalizing. However, you may still want to create a printed version of your e-book or other document-type product. And there are many cost-effective services available that will help you do just that.

When I decided to publish a print version of one of my handbooks, I opened an account with online printer Mimeo.com. They handled everything from printing my handbook to my exact specifications to shipping the orders to my customers all over North America.

In addition to Mimeo.com, there are many other services that specialize in helping "info-preneurs" print and ship information products.

- Speaker Fulfillment Services (www.speakerfulfillmentservices.com)

- Fedex Office (www.fedexoffice.com)

- The UPS Store (www.upsstore.com)

- LJ Fulfillment Services (www.ljfulfillment.com)

- Webgistix (www.webgistix.com)

Some of these companies also provide CD and DVD creation and duplication in addition to printing services, providing you with a full-service solution to your information product creation and shipping needs.

Creating Audio Products

Good news! The days of having to spend hundreds of dollars per hour to hire a sound studio and engineer are over. You can create a good-quality audio product quickly and cost-effectively using the many services available on the Internet. Check out the list below. Some of these companies are teleconference services that offer good-quality recordings, while others specialize specifically in helping web-based business owners like you create audio products.

- AudioAcrobat (www.audioacrobat.com)

- BYOaudio (www.byoaudio.com)

- AccuConference (www.accuconference.com)

- FreeConference (www.freeconference.com)

- Great Teleseminars (http://greatteleseminars.com)

- Planet Teleclass (http://planetteleclass.com)

- Teleclass International (http://teleclassinternational.com)

The service I use most often to create my audio products is AudioAcrobat. I simply log in, follow the simple on-screen instructions, and record my audio using a good-quality computer microphone. The system automatically creates everything I need to post the recording on my website, sell it as an MP3 file, submit it as a podcast, or create a CD. The sound quality is not at a professional studio level, but it's pretty darn close! I've never had a single customer complain.

Another of my favorite ways to create an audio product is to do a teleclass. This is a class that you teach over a phone via a teleconference line. You can have dozens of students attending, who can ask questions and participate in group discussions. The recording can then be sold as an audio class.

Producing Audio-Visual Products

An audio-visual product is, of course, something that your customer can see and hear: a webinar, an online video, a DVD. By its very nature, it's more time-consuming and costly to produce.

A webinar is, perhaps, the simplest format to produce. If there are publications or associations in your industry that produce webinars, try to get yourself invited as a guest speaker. Then ask for a copy of the recording for your own use.

You can also produce a webinar on your own using the many online services available.

- WebEx (www.webex.com)
- GoToWebinar (www.gotowebinar.com)
- Communique Conferencing (www.communiqueconferencing.com)
- Microsoft Live Meeting (www.microsoft.com/smallbusiness/products/livemeeting)

If you want to go Hollywood with a video product, then things get more complicated. Although information product buyers are forgiving of audio products such as teleclass recordings, they expect videos to be more polished. I suppose that's because we're so used to watching professionally produced television shows. So for video products, I suggest you hire a freelance videographer; someone who can shoot and edit your video so that it looks and sounds great. You can find videographers and other creative free-lancers at www.elance.com or www.guru.com.

Selling Other People's Information Products

So far in this chapter, I have focused mainly on selling e-books, audio programs, videos, and other information products that you create yourself. However, you don't have to self-publish to sell information on your website. You can do very well with other people's products.

Say the target market of your site is cat lovers. Instead of creating the definitive guide to homemade toys for a tabby cat, you could research the Internet for books, audio programs, and videos on that topic. You'll likely find several. Then you can investigate how you can sell these same products on your website.

There are basically two options for doing this.

The Affiliate Option

Selling affiliate products is so common that Chapter 6 is entirely dedicated to this option. Basically, you sign up for the affiliate program of the website or company offering the product you want to sell. Then you are provided with a trackable link that you use on your website and in your e-mails. When someone clicks on the link and buys the product, you get a commission.

Selling affiliate information products is a smart idea, even when you create your own. Let's face it—you can't develop products for all the information your target market is looking for. Affiliate products are a profitable way to fill in the gaps.

The Licensing Option

As a product affiliate, you're given a trackable link—not the product itself. Buyers are taken away from your website or e-mail and to the product's website to complete their purchase and receive delivery.

As a product licensee, by contrast, you receive the product itself and are free to sell it under the terms of the licensing agreement.

Warning!

Keep in mind that licensing arrangements vary widely. For most information products, you'll be given the master documents and audio or video computer files only. Unless the product is going to be available as a download only, you'll need to arrange for printing and shipping.

For example, say you're interested in selling the e-book *Dog Training in 5 Minutes Per Day*. You discover that a licensing agreement is available where you pay a flat fee of $1,000 and can print and sell as many copies as you wish for a three-year period. If the guide sells for $39, and you're reasonably comfortable that you can sell about three copies per month from your website, then this might be an excellent deal for you. You will have earned more than $4,000 in revenue before the licensing period runs out—perhaps far more than you would have earned as an affiliate.

Protecting Yourself with Fine Print

A customer purchases your e-book. He eagerly downloads the document, which you have published conveniently as a PDF. Then, impressed by your great content, your customer decides to e-mail a copy to all his friends … friends who may have been willing to purchase the product from you if they hadn't gotten it for free!

Try as you might, you'll never be able to prevent dishonest people from illegally distributing or stealing your information product. However, many of your customers will not even be aware that what they are doing is at best dishonest and at worst illegal. A fellow web-based business owner I was speaking with recently discovered a video he was selling had been placed on YouTube.com! When he eventually tracked down the culprit, that person was astonished that doing this was wrong!

So it's important to educate those who purchase your product on how they can use and share the information.

In my information products, I have the following statement clearly printed on the main inside title page:

> *A note to the reader:*
>
> *This is NOT a free publication! If you have received this how-to guide without purchasing it from the publisher, it constitutes piracy and is illegal. No part of this publication may be reproduced or distributed in any form or by any means without the prior written permission of the publisher.*
>
> *© Copyright 2008, Steve Slaunwhite. All rights reserved.*

Success Tip

Copyright laws vary around the world. While some countries require a copyright registration of some sort, others merely require you to state that the original work is yours. Check with the government department that handles copyright issues in your jurisdiction. Make sure your original work is protected!

You'll never stop thieves from being thieves. However, this statement does explain to the reader that the publication is protected by copyright and cannot be illegally reproduced or distributed. Many people innocently think they can.

The Least You Need to Know

- ◆ Information products are popular sellers on the Internet.

- ◆ Select topics that your website visitors are hungry for; feature information that is not readily available for free.

- ◆ Take advantage of the online services available that make creating information products easier and more cost-effective.

- ◆ Consider affiliate programs and product licenses as an alternative to creating your own products.

Chapter 5

The Goods on Physical Products

In This Chapter

◆ Finding physical products to sell on your website

◆ Dealing with the complexities of packaging and shipping

◆ Outsourcing manufacturing and finding drop ship wholesalers

Although the Internet is an electronic marketplace, the overwhelming majority of online stores sells and ships physical goods. In fact, the first really successful e-business was an upstart online bookstore called Amazon. com. (Heard of them?)

Selling physical products online is a much more complicated process than software, subscriptions, and other products that can be digitally delivered. You have to source or create the product, then promote and sell it, then get it shipped to the customer. On the plus side, websites that sell physical goods tend to have less competition than those that sell, say, e-books. So if you learn the ropes, and have a popular product that can be sold profitably online, you can do very well.

The Basics of Selling Goods Online

I sell two types of products on my website:

♦ Short audio classes and how-to guides available in digital format. They don't have to be delivered in the traditional sense. When customers purchase these products online, they simply download their order from a special website page.

♦ Home study courses typically comprised of a thick binder of materials and a set of CDs. This is a physical product. Selling these courses is a little more complicated for me because I have to deal with manufacturing, inventory, packaging, and shipping.

So the first thing you need to realize about selling physical products online is that it requires more work and all-around hassle than the other ways a website can make money: digital products, services, and advertising and affiliate programs.

def•i•ni•tion

Order fulfillment refers to the process of delivering the merchandise to the customer. It involves such activities as inventory, packaging, filling out the appropriate forms, shipping, and tracking. An order is fulfilled once the customer has received the merchandise he or she has purchased.

Yet, if you work everything out and get your *order fulfillment* processes running smoothly, selling physical products can be very profitable.

And as you'll learn later in this chapter, there are other ways to profit from physical products that don't require you to handle inventory, packaging, and delivery.

There are four questions you need to answer before you can sell physical products on your website:

1. How will I acquire or make the products?

2. Where will I store the products until they're sold?

3. How will I get product orders shipped to my customers?

4. Can I sell the products profitably on my website?

The third question, concerning shipping the goods, is covered in more detail in Chapter 13. The answers to the other questions I covered right here, in this chapter. So stayed tuned!

Sourcing Products to Sell

Let's assume that you're not going to manufacture a product from scratch. How do you find products that you can sell on your website?

Say, for example, you plan to build a web-based business selling custom silk flower arrangements for special events such as weddings, funerals, home décor, store displays, and so forth. You're going to need an inventory of various types of silk flowers, stems, mounts, and adornments.

The worse mistake you can make is to simply purchase these materials from a retail store. If you do, you'll be paying retail prices and it would be very difficult, if not impossible, to make a profit reselling those materials online—even if you're adding value by making the custom flower arrangements.

What you want to do is buy your silk flowers and other materials at the same price as that retail store pays.

How do you do that? You've probably heard the term *wholesale price* before. That's the price you need to be able to pay. And you get that price, of course, by going through a *wholesaler.*

def•i•ni•tion

A **wholesaler** is simply a manufacturer's representative. They may operate as a regional warehouse shipping goods to retailers and online stores (like yours) in the area. Or they can be a small operation of just a few staff members or even just one person. The role of the wholesaler is to work with retailers in a particular area on behalf of the manufacturer who may be located across the country or even overseas. When you buy products for re-sale on your website, you must buy at the **wholesale price.** Otherwise, you won't make a profit.

The typical arrangement with a wholesaler is this:

◆ You contact the wholesaler and inquire about opening a retail account.

◆ You will be offered a plan where you pay wholesale prices for the products you want to sell on your website.

◆ You open an account.

◆ You place an initial order.

◆ You start selling!

When buying wholesale, you won't be ordering one silk flower at a time. The typical requirement is to buy in bulk. In fact, depending on the wholesaler, the pricing may fluctuate depending on the size the order—100 units, 500 units, 1,000 units, and so forth. And it is not uncommon for wholesalers to have minimum order requirements.

Why can't you just buy direct from the manufacturer? Sometimes you can. Not all manufacturers work through wholesalers, but most do. Typically, the larger the manufacturer the more likely it is they will have a wholesaler network.

Finding Wholesalers

An easy way to find a wholesaler is to contact the manufacturer of the product you want to sell on your website. Ask to speak to the sales manager. He or she will be able to provide you with the names and contact information of wholesalers in your area.

Another way is to search through the many online directories and databases available on the Internet. Wholesalers want to be found! So they do a good job of getting themselves listed in every directory that potential resellers (that's you) may be searching.

Here are some places to start:

- Wholesale Directory (www.wholesaledir.com)
- Hoover's (www.hoovers.com) (This is a general company directory. Do a specific search for wholesalers.)
- eSources.co.uk (www.esources.co.uk)
- WholesaleCanada.com (www.wholesalecanada.com)
- Aid & Trade (www.aidandtrade.com)
- Daily Trader (www.dailytrader.com)
- WholesaleCentral.com (www.wholesalecentral.com)
- Wholesaledistributors.net (www.wholesaledistributors.net)
- USA Wholesalers (www.usawholesalers.com)
- Giftware Index (www.giftwareindex.com)
- Tech Wholesalers (www.techwholesalers.com)
- SaleHoo (www.salehoo.com)
- Wholesalesuppliers.net (www.wholesalesuppliers.net)

- Wholesalers Network.com (www.wholesalersnetwork.com)
- EbizOnline Dropship Source Directory (www.ebizdropship.com)
- Top Ten Wholesale (www.toptenwholesale.com)
- WholesaleBusinessConnection.com (www.wholesalebusinessconnection.com)
- TradeMama.com (www.trademama.com)
- Worldwide Brands (www.worldwidebrands.com)
- WholesaleU.com (www.wholesaleu.com)
- Shopster (www.shopster.com)

Another good resource is ThomasNet.com. It's a directory that cross-references products with manufacturers, distributors, and wholesalers. Very handy!

And don't forget to look in local business directories in your area, including the world's most popular: the Yellow Pages. Most of these directories have a category called Wholesalers, which makes it easy.

Making Your Own Products

When most people think of manufacturing, they think of making something from scratch. But that isn't always the case. Any type of assembly, or customization of an existing product, is considered manufacturing.

In my earlier example, the website owner was selling custom silk flower arrangements from supplies purchased through a wholesaler. That is, in fact, a type of manufacturing. You are treating a product, in this case silk flowers, as *raw material* for something else you are creating—custom silk flower arrangements. You could potentially do the same for snowboards (custom etching), coffee cups (logo embossing), and coffee beans (repackaging for consumer use from larger wholesale bags).

Making your own products requires a lot of preparation. You need, at the very least:

- A source of raw materials. (Ideally from a wholesaler or manufacturer.)
- The space to manufacture the goods.
- Equipment and tools.
- Required skills.
- Storage space to inventory the goods once completed.

def•i•ni•tion

Raw materials are anything that you use to create the final product that is shipped to the customer. If your website sells gemstone jewelry, for example, then the gemstones, jewelry wire, and other adornments you use to make each product are the raw materials.

Manufacturing your own stuff requires a significant up-front investment, even if your product is relatively simple to make—such as knitting instructions. Even that product may require an illustrator and writer to create the instructional sheets and printing. That investment doesn't begin to be recovered until you've opened the doors to your web-based business and started getting orders.

Before you take the leap, you should at least explore sourcing products through wholesalers, finding drop ship wholesalers and manufacturers, or outsourcing manufacturing to another company. All these topics are explained in this chapter.

Still, if manufacturing your own product makes sense for your web-based business, go for it. Just keep in mind that your per-unit costs are probably going to be higher at the beginning of your business. It takes time to learn and refine a manufacturing process to minimize costs.

Maintaining a Product Inventory

In order to ship a product promptly to customers, you need to have that product available. Unless you've made a prior arrangement with customers who place an order—such as you might with customization—then you can't wait for a product to be shipped from your wholesaler. Your customer is going to want it right away.

In fact, you might be surprised at how quickly online customers expect their orders to be shipped. At my online business, ForCopywritersOnly.com, we recently received a call from a customer demanding to know the delivery status of his order … an order he placed just three days earlier!

You need a place to store your products that is safe and secure, and where the chances of your stock being inadvertently damaged are minimal. If product is stored in your garage, for example, with lots of other family items, damage could occur in a variety of ways. (I once bumped my car into a box of books while parking.) You want to make sure merchandise can't easily be stolen. And you want to make sure it's protected from the weather and other environmental damage. A basement, for example, could flood and destroy thousands of dollars in inventory.

> **Warning!** _____
>
> Many home insurance plans do not protect you against the loss of business assets such as product inventory. If yours doesn't, check with your insurance company or advisor and ask about special business insurance or a business rider to your existing plan. Just like losing your home without insurance would be a financial catastrophe, so would losing your product inventory or other business assets.

Here are some suggested places for storing inventory:

- ◆ **A special room in your home.** Make sure it can be locked. For the reasons noted previously, the garage isn't always the best place.

- ◆ **Self-storage facilities.** There are self-storage companies in just about every major town and city in North America. Typically, they charge a monthly fee for space ranging from the size of a small closet to a large garage.

- ◆ **Commercial warehouse space.** Check out the ads in your local newspaper. Chances are, there are several that advertise commercial warehouse space for lease.

- ◆ **Shared warehouse space.** Do you know someone who has a business with warehouse space? Make an arrangement to rent a section. You may only need 100 sq. ft. to start—about 10 ft. × 10 ft.

- ◆ **Contract warehousing.** (Also referred to as public warehousing.) These are companies that warehouse goods for a variety of businesses on a contract basis. Typically, they handle receiving your goods and store them until you're ready to access them to fulfill customer orders.

Make sure you ask a lot of questions before signing up with any storage or warehousing service. You want to make sure they have insurance to protect your goods from theft or damage, and that you have access to your products as needed.

A friend of mine once stored his products in a local self-storage facility, only to discover that they were closed for the holidays during the last two weeks in December. During that time he had no access to his goods. Happy holidays!

Outsourcing Manufacturing

If you suspect that making your own products from scratch is going to be expensive and time-consuming—and it probably will be—then consider outsourcing to a manufacturer. There are plenty of companies that offer custom manufacturing even in small quantities.

If your product is new, many custom manufacturers will work with you to create it. Some even have design departments specifically for this purpose. You show them plans or drawings of what you're looking for and they create a *prototype* of the product for you to review. If you like what you see, you can negotiate manufacturing it in quantity. If you don't, then it's back to the drawing board.

def•i•ni•tion

A **prototype** is a sample of the product you want manufactured. In most cases it looks exactly like it will look once manufactured in quantity. However, because it's usually handmade, there may be some differences. The purpose of a prototype is to see the product as customers will see it before you commit to signing a manufacturing contract. Always ask for a prototype. You just can't get the perspective you need from a drawing.

A friend of mind once had a novelty item—a stuffed animal—custom manufactured by a company in China. He went through two or three prototypes before finally coming up with a product he liked. Then he placed his order and received his first shipment of the new toys in about seven weeks.

Where do you find a custom manufacturer? In addition to searching online and in directories of manufacturers, try MFG.com. On that website you can submit your product plans or drawings and get quotes from dozens of custom manufacturers around the world.

Drop Ship Wholesalers

The Achilles' heel of selling physical products on the Internet is that you have to package and ship the orders. That can be an expensive, time-consuming headache. Think of the last time you had to wrap up and mail holiday gifts to distant relatives!

Now wouldn't it be nice if the wholesaler you're purchasing the products from would also be nice and package and ship those orders directly to your customers?

Well, some wholesalers do. The arrangement is called *drop ship*. And it can make selling goods on your website a lot easier.

Drop shipping bypasses the traditional process where a wholesaler ships products to your location and you ship orders to your customers. Instead, with a drop ship arrangement, the process goes something like this:

def•i•ni•tion

Drop shipping is an arrangement made with the manufacturer or distributor of a product to ship the orders your website generates directly to your customers. The advantage is that you don't have to deal with shipping and handling yourself.

◆ A customer places an order on your website.

◆ You send that order information to the drop ship wholesaler.

◆ The drop ship wholesaler packages and ships the product to your customer on your behalf.

A drop ship arrangement seems so simple and convenient that you might wonder why any web-based business would even consider any other method. In fact, drop shipping is extremely popular among web-based business owners. But there are a few drawbacks.

First of all, just because the wholesaler is delivering the products to your customers doesn't mean they're paying for that expense. You will be charged for packaging, shipping, and other order fulfillment costs—either separately, or as a fee built into the wholesale product price. In most cases, it's cheaper to bring in the product and handle order fulfillment yourself. The primary benefit of a drop ship arrangement is time savings and simplicity.

Warning!

Some companies that call themselves drop ship wholesalers are actually retailers in disguise. They buy products from wholesalers and then simply provide you with a delivery service. To sell products profitably online, you need to buy wholesale, not retail! So make sure the drop ship wholesaler you select has direct relationships with the product manufacturers.

Also, not all wholesalers offer drop ship programs. So the products you want to sell may not be available within this arrangement.

Still, drop shipping is an ideal solution for those web-based businesses that don't have the resources to inventory products and fulfill customer orders themselves. The profit margins are a bit less, but the lower required upfront costs of getting started, along with the simplicity of this arrangement, often makes it all worthwhile.

Where do you find a drop ship wholesaler? Many of the companies and wholesalers listed earlier in this chapter offer drop ship programs. In addition to those, check out these online directories and resources.

- PSP Drop Ship (www.pspdropship.com)

- Dropship Area (www.dropshiparea.com)

- Dropshipper Network (www.dropshippernetwork.com)

- DVDdropship.com (www.dvddropship.com)

- Get Dropshippers.com (www.getdropshippers.com)

- 123Dropship.com (www.123dropship.com)

- Doba (www.doba.com)

Many of these sites do more than just help you find drop ship wholesalers. Some, in fact, are set up like a one-stop shop. They will make the drop ship arrangements with the wholesalers on your behalf, integrate with your online business to get order information (so you don't have to send it manually), place the orders with the wholesalers, and provide your customers with shipment tracking numbers.

And here's a tip. Not every wholesaler makes it obvious, even on their website, that they offer drop ship services. So if you find a wholesaler with a product you want to sell on your website, call and ask if they have a drop ship program. They might!

The Least You Need to Know

- Selling physical products online is complicated but can be very profitable.

- You can manufacture products yourself, but you should at least consider outsourcing manufacturing.

- You can avoid having to deal with shipping by working with wholesalers that offer drop ship services.

Chapter 6

Making Money with Advertising and Affiliate Programs

In This Chapter

◆ The basics of making money with advertising and affiliate programs

◆ Where to find the right affiliate programs for your web-based business

◆ How to sell traditional advertising space on your website and in your e-newsletter or blog

So far in this book I've focused primarily on selling products and services that you must provide in some manner to your online buyers. But that isn't the only way to make money with your website. In fact, you don't have to sell anything at all—at least not in the traditional sense. If your website is popular and gets lots of traffic, you can do very well by either recommending affiliate products to your website visitors, or allowing other companies to place ads on your web pages, or both.

There are numerous examples of web-based business owners who have generated enviable incomes entirely through affiliate products and advertising. And even if you do plan to offer your own products and services, this chapter will enlighten you on how these two revenue channels can provide a great secondary source of income.

The Basics of Advertising and Affiliate Programs

Chances are, you've been on the buying end of an affiliate transaction and didn't even know it.

Say you're a running enthusiast preparing for your first marathon. You want to learn more about how you should train so you Google "marathon training programs" and visit several websites. One of these sites contains great articles and free training programs that you can download. You hit the how-to information jackpot!

As you explore the site, a book recommendation for a beginner's marathon training guide catches your attention. You click on the link, are taken to an Amazon.com page, and place an order.

You may not have realized it at the time, but you just earned that website owner some cash. He is an Amazon.com associate (their preferred term for affiliate) and the link you clicked on is an *affiliate link*. That website owner will be paid a percentage of the purchase price of the book you just bought.

def•i•ni•tion

An **affiliate link** is a special link that tracks clicks and sales of affiliate products or advertisements that you showcase on your website pages or e-mails. It ensures that you get credit for the clicks and revenues you generate for the affiliate whose program you've joined.

The website owner generated income—without having to stock or deliver the product, deal with the financial transaction, or handle any aspect of the shipping and after-sales service.

Sounds like a good deal, doesn't it? And for the most part it is. But there are some important pros and cons you need to consider before you decide to promote affiliate products or place advertisements on your website. Before we get into that debate, however, let's take a look at how affiliate programs work.

How It All Works

Say your website sells custom embroidered knitted sweaters. You make and ship those sweaters yourself; however, you notice that a lot of your customers are asking you about knitting books and supplies—products you don't sell. Your customers are buying these somewhere else, which means that potential profits are literally clicking away from your website.

How do you remedy this? That's simple. You find a website that sells knitting books and supplies and you sign up for their affiliate program. You create a special page called "Stuff For Knitters" and feature a list of their products (being sure to use the affiliate links that the company has provided you with). Then when a customer visits your website to buy a sweater, they can also review the knitting books and supplies and purchase some of those, too.

Success Tip

Affiliate programs aren't always called affiliate programs! Some websites use other terms instead, such as referral programs, associate programs, partner programs, and advertising programs. However, the way they all work is essentially the same. You are provided with a trackable link to the products you want to recommend on your website—or to the advertisements you want to place. Then when a website visitor clicks and buys, you make money.

The cornerstone of an affiliate program is the affiliate link. This can either be in the form of a simple text link that you put on your web page or in your e-mails, or an online advertisement (often referred to as a banner). It can even be in the form of a small online video—similar to a television commercial—an Internet advertising format that has recently become popular.

For example, if you were an affiliate for my how-to guide *Pricing Your Writing Services*, you could either mention it on one of your web pages like this:

> *Do you struggle to quote freelance writing or copywriting jobs accurately? If so then check out this month's recommended resource: a new guide called* Pricing Your Writing Services.

Or you could place an advertisement on your website like this:

Example of a banner advertisement.

In either case, the embedded affiliate link would be the same; a special link that, when clicked, takes the website visitor to my site to learn more about the product and (hopefully) place an order, and tracks that activity so that you get paid your commission for the sale.

Should I or Shouldn't I? The Pros and Cons

Generating revenue with affiliate and advertising programs seems so simple, especially when you compare this approach to the complexities of sourcing and selling your own products. But before you consider stuffing your website with affiliate links and banner ads, you first need to carefully weigh the pros and cons.

Let's start with the advantages.

It takes virtually no time at all to start selling affiliate products. Once you've signed up for a program and received your affiliate links or banners, all you have to do is place them on your website or in your e-mail newsletter. You can be up and running—and possibly even making money—in less than an hour.

Some affiliate programs even have special programs that automatically post relevant advertisements on your web pages. You just plug in the snippet of code that the affiliate program provides you, and they handle the rest.

In addition, you don't have to worry about the traditional headaches associated with selling your own products and services. You don't have to accept payment. You don't have to deal with credit cards. You don't have to stay up late at night wrapping parcels and filling out courier waybill forms. The company with the affiliate program takes care of all those pesky details.

Finally, affiliate products can fill gaps in your own product line. If you sell coffee beans online but not coffee machines, you can sign up as an affiliate of a coffee machine company. Your customers probably shop for this equipment anyway. Why not earn extra money pointing them in the right direction?

But before you get too excited, there are a couple of important disadvantages you should consider.

> **Warning!**
>
> When you promote an affiliate product, you are also promoting the other website. If they have complementary products to your own, this might mean lost sales to the competition. So be careful which affiliate programs you sign up for. You want your customers to keeping coming back to your site, not someone else's!

First of all, affiliate products are, of course, not your own. But your website visitors may not see it that way. If they clicked a link on your site to purchase a product and become unhappy with the quality or after-sales service, they might blame you. Sure you can explain, "I'm just an affiliate!" But by that time you would have already been tarred with the same brush. That's why it's important to select only those affiliate products that you can recommend with confidence.

Secondly, when a customer clicks on an affiliate link on your website, guess what happens next? They get taken to someone else's website business! (Internet marketers call this "click and bye.") Will they return to yours after making the purchase? Maybe. Maybe not. So an affiliate link is not just an income generator, it's also an exit sign.

Yet, despite these disadvantages, it makes sense for most website businesses to offer at least some affiliate products in the form of links or advertisements. You just need to select affiliate programs carefully to ensure that the recommendations you're making to your website visitors reflect positively on you and help to build your business.

Finding and Profiting from Affiliate Programs

There are tens of thousands of affiliate programs on the Internet representing millions of products. Finding the best ones for your website can be like finding toothpicks in a haystack (which, by the way, is a lot harder than finding needles!). Where do you start? Your first step is to decide what types of products you want to recommend or advertise.

Take a look at your website product offerings. Are there gaps in your product line that need to be filled? One of my website businesses, ForCopywritersOnly.com, offers e-books, courses, and other educational materials for freelance copywriters. I have developed a lot of my own products; however, one product I didn't have was a guide to speechwriting. So I signed up as an Amazon.com affiliate, and now I make extra money by providing my website visitors and customers with a list of recommended books on the subject.

If your website is essentially an information site, then look for affiliate programs of closely associated products. Say your website features articles, stories, and other resources of interest to kayaking enthusiasts. You could sign up as an affiliate of a kayaking equipment company. An affiliate advertisement for safety helmets next to an article on whitewater kayaking would probably get a few clicks—and make you some money!

Another strategy is to ask your website visitors. Find out what kinds of products or services they are shopping for on the Internet. Then sign up for those affiliate programs.

Success Tip

Want to ask your website visitors about which products they shop for most on the Internet? It's relatively easy to put a survey form on your website or in your e-mail newsletter. My favorite tool for doing this is SurveyMonkey.com. The basic service is free and you can set up simple survey questions in just a few minutes.

Once you have an idea of the types of product recommendations and advertisements that make sense for your website business, your next step is to find the right affiliate programs.

First, check out the big guys! Just about every major web-based company has an affiliate program, from Amazon.com to Dell Computers. If there's a big player in your niche, then chances are your website visitors are already comfortable buying from them. You can take advantage of that fact, as an affiliate, by offering convenient links to recommended products.

And of course, affiliate programs are not just for the big guys. Just about every website business these days has an affiliate program of some kind. (And, as I'll discuss in Chapter 23, you should, too.) On any company's website, look for a link called affiliate program, associate program, partner program, earn cash, or something similar. There you'll find information on their affiliate program, including such vital details as how to join, how it works, and how you make money.

Another good source is affiliate program directories. These are websites where companies list their affiliate programs in the hopes of attracting good affiliates—like you! Here are some of the most popular.

- AffiliateSeeking.com (www.affiliateseeking.com)
- ClicksLink.com (www.clickslink.com)
- AffiliateScout (www.afflilatescout.com)
- JamAffiliates.com (www.jamaffliliates.com)

- Affiliate Online (www.affiliateonline.net)

- WhichAffiliate.com (www.whichaffiliate.com)

- Affiliate Programs Locator (www.affiliateprogramslocator.com)

- Affiliate Ranker (www.affiliateranker.com)

- Top Affiliate (www.top-affiliate.com)

Finally, take a look at the many affiliate networks available. These companies run affiliate programs on behalf of their clients—often web-based business owners just like you. On their websites you can usually sign up as an affiliate for free. The affiliate network company will then help you find appropriate advertisements that match the content and target audience of your website. Here are some of the most well known:

- ClickBank (www.clickbank.com)

- Commission Junction (www.cj.com)

- ShareASale (www.shareasale.com)

- LinkShare (www.linkshare.com)

- Logical Media (www.logicalmedia.com)

- CPA Storm (www.cpastorm.com)

Each of these affiliate networks operates a little differently and have varying requirements. Be sure to read all the information about the program before you decide to sign up.

Success Tip

Affiliate networks will often refer to you as a "publisher" rather than an affiliate, in reference to the fact that you publish a website. Their clients, the companies that want their links and advertisements on your website, are known to them as "advertisers." So when looking for information on becoming an affiliate, find the link for publishers.

If you're new to all this affiliate stuff, I suggest you tip your toe in the water by starting with just one or two products from a single affiliate program. Get a feel for how this method of earning income works and become savvy at using affiliate links and banners, and tracking your clicks and sales. Once you've gained more experience, you can start adding more products from more affiliate programs as appropriate.

Selling Your Own Ad Space

So far we've talked about placing links and advertisements on your website as part of a traditional affiliate program where you get paid a commission for clicks or sales. But there's no reason why you can't sell ad space on your site the old-fashioned way: by charging a flat fee.

Hey, newspapers and magazines do it all the time!

Selling ad space, of course, involves getting paid by an advertiser to put a banner ad on your site for a specific period of time—say, one month. For example, if your website features information and advice for expecting mothers, then a baby wear store might be very interested in advertising on one of your pages or in your e-mail newsletters.

To generate advertising revenues in this way, create a link on your website that contains information on your advertising program. Potential advertisers will need to know the following:

♦ The types of advertising opportunities available on your website and in your e-newsletter.

♦ The specific locations on your website where space is available for banner advertisements.

♦ The size of banner ads you accept. This is typically conveyed in pixels. For example, 234 pixels by 60 pixels is a standard small banner.

♦ Guidelines for text advertising in your e-mail newsletter. You need to place restrictions on the length of the headline and the word count of the body copy.

♦ Restrictions on banner ad special effects. You may not want a banner ad that expands across the page or plays a distracting video when someone hovers their mouse over it.

♦ Restrictions as to the type of advertisements you will accept. Will you accept competitor product ads? Sweepstakes ads?

♦ A price list. Advertisers often refer to this as a rate sheet. The typical arrangement for a banner is a flat fee per month. For an e-mail newsletter ad, it is a flat fee per issue.

For example, I recently wanted to place an advertisement on a popular website for graphic designers. I visited the site, clicked on the advertising link, and learned about their program. I discovered that they accept only two sizes of banner ads and the cost was $250 per month. After making the financial arrangements, I sent them the banner graphic along with the URL I wanted the ad to be linked to.

Running your own advertising program can be very profitable. However, you have to deal with ad sales, payments, client relationships, posting ads, and more. In essence, you're in the advertising business.

Making It Automatic with Google AdSense and Similar Advertising Programs

Another approach is to sign up with Google AdSense or a similar program that automatically displays advertisements on your website that are relevant to its content. In Internet marketing lingo, this is often called contextual advertising.

You've probably seen these types of ads before. Google AdSense (www.google.com/adsense) is the most familiar because of the distinctive way the text ads look on a web page and the familiar "Ads by Google" logo. But there are many other companies in this space, too.

- Yahoo! Publisher Network (http://publisher.yahoo.com)
- Clicksor (www.clicksor.com)
- BidVertiser (www.bidvertiser.com)
- ValueClick Media (www.valueclickmedia.com)
- Targetpoint Inc. (www.targetpoint.com/index.html)
- AdBrite (www.adbrite.com)
- AdForce (www.adforce.com)
- RevenuePilot (www.revenuepilot.com)

When you sign up for one of these programs, advertisements will be placed based on the preferences you set up and the content of your web page. So you don't have full control over which ads will appear. In fact, with Google AdSense the ads may vary with each new visitor! You can, however, prevent undesirable advertisements from being placed on your site. You might not want, for example, to see a competitor pitching his goods to your hard-won website visitors!

Sales Builder
Google AdSense or other similar advertising programs can place ads on your site in the form of text, banners, and even videos. Eye-catching and unique, online video tends to get more clicks which may mean more advertising revenue for you.

Most advertising programs like this work the same way Google AdSense does: you get paid when someone clicks on the ad. However, there are some programs that pay on a Cost-per-Impression (CPI) basis, which is usually a flat fee paid for every thousand visitors who see the ad. As with any advertising program, be sure to read the "How it works" and "How you earn money" sections carefully.

Using Affiliate Links Creatively to Make More Money

You signed up for an affiliate program and now you have access to a range of affiliate product links and advertisements that you can use to generate revenue for your website. If you place these on a few key web pages, you'll probably do fairly well. You'll generate some clicks and make some money. However, you'll earn even more affiliate dollars if you follow these suggestions.

Create a recommended resources page. Your website visitors are looking for resources associated with the products, services, and information your website provides. So why not oblige them? If your site sells gourmet cooking supplies, sign up for the affiliate programs of products and services you would recommend to your target audience. Then list these on the web page.

Leverage your e-mail newsletter. If you use an e-mail newsletter to keep in touch with website visitors, feature recommendations or ads for the affiliate products you represent. Some web-based business owners report they earn more affiliate income with their e-mail newsletter than they do their website.

Affiliat-ize your backend. When a customer purchases one of your products, recommend other affiliate products they may be interested in. This strategy alone could double your income on the sale. You can recommend products on one of the checkout pages, in the "Thank you for your purchase" e-mail, or in the information shipped with the product. Amazon.com does this all the time.

Write a review. Provide a candid review of a product or service, and then provide your affiliate link to it. People are always looking for reviews as a way to make purchasing decisions. Just be sure to give your honest opinion. Never tell your website visitors that you like a product when you really don't, just because you're an affiliate. (And if you don't like the product, should you really be an affiliate?)

There may be other ways you can think of to use affiliate links and advertisements, too. Use your imagination. Look for opportunities to show your affiliate link at those moments when your website visitor or customer may be interested in that product. The more clicks you get, the more affiliate income you earn.

The Language of Getting Paid

Throughout this chapter I talked primarily about sales commissions, because that is how most affiliate programs work. Someone clicks on your affiliate link or ad, buys the product, and you get a cut. However, not all affiliate programs work this way—and even among those that do, there are many variations. So it's important to know the language of affiliate and advertising income so you can fully understand how a particular program is going to compensate you for your efforts.

Affiliate Commission. This is the most common type of affiliate payment. Basically, you get paid a percentage of the purchase price when someone clicks your affiliate link or advertisement and buys the product. How much commission? As a rule, physical products such as books and electronics pay 5 to 25 percent. Downloadable products and online services typically pay more because there are no manufacturing or shipping costs involved; usually you receive 10 to 35 percent, although I've seen commission rates as high as 50 percent.

Residual Earnings. This is a commission paid when your website visitor clicks on an affiliate link or advertisement for a particular product but goes on to purchase other products from that company, too. It's a nice deal—look for this feature in affiliate programs you are considering joining.

Sales Minimums. These are earnings plateaus you have to reach before you receive an affiliate payment. For example, Amazon.com will only pay you with an Amazon Gift Certificate if your monthly sales are below $25. Other programs won't pay you at all if you don't reach certain minimums. Read the fine print carefully.

Cost-per-Click (CPC). This is an affiliate program that compensates you whenever someone clicks on your affiliate link or ad. You get paid regardless of whether or not that person ultimately buys the product. Google AdSense pays based on CPC.

Cost-per-Impression (CPI). This is an affiliate program that pays based on a flat fee per thousand people who see the banner on your website. These programs are usually only available to websites with very high traffic.

Cost-per-Action (CPA). You get paid when someone clicks the ad and then takes some specific action on the other website, such as signing up for an e-mail newsletter or downloading a free report.

Two-Tier Referral Program. This is a feature within an affiliate program that rewards you when someone clicks on an ad and then goes on to become an affiliate of that program themselves! Some website owners make the extra effort of actually trying to persuade visitors to become affiliates, just to get two-tier commissions.

Most reputable affiliate programs will provide you with a means of checking reports that display such important information as the number of clicks and sales your affiliate links and banners are generating. I suggest you check these statistics weekly so you can monitor the success of your affiliate efforts and, if necessary, make adjustments. You also want to monitor how much money the program owes you so you can make sure the payments to you are accurate.

The Least You Need to Know

- The easiest way to make money promoting other people's products on your website is by joining an affiliate program.

- The best way to find affiliate programs is to check out the websites of products you want to promote. Most will have an affiliate program.

- You can sell advertising space on your website or in your e-mail newsletter. You can also have ads automatically displayed on your site by signing up for Google AdSense or another similar advertising program.

- Be sure to understand how the affiliate program you join works. You need to know exactly how you will earn money; what restrictions there are, if any; and when and how you will get paid.

Part 3

Creating a Website That Sells

How do you create a website that persuades people to place orders online, or click on your ads or other affiliate links? That's what this part of the book is all about. I'll show you how to dream up and register a great domain name, plan your site and get it designed, and write motivating web copy. Then I'll walk you through the process of finding a web host and uploading your site. Once your website goes live, you're in business!

Chapter 7

Playing the Domain Game

In This Chapter

- ◆ How to select the ideal domain name for your web-based business
- ◆ The basics of registering and using your domain name
- ◆ Options when the domain you want is already owned by another person or company

Think of the most successful web-based businesses you know. Chances are, what come to mind are their domain names. Amazon.com. Ebay. com. iTravel.com. Choosing the right domain name for your business can mean the difference between a successful and profitable site and one that struggles to get noticed and attract visitors. Think about it. Which website are you most likely to remember and go to if you are a woman looking for fun and accurate information on backyard gardening: YouGrowGirl.com or AcmeGardenProducts.com?

A great domain name is the cornerstone of your web-based business. It identifies you, communicates (ideally) what your website is all about, and tells potential customers where to find you. It's your name, address, and brand statement all rolled up into just two or three words. So it makes sense to spend the time necessary to get it right. This chapter will show you how.

Selecting a Domain Name

There is a cycle of frustration in selecting a domain name for your business that I strongly suggest you avoid. It goes something like this. You dream up a fantastic domain name, you get excited, you go online to check if it's available, your heart sinks when you find out that it isn't, and then you panic. Not fun! The danger is that you'll get so frustrated you'll end up registering the first name that is available—even if it's not ideal for your business. Or you'll settle for a weird alternative of the name you really wanted, like flowrs4u.com, in the hopes that people will be able to remember it, spell it, and find you online. (Most won't).

Relax. Take a strategic approach to selecting your domain name. Even if another person or company has already registered the domain you want, there are still options available to get it or at least a suitable variation on it, as we'll discuss throughout this chapter.

The Fun Part! Brainstorming Domain Name Possibilities

Your first step in the process of coming up with a domain name for your business is to create a long list of options. Grab a pen or pencil, a notepad, and a big mug of coffee. (Caffeine is an important part of this process!) Then use the following questions to help you brainstorm domain name possibilities and interesting variations of those names.

At this point in the process, don't be concerned about whether or not a domain is already taken. You can check that later. Just have fun dreaming up all kinds of interesting names for your web-based business.

You should aim for a brainstorm of at least 20 words and phrases for each one of the points below. Don't hold back. The longer the list, the better.

Think about your website. What words describe it best? How is it unique from other similar sites? What information will visitors find on your site? What is the main theme of your site? Does your site have an attitude?

Think about your product or service. What is it? What does it look like? What is it made of? What does it do? What are its benefits? What is so advantageous about it? What sets it apart from other similar products or services?

Think about your target audience. Who are they? What are they like? What are their dreams and aspirations? What are their problems and concerns? What is their style and attitude?

Find the most popular keywords associated with your website and its products. For example, according to Google's keyword research tool, there are over 90,000 searches per month for the phrase "guitar sheet music." If your domain name contained those words, then thousands of potential customers would know they had found the right place. (More on researching keywords in Chapter 17.)

Expand your list by using word tools. Dig out your dictionary, thesaurus, synonym finder, and rhyming dictionary. You can easily double or even triple the amount of domain name possibilities that way. Unless you're a semanticist, you probably don't have all those books on your shelf. Don't worry. There are plenty of free online versions: RhymeZone.com, VisualThesaurus.com, Merriam-Webster.com, Synonym.com, and Thesaurus.com.

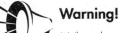

Warning!

When brainstorming domain names, don't make quick judgments. Write down as many possibilities as come to mind, no matter how silly or unsuitable they might seem at first glance. Can you imagine if the folks that came up with GoDaddy crossed that seemingly ridiculous name off their brainstorming list? That domain is now one of the most familiar on the Internet!

Play with the words and phrases you've brainstormed. Move them around. Discover interesting ways you can put them together. If your site is focused on information for moms who want to start a home-based business, then obvious words that come to mind are: *mother, mom, entrepreneur, business, biz, making money,* and *home-based.* Using a little imagination, these words can yield numerous domain possibilities: *mompreneur, mommybiz, moneymakingmommies,* and so forth.

At this point, you should have at least 50 to 100 words and phrases. Go through this list and create as many domain name possibilities as you can. You should be able to come up with at least a couple of dozen.

Creating a Shortlist

Now comes the tough part. You have to whittle your list down to about 10 finalists. There will be some names that will be easy to drop off your list because, for any number of reasons, they are obviously not suitable. For other names, however, the decision will be harder.

Here's a technique that works well for me. Imagine that you're a boss interviewing candidates for a very important job—the job of being your business's domain name!

Ask each one of these would-be domains the questions listed below. Those domain name candidates that give you the best answers will make it to your shortlist.

Are you memorable? Ideally, you want customers looking for your type of products, services, and information to be able to easily recall the name of your website.

Are you easy to say? Will people understand your domain name when they hear it on the radio, in a voice-mail recording, or at a trade show?

Are you easy to spell? Will people be able to type in the domain name correctly when looking for your site online? Flowrs4u.com, for example, can be misspelled any number of ways.

Do you communicate what the site is all about? Unless your domain name becomes a well-known brand, such as Amazon.com, you'll want a name that indicates what your site is all about.

Consider CoffeeDetective.com, the website of my friend and fellow web-based business owner, Nick Usborne. His domain name meets all of the criteria. It's memorable. It's very easy to say and spell. And it helps to communicate what the website is all about: information on gourmet coffee beans, brewing machines, and accessories.

Sales Builder
Make sure your domain name attracts the right visitors. If your website features the latest in outdoor wear and you call it CampyClothing.com, you'll attract the camping crowd alright. But you'll also get the attention of people looking for avant-garde, or "campy," apparel.

By the way, don't go through this process alone. Enlist some friends and colleagues to help. Circulate your shortlist and ask for their candid opinions. You might even get a few domain name suggestions that you would have never come up with on your own.

By this stage, you'll probably have four or five good domain name candidates. Your final choice will probably come down to whether or not a domain is available to be registered and, if it isn't, whether or not you can purchase it from the owner or register a suitable variation.

Checking Availability and Registering Your Domain Name

There are hundreds of websites where you can check the availability of a domain name and, if available, register it.

Registering a domain name is a little like registering a corporate name. Once you do, no one else can use that domain name for their website. It's yours—for as long as you continue to pay the renewal fees.

For example, a few months ago I registered the domain name for my new web-based business, a blog called TheWealthyFreelancer.com. The procedure was fairly straightforward. I went to GoDaddy's website (www.godaddy.com), checked the availability of the name, and then went through the simple steps to register it. The whole process took just a few minutes.

I use GoDaddy for obtaining my domain names, but there are plenty of other *domain name registrars* that you can use. Here are the most popular:

Warning!

Domain names are registered for fixed periods, usually one to five years. So be sure to renew your domain name well before it expires. If it does expire, that domain quickly becomes available on the open market for anyone to grab. Even if your website is well established, it will go "off the air." And getting a domain name back from a new owner can be difficult, if not impossible.

- ◆ DomainPeople, Inc. (www.domainpeople.com)

- ◆ NetworkSolutions (www.networksolutions.com)

- ◆ GoDaddy (www.godaddy.com)

- ◆ eNom Inc. (www.enom.com)

- ◆ Register.com (www.register.com)

- ◆ MyDomain.com (www.mydomain.com)

- ◆ Domain Direct (www.domaindirect.com)

You can expect to pay $5 to $40 to register a domain name. However, the average these days is about $10 for a one-year registration. That's not much more than a caffé mocha at Starbucks—and a real deal considering the value a domain name can represent for your business.

Once you register your domain name, what happens next? Like GoDaddy, most registrars will send you a confirmation e-mail stating that your domain name has been registered successfully. So watch for that happy news in your inbox. That e-mail will also contain other important information, such as a username and password to sign into your account and make changes.

def•i•ni•tion

A **domain name registrar** is a company that has been given permission by the Internet Corporation for Assigned Names and Numbers (ICANN) to register top-level domains such as .com, .net, and .org. Some websites that sell domain names are only brokers, not registrars. You can view the official list of registrars at www.ICANN.org.

Within the next few days, your registration information will appear on a public record called the Whois directory. This tells the world who owns the domain name, when it was registered, when it expires, and other information. You're required to keep the information in your Whois directory up-to-date, so if you change your company or contact information, be sure to contact your registrar and let them know.

You can view the Whois directory at www.internic.com/whois.html.

Carefully Consider the Little Extras

Most domain name registrars are for-profit companies—so in the same way McDonald's often asks, "Do you want fries with that?"—they are motivated to up-sell you a lot of additional services while you register your domain name. Don't be surprised when, as you're checking your domain name availability and going through the registration steps, you are offered all sorts of deals and options along the way.

- ◆ Discounts for registering your domain name for multiple years instead of just one.

- ◆ Deals on hosting your website. (Hosting is covered in Chapter 11.)

- ◆ Options for registering your domain name with multiple extensions, such as .net, .org, and .mobi.

- ◆ Savings when you register variations on the spelling of your domain name.

- ◆ Offers to automatically renew your domain name at the end of each registration period.

- ◆ Opportunity to "private register" your domain name. This is an option that keeps your name and contact information off the public Whois directory.

These "deals" can add hundreds of dollars to your domain name registration. But they can also save you money and help your business in other ways, too. So consider each offer carefully.

When I registered my blog domain, TheWealthyFreelancer.com, I took advantage of an offer to also register the variation, WealthyFreelancer.com, at a significant discount. (Just $2.99!) This made sense to me because I wanted people to be able to easily find my site, and it's conceivable some would forget the "the" and type in WealthyFreelancer.com instead. I wanted those people to still find my site and not end up at someone else's!

If it's a great deal, and you really need the service or option, grab it. However, don't be pushed into signing up for something you don't need or understand. It's perfectly okay to just register the domain name and worry about any other service or option you may need later on.

What if Your Domain Name Is Already Taken?

You select a terrific domain name. You go to a domain name registrar's website, type it in, click **check availability,** and—damn!—a message pops up on your screen saying that the domain name is already taken. All is lost.

Or is it?

Just because a domain name has already been grabbed by someone else doesn't necessarily mean there isn't a way to acquire that domain name or use a variation of it. Take a deep breath. You still have options.

Using a Spelling or Extension Variation

Say you're planning to create an information website for people who want to experience the adventure of teaching English in China and other parts of the Orient. On your shortlist of domains is TeachInTheOrient.com. But when you check the availability of that name, you despair. It's taken.

One possible solution is to use a different extension. The .com version of the name is gone, but the .net or .org versions may still be available. There are also .tv, .biz, .me, or .info. These can all be viable options, especially if the domain you want is registered but not being used as a website. (People register domain names all the time and never get around to using them. I own over 100!)

If your website is going to target only those who live in a specific country, then you might consider a country-specific domain name extension. In addition to the global extensions that we're all used to seeing—.com, .net, .org—each country has its own unique extension. In the United States, it's .us. In Canada, it's .ca. In the United Kingdom, it's .co.uk.

BuildingWealth.ca is the website of Canadian financial author Gordon Pape. I'm sure that the .com version of that name was long gone when he originally created his website. But since Gordon focuses on information primarily for Canadian investors, that didn't matter. The .ca version gave him a highly memorable name and communicates his Canadian expertise.

Sales Builder

Lock out the competition. When you register a great domain name, also register the other popular variations. For example, if you're lucky enough to grab a domain like JustLoveJogging.com, then also get the .net and .org versions as well as spelling variations like Just-Love-Jogging.com and JustLoveToJog.com. This will prevent other people from setting up a similar site with a similar name to yours.

An alternative spelling is another way to vary a domain name if the one you want is taken. Just because NeatKnitting.com is already registered doesn't mean you can't use the phrase "Neat Knitting" in your domain name. Here are just a few possibilities.

- Neat-Knitting
- NeatKnittingOnline
- NeatKnittingStore
- TheNeatKnittingStore
- ThatNeatKnittingStore
- YourNeatKnittingPlace
- TheNeatKnittingPlace
- ThatNeatKnittingPlace
- TheNeatKnittingPeople
- NeatKnitters
- Neat-Knitters
- CrazyAboutNeatKnitting

- NeatKnittingSupplies

- ForNeatKnittersOnly

- OfficialNeatKnittingSite

- NeatKnittingNet

- NeatKnittingSite

- NeatKnittingShop

- NeatKnittingNow

- NeatKnittersToday

- MyNeatKnitting

As you can see, there are dozens of alternative domain names that may be up for grabs. So turn on your imagination and do some brainstorming, using the previous list as a guide. You might be surprised to discover that an even more desirable domain name emerges from the exercise.

Buying a Domain Name from Its Owner

A few years ago, I developed a home study copywriting course called Strategic Copywriting. However, when I checked the availability of StrategicCopywriting.com, I discovered that someone else already owned the domain. I also noticed, however, that the owner did not currently have a website for the domain, nor was he using it in another way that I could determine. So I decided to approach him directly and offer to buy it.

This could be a viable option for you if the domain name you want is taken but not currently in use. There's a chance, perhaps a very good chance, that the owner doesn't have any set plans for the domain and will sell it to you for a fair price.

In the case of StrategicCopywriting.com, I looked up the owner's contact information in the Whois directory. Then I sent him an e-mail expressing my interest in purchasing the domain name.

Here's that original e-mail:

> *Subject: About your domain name: strategiccopywriting.com*
>
> *Hi _____,*
>
> *My name is Steve Slaunwhite. I noticed that you own the domain name: strategiccopy-writing.com. The reason for my e-mail is that I may be interested in purchasing that domain name from you … if you are interested in selling it.*
>
> *Are you? If so, let's talk. You can reach me during business hours at _____ or by e-mail to _____.*
>
> *All the best,*
>
> *Steve*

When I sent that e-mail to the domain name owner, I got a call back the same day. Within three days we negotiated a fair price and the domain was mine.

In my case, the process went smoothly. But of course, it doesn't always work out that way. The domain name owner might not respond to your inquiry at all. Or they might respond, but just to say, "No thanks." Even if the owner is interested in selling, he or she might demand a price that is far beyond what you think is reasonable or can afford. And what if the domain name is owned by a large company? It might be difficult to identify and reach the person with the authority to make a deal.

Still, for the short amount of time it takes to send an e-mail or make a phone call, it's worth a try. You might just get the domain name at a very reasonable price.

Success Tip

Many domain name registrars offer a service that monitors an already-taken domain name for you and then notifies you or registers it on your behalf, the instant the domain becomes available. Thousands of domain name registrations expire every day, so if you don't mind waiting, this could be a way to get the domain name you want.

If you and a domain name owner do come to an agreement, what's the next step? After you make payment arrangements, you'll have to get the domain name ownership transferred to you. It's a little like buying a car. You have to get the registration records changed to reflect the new ownership.

How do you do that? Each domain name registrar has a slightly different procedure, but in most cases, the process can be handled online. If you can't find the instructions for transferring domain name registration on the registrar's website, contact them.

Using a Domain Name Broker

Another way to purchase a domain name is through a domain name broker. These are companies that specialize in selling domain names on behalf of their clients. In fact, if you have a domain name for sale, you can list it with one of these companies and they'll attempt to sell it for you in exchange for a percentage of the final price.

There are several domain name brokers online. The most popular are:

◆ BuyDomains.com (www.buydomains.com)

◆ GreatDomains (www.greatdomains.com)

◆ Afternic (www.afternic.com)

◆ Sedo (www.sedo.com)

◆ GoDaddy's Domain Name Aftermarket (https://auctions.godaddy.com/trphome. aspx)

◆ Pool.com (www.pool.com)

◆ SnapNames (www.snapnames.com)

A domain name broker website operates much like a registrar. On the front page there is usually a place where you can type in a desired domain name or keywords associated with your website. The obvious difference is that instead of a $10 to $15 registration fee to grab an available domain, you have to pay a price to buy it—and that price can range anywhere from a few hundred dollars to over one million bucks!

When you purchase a domain name from a broker, they typically take care of all the details regarding payment and transfer of ownership.

Typically, it's expensive to purchase a domain name from a broker because most of these companies focus on highly sought-after names that lots of web-based businesses are clamoring to get their hands on. It may very well be worth spending $500, $5,000, or even $25,000 on a domain name that will play a key role in the success of your web-based business. But I strongly suggest you don't spend a cent until you've considered all other domain name options first.

The Least You Need to Know

◆ Brainstorm a long list of potential domain names for your business.

◆ Check availability with a domain name registrar. If a desired name is available, register it immediately.

◆ Consider variations in spelling and domain name extensions.

◆ If someone else owns the domain you want, see if you can buy it at a reasonable price from the owner or through a domain name broker.

8

Getting Your Website Planned and Designed

In This Chapter

◆ Creating your website plan

◆ Finding and working with a good designer

◆ Website design tips from the pros

The cornerstone of your web-based business is your website. You need to carefully plan how it's going to look and work, as well as what features, content, and other special characteristics it will have. Unless you're a do-it-yourself designer, you must then find and work with a good web designer to turn your plan into a great looking site. This chapter shows you how.

Questions to Ask Before the Design Process Begins

Meet Jill. She's a budding web-based business entrepreneur with a dream—a dream that you've seen used as an example many times in this book. She wants to create a website that sells knitting patterns online. She's done all the research. She is confident there is a large audience of potential buyers out there in cyberspace, just waiting to place orders. All she needs now is a website!

A big mistake that Jill could make, and one that many entrepreneurs make, is to simply find a good web designer and say, "I need a website. Make it for me." Then leave the entire process of planning and creating the site to that person.

Jill needs to be more proactive than that. She needs to have answers to some key questions in advance, and develop a clear plan for her website, before she talks to a designer. Otherwise, the most important determinant of her business success—her website—may not turn out the way she hoped it would.

Let's switch gears now and talk about *your* site. What questions do you need answers to before you talk to a web designer?

What Is the Purpose of Your Website?

This may seem like an obvious question. After all, this is a business. So isn't the purpose of your website to make money?

Well, at a high level, of course it is. But you have to go deeper than that. Think about your target audience—your potential visitors and customers—and what the site will provide for them and how.

This is easy to do. Just finish this sentence and review the samples I provide: *The purpose of my website is …*

> **Example 1:** *… to provide how-to information and education to freelance copywriters. How? By publishing a free e-mail newsletter, providing free articles and advice on the website itself, and selling how-to guides and home study courses.*

> **Example 2:** *… to provide great knitting patterns to knitters. How? By offering a free knitting pattern of the week club, and selling a wide range of premium knitting patterns, which can be downloaded in PDF format.*

> **Example 3:** *… to provide information, news, and reviews to people who enjoy premium coffee. How? By publishing a free e-mail newsletter and blog on the topic and by featuring articles, reviews, and the latest news on the website. The site will be supported by affiliate products that I recommend and by advertising.*

Why do you need to go through this exercise? Clarifying the purpose of your website helps to determine how the site is going to look and function. Once you've defined the purpose, you're one step closer to determining how the home page will look, the number of pages that need to be created, and so forth.

For the coffee site, for example, it's obvious from its purpose that the site will feature an e-mail newsletter and blog, will need several pages of tips and articles, and will require affiliate ads posted in strategic places throughout the site.

What Should It Look and Feel Like?

A friend of mine, a fellow web entrepreneur, once created a website that had a warm, touchy-feely look to it. The pages were filled with soft colors and soothing images. When I first visited the site, I almost expected the home page to reach out and give me a big hug!

The problem was, that *look and feel* was completely out of sync with the target audience, which were primarily self-employed professionals who were serious about business success. Her site had great content—on-target articles and terrific advice—but potential customers didn't sign up for her programs because they perceived the website as lightweight.

def•i•ni•tion

> **Look and feel** refers to the overall impression your website makes when potential customers see it for the first time. That impression could be described as funky, cool, businesslike, professional, fun, informative, warm and caring, new age, modern, geeky, or in any number of other ways. It's important that the look and feel of your website makes the right impression on your visitors. If it doesn't, your site may not be as successful as you hoped it would be.

Fortunately, she changed her website to make it look more professional and business-oriented and, as a result, her programs took off.

Like it or not, people are going to make immediate judgments about your website based on how it looks. If it looks amateurish, people may not take it seriously, no matter how great the content is. If it looks like a page out of a science magazine, and your target audience is cooking enthusiasts, then people who arrive at your site might think they're in the wrong place and leave!

How do you determine the right look and feel for your website? Start with your target audience. What are they like? As a group, what is their personality? What styles attract them most?

A quick way to find the answers is to look in magazines and other publications that target your potential buyers. For example, if you plan to sell custom engraved snowboards online, check out a few snowboard publications. You'll soon discover that the look and feel of your website is going to need to convey speed, thrills, fun, and a touch of the rebel spirit to attract this crowd.

When planning your site, make a list of words that best describe the look and feel you want to achieve. This will help you, or your web designer, stay on track during the design phase.

What Ingredients Do You Need?

Your website isn't just about layout and pretty pictures. There are a lot of other ingredients that you need to get together before you can start designing your site.

If your website is going to sell adventure travel packages, for example, then you're going to need lots of pictures. People need to see snapshots of the fun before they decide to book. Make a list of all the images you need for your site.

Another ingredient you may need is an account with an e-mail marketing service (see Chapter 22). You'll want to get this before designing your site so that the sign-up form can be integrated into the code.

> ### Sales Builder
> One of the most important ingredients to a successful website is keywords. Integrating the right keywords into the design and content will help get your website ranked high in search engine results. Use the tips and tools in Chapter 17 to build a list of keywords that your target customers are using to find sites like yours.

You also need to make a list of all the content you need for your website. Depending on the purpose of your site, that may include initial blog posts, articles, how-to tips, product descriptions, company information, copy for the home page and key landing pages, and more. Again, make a list of what you need.

Other ingredients may include:

- Affiliate program links and banner advertisements

- Blogging software

- Online payment processing solution

- Product pictures

- E-mail newsletter design

- Software for generating pop-up messages

It's important to get all these ingredients planned in advance. It will make the design phase go much more smoothly and ensure your website goes live on schedule.

Creating Your Site Plan

Once you've clarified the purpose of your website, decided on the look and feel, and determined what ingredients are needed, then you're ready to create a *site plan*.

You certainly don't need to be an architect or artist to create a site plan. Here's a very simple way to do it:

- Get a blank piece of paper and turn it sideways.

- Write "Home Page" in the middle of that page.

- Draw a line out to indicate each of the main links from your home page. For example, "Newsletter," "Free Club Membership," "Knitting Patterns," "FAQs," "How-to Tips," "About us," and "Contact us."

def•i•ni•tion

A **site plan** is simply a drawing that shows the pages on your website and how they are all linked together. You need a site plan to help you and your web designer understand what website elements need to be created and how your website is going to look and work.

Example of a site map.

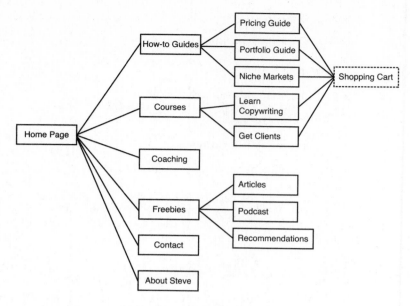

ForCopywritersOnly.com - Basic Site Plan

Now you have a basic site map. But of course, you need to go into a lot more detail because your main pages will be linked to other pages. For example, your "Knitting Patterns" page may have links to such categories as "Sweaters," "Scarves and Wraps," "Blankets," and more. So repeat the site mapping process for each of your main links.

Your site map is complete when you have a schematic of all the planned pages on your website, with a line indicating which pages are linked to which. Depending on the complexity of your website, your site plan may contain several pages.

Warning!

When creating your site map, don't forget about the "invisible" pages. These are pages that don't contain obvious links to the main website pages so they're easy to miss. Invisible pages can include the thank-you pages that customers see when their order is complete, and the download pages used for digital products, such as e-books.

If you prefer to create a site map on your computer, rather than manually, I suggest you use mind-mapping software. This will make it easier to create the schematics. There are some good free mind-mapping programs available on the Internet. Check out www.freemind.sourceforge.net, www.xmind.net, www.mindomo.com, or www.mapyourmind.com.

With a site map complete, you're ready to start the design phase.

Finding a Good Web Designer

One of the most important decisions you'll make regarding your website is selecting the right web designer. Your choice will dramatically impact how your website will look and function, and how smoothly the website design process goes.

Where do you find a good web designer? The best place to look is your own back-yard. Ask friends, colleagues, and other web-based business owners for recommendations. You'll feel more comfortable hiring someone who has been referred to you.

Also take a look at any professional membership organizations you belong to. If, for example, you are a member of a professional group for the industry you're in, on that industry website may be a list of suppliers—including web designers. As a member, you might get preferential treatment and a good rate.

Of course, searching the Internet is another effective way to find a web designer. I suggest you use some of the many websites available that help match web designers to your needs. Check out the following.

Success Tip

Designers are sometimes credited on the websites they've built. Find websites that have a design similar to what you're seeking for your own site, and then scroll down to the bottom of the home page. You might find a "Website designed by ..." credit down there with a link to that designer's website. Click and make contact!

- ◆ Elance (www.elance.com)

- ◆ Guru (www.guru.com)

- ◆ FreelanceDesigners (www.freelancedesigners.com)

- ◆ DesignFirms.com (www.designfirms.com)

- ◆ WebDesigners-Directory (www.webdesigners-directory.com)

- ◆ WebDesign Finders (www.webdesignfinders.net)

- ◆ Web-Development.com (www.web-development.com)

- ◆ GetAFreelancer.com (www.getafreelancer.com)

Many of the template companies listed in Chapter 9, plus many of the major websites that cater to online businesses such as Constant Contact, GoDaddy, and Yahoo! Small Business, maintain lists of recommended web designers. Check out the sites for more information.

Evaluating Potential Designers

You've made a shortlist of potential web designers. How do you determine which one is right for your website project?

The first step is to review their portfolios—specifically, the websites they've already created for other business owners. Contact each web designer and ask them to send you links to the sites they have created. Then visit each one to see which, if any, match the look, feel, and functionality you've planned for your own site.

Success Tip

When reviewing websites that a designer has built, be sure to ask to what extent she was involved in its creation. Don't just assume that she built it from scratch just because it's in her portfolio. Ask if she contributed to the general layout strategy, design of the masthead and logo, placement and structure of the text, installation of special features such as blogs and forums, and so forth. This will give you a better idea as to her capabilities.

You wouldn't think of hiring a home improvement contractor without asking for references. The same holds true when hiring a web designer. Ask for the names and contact information for at least two clients, and then contact those people. Ask them if they were satisfied with the working relationship and if the designer did what he promised, met deadlines, and offered good advice.

If your website requires special features, such as a blog, forum, online payment system, or streaming video, make sure the web designer has a track record of success in those areas. Be suspicious if someone tells you, "I've never done one of those before but I'm sure it won't be a problem." Some website features require a lot of technical know-how in addition to design savvy. Think about it. Do you really want that person to practice on your website business?

Finally, follow your gut. What was your impression of the web designer when you talked to him on the phone? Did you get a good feeling about him? Did he seem like someone you would enjoy working with? Did you get a good sense that he is competent, helpful, reputable, professional—and damn good at what he does?

Take your time and hire the right designer the first time. Because it will take you a lot longer to get your web-based business up and running if you have to replace a web designer midway through the project.

Getting a Project Quote

Once you've selected a web designer, it's time to talk about money. You need to get at least a ballpark estimate as to how much the design work on your website is going to cost.

While some web designers charge by the hour, the majority will quote you a project price. That price will include all the work that the designer has described to you in the *project scope*.

def•i•ni•tion

A **project scope** is a description of the work that needs to be done for a specific project. For a website, a project scope may include the creation of an initial design template, the laying out of a specific number of pages, the installation of a shopping cart program, and so forth. This information is used primarily by the web designer to provide you with a project price estimate. Any work that falls outside the project scope is typically subject to an additional charge.

I suggest you clearly communicate to the designer exactly what work you need done. Tell him or her about:

- Any special images you need developed, such as illustrations or photography.

- Whether a new logo for the website masthead is required. (Don't assume a web designer will create one of these for you.)

- The number of web pages that need to be created.

- Special pages that require additional design or customization beyond the basic design template, such as checkout pages.

- The payment system that needs to be installed and tested on the site.

- Special features that need to be installed, such as blogs and forums.

- Anything else you expect the designer to do for you.

Don't assume anything. Be sure your designer knows exactly what you want him to do—the project scope—so that he can provide you with an accurate quotation. If there is a misunderstanding on this point, it may result in additional fees later on.

In addition to getting a fee quote, you should also request a project schedule with expected completion dates for design concepts, design revisions, creation of a test site, and so forth.

Working With Your Web Designer

You've hired a web designer! Now you can sit back and relax while your site is being professionally created. Right? Wrong. Sure, the designer is going to be doing a lot of work on your behalf. That's why you hired a professional. However, you do need to play an active role.

The first thing a designer is going to do is come up with two or three concepts of the basic website template for you to review. (You can learn more about templates in Chapter 9.) Chances are, these will look nearly complete and be shown to you either as a PDF or on a web page (often called a *beta site*). The idea is to give you a clear idea of what your website is going to look like.

def•i•ni•tion

A **beta site** is a special web address where your website resides during the design phase until it's finished and ready to go live. A beta site is often hosted on the web designer's own website or a special site specifically for this purpose. A beta site allows you to view and interact with your website, and request changes and revisions, until it's finished.

For example, when I first got my web-based business site designed, I sent my web designer a list of websites that I thought were particularly effective, along with notes explaining what I liked and didn't like about each. This helped him avoid much of the guesswork and provide me with a couple of great concepts that I really liked.

At this point in the process, it's perfectly okay to request changes and revisions, even if they are major. So if you're unhappy with the design of the masthead, size of the text, placement of images, color of the headlines, or any other element of your site, say so. The web designer may disagree with you, and a good designer will tell you why. If you think his or her suggestions are sound, by all means follow them. However, at the end of the day, it's your website. Make sure it's exactly what you want.

The Least You Need to Know

- Clarify the purpose of your website, the look and feel you want for it, and the ingredients that are required to make it work.

- Create a site plan that contains all the planned pages and links.

- Select a web designer with care. Then work closely with that person or firm while your website is being created.

Chapter 9

Building Your Website Yourself (Or with a Little Help)

In This Chapter

- ◆ Creating and working with a website template
- ◆ Making it easy with ready-made templates
- ◆ Taking advantage of site-builder programs

Are you a do-it-yourselfer? If you want to build your own website, you'll need to learn the basics of creating a website template, and working with it to place your text, images, and other needed elements (such as sign-up forms). You can create an original template from scratch using a good web design program. Or take advantage of one of thousands of ready-made templates available online.

Your ultimate goal, of course, is to create a website that looks great, works great, and sends the right message to your potential customers.

Doing It Yourself from Scratch

When I created my first website many years ago, there weren't many ready-made templates available. And I didn't have the budget to hire a professional web designer, who in those days were very expensive. So I attempted to design the thing on my own.

I admit, I was like a homeowner building a backyard deck for the first time. I was all thumbs. I used Microsoft FrontPage as my web design software and did the best I could. It took me a long time just to figure out how the software worked! In the end, my website looked okay—but far from the professional look I was striving to achieve.

As you'll discover later in this chapter, I suggest you use a ready-made template to create your website. Especially if you don't have a lot of design experience. You'll save yourself a lot of time, and your website will look better.

However, if you have web design experience, and you feel comfortable with creating your own website from scratch, then by all means do so. It will take you many hours of work, but you'll save money.

A caveat: be honest with yourself regarding your design and layout talent. Some people have the innate ability to create effective layouts and design while others, frankly, don't. I've seen many websites designed by do-it-yourselfers that look amateurish. Not many people will trust a site like that enough to type in their credit card information and place an order!

Web Design Software

To design your own website from scratch, you need good web design software. The most popular are:

- Adobe Dreamweaver (www.adobe.com/products/dreamweaver)
- Microsoft Expression Web (www.microsoft.com/expression) (The replacement for Microsoft FrontPage.)
- Adobe GoLive (www.adobe.com/products/golive)
- CoffeeCup (www.coffeecup.com)
- Web Studio 4.0 (www.webstudio.com)
- PersonalWebKit (www.personalwebkit.com)
- SiteSell.com (www.sitesell.com)

♦ iBuilt (www.ibuilt.net)

♦ Evrsoft First Page (www.evrsoft.com)

The first two on the previous list are used by most professional designers. Dreamweaver and Expression Web are a bit difficult to learn, but once you've mastered the features, you'll be impressed by what you can do.

Some of the others on the list are designed specifically for the novice. SiteSell.com, for example, walks you through the process of building your website and getting it up and running. You don't need any previous web design experience to use it.

Many of these programs also include a variety of professionally designed, ready-made templates that you can take advantage of.

Creating and Using a Website Template

Regardless of which web design software you use, the basics of building a website are relatively simple. Your first step is to create or choose a template, which is the basic layout and design of your website.

If you look closely at other websites, you'll probably notice that each page has many of the same elements. Take a look at ForGraphicDesignersOnly.com, for example. You'll see that each page has the same logo and navigation bar along the top and the same thin column down the right side (which contains a sign-up form for the e-mail newsletter). The only thing that changes when you click around is the text in the thicker main column.

That's an example of a simple yet very effective website template.

Although a website may contain dozens or even hundreds of pages, it may only use one or two templates. (Some websites have a slightly different template for their inside pages than they do for their home page.)

So the first step in building your site is to create or select the template. This is usually comprised of a *masthead*, a thick column for the main text of the page, and one or two other thinner columns.

*Screen shot of http://
forgraphicdesignersonly.com.*

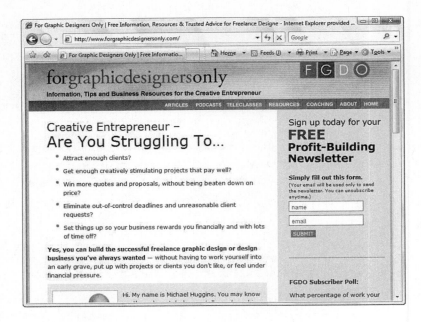

def•i•ni•tion

In web design lingo, a **masthead** is the area that runs horizontally across the top of the page and typically contains the business name and logo, and sometimes also the navigation bar. A column is an area that runs vertically below the masthead. Typically, there is a thick column for the main text of the page, and one or two thinner columns for the navigation bar, advertisements, and other information. However, there are a lot of variations!

How do you decide which basic template structure will work best?

Think about the types of information you need to present on your site. If, for example, you have just a few products or services, then you may only need one or two columns. If, however, you plan to feature a catalog of products, or if you need space to place affiliate advertisements, then you might need two or even three columns.

You may be a brave do-it-yourselfer. And if you are, I applaud you for it! But I suggest that you hire a professional designer to, at least, create the masthead for you. While you can probably create the basic template structure on your own, and learn to place text and images effectively, the masthead design requires a professional's touch.

Take a look at ForGraphicDesignersOnly.com once again. Notice that it's the masthead that has the most impact on how the site looks. Now imagine if that masthead looked plain or amateurish. That would be a serious turn-off for potential customers (who, by the way, are all designers)!

The topic of web design is a book in itself. I suggest *The Complete Idiot's Guide to Creating a Website* (Alpha, 2008).

Once you have your basic template created and designed, your next step is to fill in the text, images, and other elements of your site.

Working With Text

Text is the voice of your website, so it's important to make it easy to read. After all, if a potential customer has difficulty reading your web copy, he's not going to learn about all your wonderful products or services and place an order.

Your first step is to select the right font, font size, and color.

Font refers to the style of type used to create the text. Your word processing program, for example, probably has Times New Roman or Arial as the default font. Although there are literally hundreds of fonts to choose from, I suggest you use Verdana or Arial. Studies have proved that these are the easiest to read on the Internet.

Font size, of course, concerns the size of the font. This is tricky because most Internet web browsers, like Foxfire, allow users to adjust the size of the text for optimum readability. Ideally, you want your website copy to be the print-equivalent of at least 10pt for the main body copy and 12pt, 14pt, or 18pt for the headlines. Your web design software may use a numerical system of 2, 3, 4, and 5 to denote these font sizes. Be sure to check.

As for font colors, the best are black or dark gray for the main text. For some reason, I find that dark gray looks more gentle and eye-friendly, and therefore more inviting to read. Red and blue are effective for headlines.

Warning!

Choose the background color for the main text area of your web page carefully. Darker colors can make the text difficult to see and read. The rule of thumb is black or dark gray text against a white or light beige background. Also, avoid using fancy designs or pictures as backgrounds to text areas on a page. That's never a good idea!

One final tip. Always left justify your text—which means the text is aligned straight on the left and jagged on the right. Full justification, with both sides aligned straight, can work well in some print communications—but never on the web.

A Picture Is Worth a Thousand Words

You want to place a big picture of a smiling woman on your product page. Why? Because it looks great! But is that a good enough reason to use that image?

Eye path studies prove that the attention of website visitors are naturally drawn to a picture or other image on the page. If that graphic doesn't help to explain something more clearly, tell the story better, enhance the presentation of the information, or otherwise help communicate what you're trying to say in your web copy, then don't use it. It will only be a distraction.

That being said, how do you work with images?

Your first step is to source the images you want to use on your website. You can get stock pictures and clip art from a variety of sources on the web. I suggest checking out comstock.com, stockvault.com, and freephotosweb.com for stock pictures and clipart. com and office.microsoft.com/clipart for clip art.

You can also capture images yourself with a digital camera or scanner.

Success Tip

In web design, the most common formats for images are GIF (Graphic Interchange Format) and JPEG (Joint Photographic Experts Group). Both formats are compressed versions of the image so that it downloads quickly to the web page. JPEG is preferred for large photos and complex illustrations. GIFs are ideal for simpler images such as banners that contain only a background color and some text.

The process of placing the images where you want them on a web page varies from one web building software to another. Some make it easy by providing you with a simple Insert Image command that places your image where you indicate on the page. Other programs require you to type in the HTML code or select the appropriate CSS command.

I use WordPress (a web builder software) for one of my websites, which has an Insert Image feature. It works like this:

◆ Position your cursor in the text where you want your image placed.

◆ Click on the **Add an Image** icon on the toolbar.

◆ In the pop-up box that appears, click **Choose Files to Upload.**

◆ Select the appropriate image file on your computer. Once uploaded, you will see the image in the pop-up box.

◆ Use the tools in the pop-up box to edit your picture. You can adjust the size, add a border, make it clickable to another page, add a caption, and more.

◆ Click **Save All Changes.**

Once the image is placed on the page, you can fine-tune how it looks by clicking **Insert/Edit Image.**

Other web builder programs allow you to work with images in a similar fashion.

Making Your Site Easy to Navigate

You want to make the information on your site easy for the website visitor to locate. The last thing you want is for a potential customer to get frustrated trying to find a particular product and then leave. You've just lost a sale!

Start with your navigation bar. The navigation link titles should be clear and descriptive. If your website sells products, for example, then you should have a link that's called simply "Products" or "Store." Don't be cryptic with navigation link titles!

The best location for your navigation bar is either across the top of your page directly under the masthead, or down the side in the left column. Don't place it on the right or at the bottom of your page. People might have trouble finding it.

When it comes to text links, avoid being creative. Website visitors have an expectation of what is "clickable" and what isn't. We all know that if a line of text is underlined or is bright blue (or both) then it's probably a link. Make yours like that. Don't try to be a rebel by making your links green. Conform!

Making It Easy with Ready-Made Templates

One of the most popular options for getting a website created is using ready-made templates.

A website template is a website design that is virtually ready-to-go. All that's required is for you to type in your company name in the masthead and add the web copy for all the pages you need. You can add pictures and other images, too. Then you're done!

Typically, a website template comes with a home page and several inside pages pre-formatted for various functions—product descriptions, about us, contacts, etc. A product page in a template, for example, might have a spot allocated for a product picture, and dummy text placed for a headline and description.

Finding the right website template is like shopping for a house in a new home development. You walk around the showroom looking at all the home designs on the wall and pick the one closest to your needs. You do the same thing when shopping for a template. You review all the templates available, make a shortlist of those that best fit your needs—based on the plan you developed in Chapter 8—then make your selection.

There is no shortage of websites that sell templates. Here is a list to get you started.

Warning!

Don't assume that a website template is a great design. There are thousands of templates for sale on the Internet, and not all of them are effectively designed and laid out. In fact, many templates available are several years old and out-of-date. It's the online equivalent of wearing a thick necktie from the 1970s! Shop carefully. Make sure the template you select looks modern and professional.

- ◆ Template Monster (www.templatemonster.com)
- ◆ The Template Store (www.thetemplatestore.com)
- ◆ WebSiteTemplates.bz (www.websitetemplates.bz)
- ◆ PixelMill (www.pixelmill.com)
- ◆ Dream Template (www.dreamtemplate.com)

Most of the web design software listed earlier in this chapter also includes a gallery of templates.

Some templates are specifically designed for a specific web design program. For example, you can purchase a template that works with Adobe Dreamweaver, Microsoft

Expression Web, or WordPress. You simply follow the instructions to import the template design into the software program and then add in your text and images.

One of the main drawbacks of a template is it's just that—a template. It's not a website created just for you. It's a compromise between what you want and the template designs available on the market.

Templates can, of course, be customized with your own logo, web copy, and pictures. But if you want to significantly change the fundamental design elements—the color schemes, the column widths, and so forth, it's very difficult to do that on your own. In fact, it's discouraged.

That's where a freelance web designer can help. He or she can take your template and, to a degree, customize it the way you want. This is a cost-effective alternative to hiring a designer to build a website for you from scratch.

Taking Advantage of Special Site Builder Programs

Some of the major companies that cater to the needs of web-based business owners, such as GoDaddy and Yahoo! Small Business, offer their customers online site builder programs. Typically, these programs include easy-to-use web design software and a wide range of templates.

GoDaddy's WebSite Tonight product, for example, is one of the most robust. And it's fairly typical of other site builder programs. Here's how it works:

- ◆ You begin by filling in an online form, which includes a series of questions that tell the system what type of site you want to create.

- ◆ The system automatically creates the home page and inside pages you need, along with other required elements.

- ◆ You select from a range of templates available.

- ◆ You customize the template colors.

- ◆ You upload any images you want placed on your website, including your logo. (WebSite Tonight gives you free access to a gallery of more than 8,000 images. Isn't that handy!)

- ◆ You drop in the text and format it using the tools provided. Like a good word processing program, Website Tonight offers a full range of formatting options: bullets, highlights, numbered lists, links, the works.

- The system walks you through the process of optimizing your site for the search engines.

- You do a final check of your site to make sure it looks great and functions correctly.

- You upload your site using one of GoDaddy's web hosting plans. Now it's live!

Website Tonight also lets you easily insert special website features such as blogs, forums, sound, and video.

Can you really get a website up tonight, as GoDaddy's web builder product suggests? You can, if you have everything else done in advance, such as sourcing your images and writing your web copy. But, depending on the complexity of your site, it might be a long night!

Other web hosting companies that offer website builder programs and services include:

- iPowerWeb (www.ipowerweb.com)

- Act Now Domains (www.actnowdomains.com)

- Pro Website Group (www.prowebsitegroup.com)

- Network Solutions (www.networksolutions.com)

- VodaHost (www.vodahost.com)

- Yahoo! Small Business (http://smallbusiness.yahoo.com)

Keep in mind that building your website isn't a one-time event. To stay competitive, respond to changes in your marketplace, and improve the effectiveness of your site, you're going to be continuously updating, changing, and tweaking your website.

So get good at it!

The Least You Need to Know

- Familiarize yourself with the basics of creating and using a template before building your site.

- Consider taking advantage of ready-made templates. It sure makes building a site a lot easier!

- There are many web design software programs available that make getting a site built a lot easier. Check them out.

Chapter 10

Writing Persuasive Web Copy

In This Chapter

- ◆ The types of copy you need written for your website
- ◆ The basics of writing effective web copy
- ◆ How to work effectively with freelance writers and editors

Recently, a friend of mine was looking for advice on time management for busy self-employed professionals. So she did a Google search and visited several websites that offered coaching programs in this area. There were dozens. She reviewed all the websites carefully, became impressed with one coaching program in particular—"It seemed like the perfect fit for me," she said—and ultimately signed up.

The interesting thing is, she made her purchase without ever talking to anyone. The words on the web pages—the copy—did all the work in making the sale.

There's no doubt about it. The more persuasive your marketing copy, the more products and services you will sell. So it makes sense to learn how to develop the most effective copy possible for your product descriptions, web pages, landing pages, e-mails, sign-up forms, and other elements of your site. This chapter will show you how.

Deciding What You Need Written

You're staring at your website plan, and all you see is a lot of blank pages. You need to get this thing written! Where do you start? Your first step is to understand the kind of web pages and other website elements that you need words for.

Chances are, you've reviewed many different types of commercial websites in your quest to start a successful web-based business. So you've probably noticed that there are basically two types of writing at work.

The first type is called *content*. This includes articles, tips, resources, advice, opinions, and other information that is nonpromotional in nature.

But content alone can't sell a website's products and services. That's where the second type of writing—*copy*—comes in. Copy is the friendly, knowledgeable salesperson of your website. It's the copy that persuades your visitors to click and buy.

In the world of online business, content and copy work together to attract visitors to your website and convert them into customers. People won't stay long on your site, nor are they likely to return, without great content. And those same people are not likely to be motivated to make a purchase without compelling copy.

Content and copy. They are the twin pillars of persuasion for your web-based business.

Success Tip

Customers aren't the only creatures who are attracted to sites with great content. Search engine spiders—those invisible programs sent by search engines to evaluate your website—are also fans. Your site will tend to rank higher in search results if it contains lots of valuable, nonpromotional information. And, of course, the higher your website is listed in the search results of Google, Yahoo!, MSN, or other popular search engines, the more traffic it will get.

Examples of content include free e-mail newsletters, articles, tips, customer forums, blogs, podcasts, online videos, free e-mail courses, success stories of happy customers or clients (sometimes referred to as *case studies*), and free special reports or white papers.

Places where persuasive copy may be required include:

Website home page. This is perhaps the most important page on your site, so it has to be persuasive. It has to assure the first-time visitor that your website has what they're looking for.

Website sales pages (also known as *landing pages*). These are pages that describe your product or service and make a specific pitch to get the website visitor to place an order.

Website sign-up boxes. This is a block of copy designed to motivate a website visitor to sign up for your e-mail newsletter, special report, or other e-mail communication. It doesn't necessarily have to be in a box.

E-mail newsletter advertisements. These are pitches in your e-mail newsletter for specific products, services, and other offers on your website. They don't necessarily need to look like a traditional ad. Some e-mail advertisements are as simple as a headline with a short paragraph of text.

E-mails. These are e-mails that make an announcement or pitch a specific offer. They are sometimes referred to as *solo e-mails* or *solo promos* because, unlike an e-mail newsletter, they are entirely promotional.

Website advertisements and banners. These are advertisements that you place on your website to get visitors to click to your sales pages. They can be as simple as a line of copy with a link or as sophisticated as a banner ad with an embedded video.

Autoresponders. These are e-mails that are sent after a website visitor makes a purchase, and usually contain a pitch to purchase other products.

Pop-ups (and -unders and -overs). These are small screens of information that typically pop up over the web page. Pop-ups are often used to make special offers, such as an invitation to subscribe to an e-newsletter.

And there are other elements of your website that may need effective promotional copy, too.

When planning your website, you need to think about what content and copy you need to develop in order to achieve the results you want. If, for example, you sell exotic Asian tea and related accessories, then you may need a persuasive sales page for each product, an e-mail advertisement, and an autoresponder e-mail to upsell buyers to a tea-of-the-month subscription.

To keep visitors interested in your website, you may also need great content in the form of an e-mail newsletter featuring articles on the Asian tea scene, tea reviews, trivia, and more.

Content and copy—they work together!

It's All About the Features and Benefits, Folks

When you're writing web copy to promote a product or service, you're basically presenting its features and benefits.

What are those?

Ask an audience of Internet marketers what a product *feature* is versus a *benefit* and you're likely to get dozens of answers, some of them contradictory! I know because I often do this exercise in my own seminars.

The simplest and most useful definition is as follows:

- A *feature* is the answer to the question: What is it?

- A *benefit* is the answer to the question: So what?

When you're writing copy to promote your website product or service, you're basically describing all the things it is or has—the features; and then explaining what those features actually *do* for the customer—the benefits.

Success Tip

When writing web copy, focus on the prospect, not just on the product. Customers are ultimately interested in what's in it for them. So no matter how amazing you think the product features are, if you don't translate those features into meaningful benefits to customers, then your chances of motivating very many of them to place an order online are low.

Here's an example:

Say you're planning a website, SilkySheets.com, that will sell high-end bedsheets at discount prices. Your most expensive sheet has 300 threads per inch. That's a feature; an answer to "What is it?" But that's not nearly enough to motivate a customer to place an order. You need to present her with a benefit, an answer to the question:

"So what?" Hmm. Three hundred threads per inch. So what? Well, the dense thread count makes the sheet more tear-resistant and durable. Therefore, it will last longer. That's the benefit!

So keeping all that in mind, you might write:

> *Our line of luxurious Amore Linens are woven with a minimum of 300 threads per inch [feature], making them tear-resistant and durable. That means your sheets will not fade [benefit] and not require replacement for several years [benefit].*

When writing copy, keep asking yourself "What is it?" and "So what?" over and over again. If you craft your web copy by providing compelling answers to those two questions, you can't go wrong.

Making Your F&B List

One of the easiest ways to ensure that you write effective copy is to create a simple features and benefits list for your product, service, or offer. An F&B list, as I like to call it, makes the writing process a lot faster, ensures you don't miss anything, and keeps your copy focused on all the compelling reasons why a customer should say "Yes!"

Making an F&B list is easy. Just create two columns on a piece of paper or on your computer. At the top of the left column, write "Feature" and in brackets next to it, "What is it?" Then put "Benefit" at the top of the right column, and next to that, "So what?"

Now comes the fun part! In the left column, list all the features you can think of for your product, service, or offer. Then, in the right column, answer the question "So what?" by writing the benefits of each corresponding feature.

Here's an example of a features and benefits list for a website that sells custom embroidered sweaters.

Success Tip

How long should your copy be? As long as it needs to be to tell the complete story of your product's features and benefits. Don't shortchange the effectiveness of your web page or e-mail advertisement just to make the copy short! You must convey all the information the customer needs to learn about your offer, be motivated to make a decision, and place the order.

Features and Benefits List for Custom Embroidered Sweaters

Feature ("What Is It?")	Benefit ("So What?")
Handmade by "Association of Knitting Professionals" certified knitters.	High-quality workmanship. Won't lose shape.
Custom embroidered.	Great idea for a gift. Your personal "one of a kind" sweater.
Free delivery.	No extra fees when you order.
All sizes available.	Customers won't be disappointed.
High-quality wool used.	Sweater will last long. Looks great for years. Won't easily wear out. More comfortable.

As you can see, once you've created a features and benefits list, the copy practically writes itself. Well, almost! In fact, most copywriting is simply a process of explaining a feature, touting its benefits, then moving on to the next feature.

Gaining Attention with Great Headlines

Unless you're reading this book very early in the morning, you have already been inundated with newsletter advertisements, e-mails, radio ads, billboards, website banner ads, and a myriad of other marketing messages all vying for your attention. The competition for the hearts (and wallets) of the online buyer is huge. That's why it's so important that your website pages and e-mails gain attention and motivate people to read the copy.

Think about it. If no one reads your web copy, then few people will learn about your products and services and be persuaded to make a purchase.

How do you gain attention? Effective *headlines*.

A couple of years ago, for example, I was asked by a client to improve an e-mail newsletter advertisement. The ad was getting about 10 to 15 clicks each time he placed it in his bi-weekly newsletter. Not great. After studying the ad, I decided to make just one change: the headline. In his next issue, clicks on the advertisement tripled and, subsequently, so did his product sales.

def•i•ni•tion

A **headline** isn't just a big block of text in an advertisement. In online marketing, a headline can be the subject line of an e-mail, subheads placed within the main body copy of a web page, the words in a small text box or callout, or any other line of copy primarily designed to gain attention and motivate website visitors to read on.

How do you write an effective headline?

The best headlines convey a benefit of some kind. That could be a solution to a problem, an offer for a discount, a fulfillment of an aspiration, or any other message that meets our definition of a benefit as discussed in the previous section.

Take a look at this headline, for example:

> *Discover the Techniques Thousands of Infertile Couples Have Used to Get Pregnant When Doctors Said They Couldn't*

This headline, written by my friend and fellow copywriter Bob Bly, packs a big promise of benefit. It is saying that if you read on, you'll discover proven techniques for getting pregnant. My wife and I faced this challenge years ago and, I can assure you, that headline would have gained our attention!

The best way to come up with headline ideas is to brainstorm. Dream up as many possibilities as possible—use your imagination! Then whittle that list down to two or three good possibilities. Here are some ideas to get you started:

- Use the words "how to" or "discover." Example: *How to attract more clients— quickly and easily.*

- Use a customer testimonial. Example: *"I love SalonSensations.net. I can buy the leading hair salon products online and get them delivered free to my home!"*

- Make a compelling offer. Example: *May we add a second HP LaserJet replacement cartridge to your order for half price?*

- Tell the website visitor that he's in the right place. Example: *Looking for unbiased product reviews of home exercise equipment? You've come to the right place.*

- Provide helpful advice. Example: *5 proven ways to prevent the onset of a migraine.*

- Make an invitation. Example: *You're invited to an exclusive webinar on how to double the win rate of your sales proposals.*

◆ Remind the reader of a pressing deadline. Example: *The 40% discount on all running shoes ordered online ends at midnight tonight.*

◆ Make a big promise. Example: *Start from scratch and make money selling information products online in less than 3 days.*

◆ Dramatize the problem. Then hint at the solution. Example: *Is adult acne making you look like an embarrassed teenager? Here's a solution that will make you feel like a grown-up again ....*

◆ Say you're number one. Prospects are attracted to the industry leader. Example: *What motivates motivational speakers? ACME EasyPoint presentation pointer is the number one choice among members of the National Speakers Association.*

When evaluating potential headlines, put yourself in your prospect's shoes and ask, "Does this headline motivate me to stay on this web page and learn more about the product?" If your answer is no, or an uncommitted maybe, then go back to the drawing board and come up with a few more alternatives.

Take the time to write a great headline. I promise you, the subsequent increase in sales will make it time well spent.

Using Belief Builders to Overcome Skepticism

Wouldn't it be nice if every advertisement or web page you read were truthful and never deceptive in any way? It would make this section unnecessary! Unfortunately, that's not how things are. People are naturally skeptical about what they read in e-mails, websites, and other marketing communications. And who can blame them? Surf the Internet for five minutes and you're bombarded with a barrage of hype, inflated claims, and outright lies.

So when an honest web-based business owner, like you, makes a product claim that is not substantiated, there is—unfortunately—a nagging element of doubt. Sorry, but a significant percentage of your website visitors just won't believe you.

For example, say your website sells industrial pumps. And you said this in your copy:

We proudly represent ACME industrial pumps, which cost less and last longer. So buy online today to save money and reduce downtime.

The claims made here are "cost less" and "last longer." Hmm. Some of your website visitors may believe you. But many will raise their eyebrows in suspicion. They're thinking, "Do your pumps really cost less and last longer? Who says so? Why should I believe you?"

You have to address this skepticism in your copy. Otherwise, it's going to be very difficult for you to convince the prospect to buy—especially online.

Now let's rewrite the copy to make it more believable:

> *According to tests by the Industrial Fluid Handling Association, ACME pumps last longer than comparable brands. This reduces your downtime. In addition, our catalog price is 22.3% lower than the leading comparable brand, so you save money as well.*

I think you'll agree that this version is much more believable—and therefore much more persuasive. And it's all because we added a couple of *belief builders* to the copy.

We mentioned an independent organization, which added credibility to our claim that the pumps last longer. And we pointed to a specific fact, the listed catalog price, to show our prices are indeed lower.

Belief builders reassure your website visitors that the claims you are making are accurate and make them more comfortable in placing an order. The more of these you have in your web copy, the more persuasive it will be.

def•i•ni•tion

A **belief builder** is anything you add to your web copy to make it more believable to the reader. That could include verifiable facts, customer testimonials, product reviews, endorsements, statistics, surveys, studies, and other evidence that what you're saying in the web copy is true.

Gathering Testimonials

Testimonials of satisfied customers are the most common, and effective, belief builder of them all. Let's face it. Website visitors expect you to be a little biased in the copy. After all, you want to make the sale! But they will trust their fellow customers to tell it like it is.

How do you get customer testimonials? One of the best, and often overlooked, ways is to pay attention to your phone calls and e-mails. Customers who contact you—even when it's to complain!—will sometimes make positive comments about your website or its products and services. When that happens, immediately ask for permission to use what was said as a testimonial. In my experience, most will say yes.

Another way to get customer testimonials is to ask for them. It's easy. Simply make a list of customers who have purchased regularly over the past year. (If they're repeat buyers, there is a good chance they are fans of your site!) Then send them an e-mail requesting that they provide you with a testimonial.

Here's a template you can use.

Subject line: May I ask you for a favor?

Dear _____,

Thank you for being such a valued customer over the past few months. I really appreciate your support.

May I ask you for a favor?

I'm compiling a list of testimonials from satisfied customers like you. Would you please reply to this e-mail and let me know what you think of our website and its products and services?

I look forward to reading your positive comments … but if you have a criticism, I want to know about that, too.

Thank you in advance for helping me out. If you have any questions, don't hesitate to contact me personally.

All the best,

Steve Slauwnhite

Publisher, ForCopywritersOnly.com

Although I receive plenty of unsolicited testimonials from my customers, I also use this technique. It gets a great response. Satisfied customers want to say nice things about your website, if only you would ask them to.

Getting to Yes with the Motivating Sequence

There are a lot of step-by-step formulas for writing effective web copy, but the one that I find works best is *the motivating sequence*.

The motivating sequence was developed by famed copywriter Bob Bly and writing expert Gary Blake. It is easy for the nonwriter to follow and almost always assures that your copy will impact readers and get the results you need.

Here are the steps in the motivating sequence adapted for use in website and e-mail copywriting:

1. Gain attention with a great headline.

2. In the body copy, begin by highlighting the reader's problem or aspiration.

3. Next, bring in your product, service, or offer as the solution to that problem or the means to fulfill that aspiration.

4. Prove the claims you make by using belief builders.

5. Ask for action. That could be anything you are trying to get the reader to do, such as click on a link to more information, fill out an online form to sign up or register, or pull out their credit card to make a purchase.

The motivating sequence is based on tested strategies in persuasive communications. I won't get into all of the psychology of it here; just know that this formula works very well and is used—in one form or another—by many of the top copywriters in the business.

So when you sit down to write a short blurb pitching your website, or an e-mail newsletter advertisement to promote a new product, or a longer sales page to motivate website visitors to click and buy, follow those five simple steps. It will ensure your copy is structured for maximum impact and effectiveness.

Here's an example of the motivating sequence in action on a web page promoting a seminar for freelance writers:

> *How to Earn $75–$125 Per Hour Writing Promotional Materials*
>
> *Do you struggle to earn a decent income from your writing?*
>
> *If so, then take a closer look at copywriting, one of the most lucrative specialties in the freelance writing field. It's not unusual to earn up to $125 per hour handling projects like sales letters, ads, web pages, e-mail promotions, brochures, blogs, and more.*
>
> *So how do you get started?*
>
> *The next PWAC Presents seminar will show you how. Copywriting expert Steve Slaunwhite, author of* The Everything Guide to Writing Copy *and* Start & Run a Copywriting Business, *will teach you:*
>
> - *All the basics of writing effective promotional materials.*
> - *Techniques for rapidly building your portfolio.*

◆ *Who hires freelance copywriters and how to get the work.*

◆ *How to start your copywriting business, part-time or full-time.*

And much more.

According to a recent study by Robert Half & Associates, copywriting ranks among the top 5 in-demand professions of 2007. So, if you love to write—and make good money—this could be your ticket to success.

Only 25 spots are available and this seminar is expected to fill up fast. Click the registration link below to reserve your spot today.

Notice how that web page copy closely follows the motivating sequence? It gains your attention with a compelling headline, highlights the problem in the opening sentence, positions the seminar as the solution to that problem, provides proof by touting the seminar leader's credentials and the independent study, and, finally, tells the reader what to do next.

Want to motivate more website visitors to buy your products and services? Make sure the copy follows the motivating sequence!

Working With Freelance Writers and Editors

There's no getting around it. Writing web copy is damn hard work. It requires planning, brainstorming, writing, editing, polishing, and, sometimes, writing some more! You can expect to spend two to eight hours crafting a basic website sales page. So it makes sense to consider working with a freelance writer or editor to help you get the job done faster—and better.

You can work with a freelancer to write the entire site for you from scratch. In this case, she would interview you, review the information you provide about your website and its products and services, and then write a draft of the web copy for your review. After that, it's back and forth with revisions until the copy is complete.

Another alternative is to write a rough draft of the web copy on your own, and then get a professional copywriter to revise and polish it for you. This is sometimes referred to as a *copy makeover* or *substantive edit*. The writer reviews your rough draft and, as famed television chef Emeril often says, "kicks it up a few notches." You can expect a good writer to revise your headlines, tighten the text, move things around, take things out, add things in, and do anything else necessary to create an effective polished draft of your web copy.

A copy makeover is cheaper than a write-from-scratch job, usually by 50 to 75 percent. So it's an ideal option when you're starting your web-based business on a tight budget.

And speaking of fees, there are a lot of writers out there who are willing to work for peanuts. However, they often don't have the skills or experience to do a decent job on your web copy. You'll be disappointed and may have to get the job done all over again by someone more qualified. So resist the urge to go with a freelancer charging bargain-basement rates. As the saying goes: you get what you pay for.

> **Success Tip**
>
> Freelance writers who specialize in writing sales and marketing copy are often called copywriters. So when you're looking for help developing copy for your website and e-mails, making sure the professional you hire refers to himself or herself as copywriter is a good place to start.

Where to Look

If you plan on hiring a freelance writer to help you write or revise your website pages and e-mails, I highly suggest you select someone who has a demonstrated ability to craft effective marketing communications. A would-be novelist may be able to write well, but can she create an e-mail newsletter article that generates clickthroughs or a sales page that actually does sell? You want someone with demonstrated skills and experience writing the type of web copy that captivates your website visitors and motivates them to buy.

Where do you find such writers? There are several websites that can help you:

◆ Elance (www.elance.com)

◆ Guru.com (www.guru.com)

◆ DirectResponseJobs.com (www.directresponsejobs.com)

◆ ASJA Freelance WriterSearch (www.freelancewritersearch.com)

◆ Writers.ca (www.writers.ca)

◆ iFreelance (www.ifreelance.com)

◆ SoloGig (www.sologig.com)

◆ GoFreelance (www.gofreelance.com)

Many of these sites provide you with the means to post your project description and invite bids and inquiries from qualified writers.

Another way to find a good writer is to tap your network. Contact friends and colleagues and ask them if they know of a good web copywriter. Chances are, you'll get several excellent recommendations.

The Least You Need to Know

- ◆ Effective copy is essentially a presentation of the features and benefits of your website and its products and services.

- ◆ Gain attention with great headlines.

- ◆ Online shoppers are skeptical. Make sure you prove all the claims you make in your copy using belief builders.

- ◆ Use the motivating sequence to structure your web copy for maximum readability and persuasion.

- ◆ Consider hiring a qualified freelance copywriter to help you.

Chapter 11

Selecting a Web Host and Going Live

In This Chapter

◆ Understanding the role a web host plays in the success of your business

◆ How to find the best web host for your website

◆ Signing up with the right plan and additional features

If you were starting a traditional retail store, one of the most important decisions you would need to make is leasing the right space. You'd want to make sure that you have plenty of room for your inventory and displays, and that the services provided to you—lighting, maintenance, utilities, special features—support the success of your business.

In the online world, the equivalent is your choice of web host. You want to make sure the web hosting provider you select is able to give you the services you need at a price that fits your budget. This chapter will help you make the right decision.

What Does a Web Host Do?

You've worked hard to plan your website and get it created. The design is magnificent. The copy is great. All the links have been checked and go where they are supposed to go. Your new website looks and works wonderfully—on your computer! But how the heck do you get it to display on the Internet?

That's where a *web host* comes in.

A web host is a service that provides and maintains computer *servers* that are permanently linked to the Internet. When you sign up with a web host, you are allotted a certain amount of space on its server for your website. It's a little like leasing retail space in a shopping mall. Once you upload your website files into that rented space, it becomes live on the Internet to a world of potential visitors and customers. You're in business!

def•i•ni•tion

A **server** is basically a computer with a massive memory that stores multiple computer files and programs. A **web host** company can have several servers in its facilities, each hosting dozens of websites like yours.

A web host is important to your business because it is, literally, your connection to your customers. If something goes wrong with your web hosting company and your website is no longer displaying on the Internet, then your entire business comes to a grinding halt. People can't see your site. Transactions can't occur. For all intents and purposes, your business ceases to exist—at least from the prospective of a customer.

So the web host you select must be reliable and provide you with all the services you need to launch your business and support its growth throughout the years.

How to Find a Web Host

When I launched my first website many years ago, I signed up with the first web hosting company I could find that offered hosting at a decent price. The company was local, so I also figured I'd be able to easily get the support I needed when I needed it. I got lucky. That particular web host turned out to be an excellent choice. But I wouldn't suggest you select your hosting service in the same casual way I did. It's too important of a decision.

Take your time and explore the numerous web hosting services available that cater to small web-based businesses. Here is a list of popular companies to consider:

- Web.com (www.web.com)

- Verio (www.verio.com)

- BlueHost (www.bluehost.com)

- 1&1 (www.1and1.com)

- Globat (www.globat.com)

- IPower (www.ipower.com)

- Hostway (www.hostway.com)

- GoDaddy (www.godaddy.com)

- Lunarpages (www.lunarpages.com)

- StartLogic (www.startlogic.com)

- HostMonster (www.hostmonster.com)

- Dot5 Hosting (www.dot5hosting.com)

- IX Web Hosting (www.ixwebhosting.com)

- Network Solutions (www.networksolutions.com)

When you visit these sites, you might be overwhelmed by the range of additional services that some of these companies offer to web-based business owners. In addition to basic web hosting, many of these sites also pitch e-mail services, domain name registration, website design, and even small business advice. It makes sense to explore these extra services. But first, you need to keep your eye on the prize. You want a web host that is proven to be reliable and that offers the web hosting services you need to grow your business.

Warning!

Don't be tempted by low-cost or free web hosting services. These companies have to keep costs down somehow to offer bargain-basement prices, and often what gets sacrificed is reliability and customer support. You might find that your website is down more often than you would like or that you can't reach anyone in the support department when something goes wrong. Issues like these can kill the success of your business. As the saying goes, you get what you pay for.

The most important feature to consider in a web host is the space available. As I said earlier, you are essentially reserving a certain amount of computer memory on a web host's server. And you want to make sure it's enough memory to accommodate your website. Remember, as your business grows, you'll be adding pages, images, and additional features to your website, as well as getting increasingly greater numbers of visitors and online transactions. You want to make sure your website has plenty of elbowroom on that server to accommodate your soon-to-be thriving online business.

How much space do you need? If you plan to offer a range of products on your website, and accept payments online, then I suggest you select a hosting plan that gives you at least 100 GB (gigabytes) of memory. This will give you plenty of space to launch a robust website and accommodate future growth.

Another feature that's important for you to consider is the amount of allowable "data transfer" you need. When someone visits your website (which resides on your web host's server), data is transferred to that visitor's web browser to display the pages, just like the cable company delivering TV shows to your television screen. Many web hosting plans set limits on how much data can be transferred per month—and will charge you extra when you exceed that limit.

Warning!

Do you plan to have a lot of high-resolution pictures or other graphics on your website? Will your customers be buying digital products and downloading them from a web page on your site? Then you will need to make sure you get a high data transfer limit from your web hosting company to handle the load.

Data transfer is like the doorway to your website, and the wider that door is the more people you can let in at any given time. As your business grows, you want your website to be able to handle more and more traffic (because that, of course, means more and more customers!). So a generous data transfer limit is important.

Data transfer is usually expressed as an amount of gigabytes or megabytes per month. For a basic e-commerce website, I suggest ensuring you have at least 1,000 GB transfer.

Here is a list of other things you need to consider when selecting a web hosting service.

Uptime. No web host can guarantee that your website will be up and running on the Internet 100 percent of the time. But you do want to select a company that comes pretty darn close! GoDaddy, for example, assures its customers a 99.9 percent uptime.

CGI Bin. This is a special file that your web host should include with your web host package that allows you to install special programs and scripts. It's standard on most web hosting plans. Still, you want to make sure it has been included in the plan you select.

SSL Certificates. If you plan to accept credit cards directly from your website (see Chapter 12), then you will need to obtain an SSL Certificate from your web host. SSL stands for Secure Socket Layer Encryption, which is the standard in online transaction security. Most web hosts include it free in their hosting plans. Others charge extra. Be sure to check.

MySQL. Increasingly, many database applications such as membership lists and content management systems that you may want to run on your website require MySQL. Make sure your web host offers this capability. And, if so, find out if you have to pay extra for it.

Easy set-up wizard. If you plan to upload your website yourself and, as your business grows, other pages and updates, too, you want to make it as easy as possible. After all, you're an entrepreneur, not a computer geek! (My apologizes if you do happen to be very computer savvy.) That's why an intuitive set-up wizard is important. It should take you by the hand and walk you through the process of uploading and updating your site step-by-step.

E-mail accounts. Most web hosts provide you with the ability to have an e-mail address that includes your company name, such as yourname@yourcompany.com. However, there are still a few that don't. So make sure the web host you select offers e-mail accounts, and find out how many you get. Most web hosting plans provide you with at least five e-mail accounts. You may need more, however, if you intend to have a larger staff.

Automatic data backup. What happens if the web host server that contains your website gets damaged or attacked by a virus? Your website could be wiped off the Internet in seconds. You should, of course, make sure that you have a copy of your website on your own computer ready to upload should disaster strike. However, your web host should have a backup system in place. Check.

Support. If you run into difficulties with your website, will you get the help you need when you need it? Take a close look at the web host's support services. How easy is it to submit a support request? What is their response turnaround time? Does the web host provide an option for reaching a human being?

Review potential web hosts carefully because you want to make the right choice the first time. It's not impossible to switch to another web host if you're unhappy with your first selection, but it can be a hassle.

Virtual Dedicated and Dedicated Servers

So far we've been talking about the most popular web hosting option for small business owners: shared hosting. That's like leasing store space in a shopping mall with lots of other retailers. But if you expect your website to generate a lot of traffic very quickly, or if your website is particularly large and requires lots of server space, or both, then you may want to consider either a virtual dedicated server or a dedicated server.

A virtual dedicated server is similar to shared hosting except that special software is used to create an operating environment that is isolated from the other websites hosted on that same machine. With me so far? You're still in the shopping mall, but now you have the big box store on the end. A virtual dedicated server allows you to handle more traffic and website files, and to run website applications that may not be compatible with a traditional shared hosting plan.

A dedicated server is just that: dedicated. The server hosts your website and no one else's. It's like owning the shopping mall. Since this means you'll have access to lots of memory, and probably unlimited data transfer, too, your website will be able to handle almost any amount of website visitors, transactions, and downloads. There are benefits galore in signing up for a dedicated server but, as you'll learn in the next section, it sure ain't cheap!

Success Tip

If you're just starting out in your web-based business, start with a good shared hosting plan. You'll save a lot of money that way. Then, as your business grows and requires more server space and data transfer, you can easily move up to a more expensive virtual dedicated or dedicated server plan later on.

Most small web-based businesses can do just fine on a shared hosting plan. I have several websites that operate this way and I've never run into difficulties—even though I get plenty of traffic, accept online transactions, have download pages for audio products that require a lot of server space, and have over 100 pages per site.

Selecting the Right Hosting Plan

Few web hosts offer a single plan. Most, in fact, will pitch you a range of hosting plans to choose from—and it's not always easy to make the right decision.

GoDaddy.com, for example, offers three shared hosting options: Economy Plan, Deluxe Plan, and Unlimited Plan. The main difference between the three is the amount of server memory you get for your website—the space—and the amount of data transfer allowed per month. There are some other differences, too, mainly involving extras such as the number of e-mail accounts and the ability to host multiple websites with the same account.

GoDaddy's options are fairly typical of most web hosting companies that target small online business owners. How do you decide which hosting plan is right for you? I recommend that you review your hosting needs using the information provided in the previous section, match those needs to the hosting packages available, and then select the *next higher* option. That's right. Get more hosting than you think you'll need. Chances are, you'll need that additional elbowroom and other capabilities as your web-based business grows.

Web hosting plans, especially for shared hosting, is a very competitive market. Everyone is clamoring to offer the most attractive price. Keep in mind, however, that the reliability and features of your web host are the most important buying criteria for you to consider. Price comes second.

Pricing for a shared hosting plan can range from as little as $5 per month to up to $25 per month. The average for a good web host service hovers around $15.

Virtual server hosting plans are quite a bit higher—typically, $45 to $125 per month.

Success Tip

You can save money by purchasing an annual, rather than monthly, web hosting plan. Most web host companies offer discounts of up to 25 percent when you pay for a year of hosting, or multiple years. Depending on the web host and the hosting plan you select, that can translate into hundreds of dollars in savings.

And the crème-de-la-crème of all hosting plans, the dedicated server, will run you at least $100 per month, and in some cases up to $750 per month.

Pay close attention to potential extra charges. Many hosting companies will hit your pocketbook for more money when you go over your monthly data transfer limit, need an SSL certificate, require additional server memory, and so forth. So review the price structure of the hosting plan you're considering closely. Know exactly what your costs are going to be.

Uploading Your Site

Once you've selected a hosting package, the sign-up process is relatively straightforward. Typically you pay for the package online, then receive an e-mail with instructions as to how to log-in to your account. Once you do that, most good web host services will walk you through the process of uploading your website.

By uploading, I mean the transferring of your website files from your computer to the web host's server. The actual process of doing this varies depending on the web host you've selected and the software you (or your web designer) used to create your website.

Success Tip

Don't want to upload your website on your own? Ask your web designer to do the job for you. For a web designer, uploading a website is as simple as cropping a picture. She can do it with one hand tied behind her back. So if a web designer helped you create your website, get him or her to upload it for you as well. This will save you a lot of time and frustration.

Most web hosts accept website files via a File Transfer Protocol (FTP) program. This is basically a program that takes your website files and puts them in the right place, in the right way, on the web host's server.

If you've created your website in a popular design program such as ExpressionWeb, Adobe GoLive, or Dreamweaver, then the FTP program is already included. If the website design program you used doesn't have FTP, then you'll need to use a separate FTP program. There are many free and low-cost FTP programs available online. Check out www.filezilla.com, www.cuteftp.com, or www.goftp.com.

When uploading a website to a web host using FTP, you typically need the following information.

♦ Your website URL. For example, thewealthlyfreelancer.com.

♦ The username and password for your hosting account. This is provided to you by the web host.

♦ The FTP host. That's the address of the web host server and, like your username and password, it's provided to you by the web hosting company.

♦ The host directory. That's exactly where on the web host's server your website files will be organized. The hosting company will give you that information.

There may be other information that the web host will require as well. Most web hosting companies do a very good job of idiot proofing the process by walking you through the uploading procedures step-by-step. Many even provide an FTP program if you don't have one.

Making Sure Everything Works

Congratulations. You've selected a web host and uploaded your website. Now your web-based business is up and running.

Well, not quite yet. Your website might be on the Internet. But you still have to test it to make sure everything is working correctly.

First, type your website address into your web browser. Do you see your website? If not, don't panic. Although newly updated websites usually appear almost instantly on the Internet, that doesn't always happen. Sometimes it can take a few hours, or even as long as a day or two, for your website to become available to everyone in the world to see. There's a technical term called *propagation delay*, which basically means that it can take some time for information about your new website to find its way around the online world.

Another common reason why your website may not display after you've uploaded it is that your intended front page doesn't have the */index* file extension. Ever wonder how your web browser knows which page to display first when you type a website address? It looks for the page with */index* as its extension and shows that first. If your front page doesn't have that extension, it won't display. This is a very easy fix. In fact, your web host should be able to do this for you.

Warning!

A website can appear differently in different web browsers, and even in the various versions of the same browser! So when testing your new website, be sure to view it in Internet Explorer, Firefox, and Safari. Those are the most popular web browsers and are all available as a free download.

If your website still isn't displaying on the Internet, make yourself a cup of soothing tea. Relax. I promise you it's all going to work out. Then, contact the web host's support department. They can view your files on their server and figure out what's wrong.

Once your website is showing on the Internet, be sure to check every page—and I mean *every* page—on the site. Check that all images are showing correctly. Check that the layout of each page is as it should be. Check that all the links work and are taking visitors to the right place.

Once you've tested everything and your website is displaying and working correctly, you are truly in business online. Buy yourself a celebratory cappuccino, with extra chocolate sprinkles. You deserve it!

The Least You Need to Know

◆ To get your website online, you need to sign up for a hosting plan with a web host company.

◆ Select your web host company with care. You want to make sure their web hosting services are reliable.

◆ Start with a good shared hosting plan. Then, as your website business grows, consider a virtual dedicated hosting or dedicated hosting plan.

◆ Once your website is online, check it thoroughly to make sure everything is displaying and working correctly.

Part 4

Managing Your Web-Based Business

As a web-based business owner, you're the CEO. And the VP of Finance. And the Sales Manager. And the Shipping Clerk! Chances are, at least in the beginning, you will have to do it all.

The good news is, there are many time-saving tools and strategies that will make managing your business a lot easier. In this part of the book, you'll learn how to accept payments online, deal with product delivery, handle all the nitty-gritty administrative tasks of your business, and use analytics to track how well your website is doing.

Chapter 12

Accepting Payments Online

In This Chapter

◆ Understanding how online transactions work

◆ How to accept major credit cards and other means of payment

◆ Finding the right shopping cart for your web-based business

If you plan to sell something on your website, you have to figure out how the money is going to change hands. Unlike a brick-and-mortar store where your customer can pull out his wallet and peel out the cash, you're dealing with customers virtually. So you have to arrange to be able to accept payments via a major credit card, online money transfer service like PayPal, or another means convenient to your online customer.

Figuring out how best to accept payment can be migraine-inducing for many web-based business owners. You're dealing with banks, online payment services, transactions fees, settlements, reserves, and more. Yikes! Don't despair. This chapter will walk you through the payment alternatives available to you, and the process of setting things up and getting everything working smoothly.

How Online Transactions Work

Someone clicks the **Buy Now** button on your website. (A smile-inducing event for any web-based business owner!) An order is placed. And a couple of days later, the money gets deposited into your bank account—or, at least, most of the money, after the credit card company and other payment processing services have taken out their fees.

How did all that happen?

You don't have to understand the nitty-gritty technological details of how online payments are processed electronically. However, it is a good idea to know the basics.

Let's start with that Buy Now button. When your customer clicks on that, she is typically taken to a website checkout page of some kind. That page confirms all the details of her order and asks for her contact information and payment details. Once that's typed in, the customer clicks a final **Place Order** button and the transaction is processed. Usually, another screen comes up confirming that the transaction has gone through.

Chances are, you've placed many orders yourself online and are familiar with this process—at least from the perspective of the customer. But what happens behind the scenes?

Here's an inside look at the process:

◆ The customer fills out the *shopping cart* checkout screens and submits the order.

◆ All that information gets encrypted and then sent to your *payment gateway*.

◆ Your payment gateway checks that all is correct and then sends the transaction on to the financial institution where you have your *merchant account*.

◆ That financial institution approves the transaction and sends that information back to your payment gateway.

◆ Your payment gateway sends the approval back to your website's shopping cart system.

◆ Your customer sees an on-screen message that his or her order has been approved.

That's a lot of stuff happening, considering it all happens in just a few seconds!

def•i•ni•tion

A **shopping cart** is the system on your website that generates your checkout pages and manages your customer transactions. A **payment gateway** is like the terminal that retail stores use to swipe your credit card. It collects and encrypts the transaction information and transmits it to the appropriate financial institution for approval. A **merchant account** is your agreement with a financial institution to accept credit cards.

The process can be a bit more involved than I described. There may be other steps in the transaction approval highway, such as a bank's payment processing service provider, but unless you're a financial transaction engineer, you don't need to know all those details. (Thank goodness!) Understanding the basics is more than enough to get you started.

And the basics are these: to accept credit cards and other forms of online payments, you need to either have your own merchant account, payment gateway, and shopping cart—or, as we'll talk about in the next section, piggyback on someone else's.

Getting Started with PayPal or Google Checkout

If you are new to accepting online payments, consider sticking your toe in the water by signing up as a merchant with PayPal or Google Checkout. You don't have to apply for a merchant account or sign up with a payment gateway. And you can get started selling stuff on your website in minutes.

Let's take a look at PayPal since that is by far the most popular online payment service used by website owners, the most familiar to online shoppers, and the easiest to set up and use. However, I do encourage you to review what Google Checkout has to offer, too, as their features are similar and their rates are competitive.

To get started as a PayPal merchant, you need to sign up for a PayPal business account, which is different from the basic personal account. The process involves filling out an online application, verifying your business address and other contact information, and selecting and setting up your website payment solutions.

Once your PayPal business account is open, you're ready to go. PayPal walks you through the process of setting up your shopping cart, getting your customizable Buy Now buttons, and getting everything working correctly on your website. You can even add your company name and logo to the shopping cart checkout screens. (But, not surprisingly, you can't remove PayPal's logo!)

Warning!

When signing up for any online payment solution, make sure you understand all the fees. You can expect to be charged a transaction fee on purchases made by your customers, which is typically a small percentage of the sale. And there may be other charges, too, such as set-up fees, monthly maintenance fees, and more. Read the fine print!

Here is what your customer experiences when he or she makes a purchase from your site:

- Your customer clicks the **Buy Now** button.

- A PayPal checkout screen pops up, with the name and selling price of the product ordered already filled in.

- Your customer types in his PayPal username and password to access his account.

- If your customer doesn't have a PayPal account, he can still pay with his credit card, although, unfortunately, PayPal checkout screens don't always make this option obvious.

- Once the PayPal transaction is complete, your customer is sent back to any "Thank you" page on your website that you specify.

Where's your money? It gets deposited into your PayPal account right away, which is a little like a traditional bank account. You can keep your funds there or, with just a click or two, get it transferred to your own bank.

PayPal, as well as Google Checkout, offers your website customers a wide variety of convenient payment options, including every major credit card imaginable, bank transfers, debit cards, and even virtual checks. Of course, customers can also pay using their PayPal funds.

PayPal's two main options for online businesses are PayPal Payments Standard and PayPal Payments Pro. The pro version, which is currently available to U.S., UK, and just recently Canadian merchants, offers a richer array of features such as the ability to accept credit cards by phone and even in person.

My advice? Read all the merchant options carefully on the PayPal and Google Checkout websites so that you can make an informed decision as to which online payment option is right for you.

Other Website Payment Solutions

PayPal and Google Checkout are the big players in the online payments field, but they're not the only ones in the game. There are many other online services available that enable to you sell stuff on your website and accept payments.

- ClickBank (www.clickbank.com)

- 2Checkout.com (www.2checkout.com)

- Digital River (www.digitalriver.com)

- AlertPay (www.alertpay.com)

- TrialPay (www.trialpay.com)

- CCNow (www.ccnow.com)

- ProPay (www.propay.com)

None of these services work exactly the same way, so review the information on their websites carefully. For example, ClickBank handles only downloadable products such as e-books and special reports, while CCNow works primarily with websites that sell physical goods. There are important variations in how customizable the checkout screens are in each of these services, too.

And pay particular attention to how the money is handled. Unlike PayPal and Google Checkout, most of these services only deposit your funds into your account on a weekly, bi-weekly, or monthly basis. A few will even hold back a certain percentage of your money in reserve in case there are disputes or refund requests.

Getting Your Own Merchant Account

Compared to signing up with PayPal, Google Checkout, or some other online payment service, getting your own merchant account—which is basically permission from a financial institution to accept credit cards on your website—gives you a lot more control over how things look and work. You can select almost any shopping cart system you want and customize it to your exact requirements.

However, while signing up as a PayPal merchant takes only a few minutes, applying for a merchant account can be a considerably longer process. It involves a financial institution (and sometimes more than one) checking your credit score, reviewing your website, and scrutinizing the type of products and services you plan to sell.

Success Tip _____

Consider applying for your merchant account through your payment gateway service provider (explained in the next section). They know how the banking and credit card systems work and can greatly simplify the process of helping you get accepted by Visa, MasterCard, American Express, and other credit card companies, and can also help set you up to handle debit cards and virtual checks.

For obvious reasons, banks and credit card companies only want to approve reputable web-based business owners who sell merchandise with a low risk of returns. They don't want their customers complaining about improper charges or product guarantees that were not honored. As a result, it can take two to four weeks to get approved.

Here is a list of websites where you can apply for your merchant account. Some of these companies are also payment gateways, while others use a third-party gateway like Authorize.net.

- Merchant Accounts Express (www.merchantexpress.com)
- PSiGate (www.psigate.com)
- CollectivePOS (www.collectivepos.com)
- Gotmerchant.com (www.gotmerchant.com)
- Flagship Merchant Services (www.cardservicesales.com)
- Merchant Warehouse (www.merchantwarehouse.com)
- ElectronicTransfer, Inc. (www.electronictransfer.com)
- FreeAuthNet.com (www.freeauthnet.com)
- Total Merchant Services (www.totalmerchantservices.com)
- WorldPay (www.worldpay.com)
- Verotel (www.verotel.com)

When I applied for my merchant account, I double-checked to make sure my website was the picture of reputability: a clearly stated refund policy, a privacy policy, a working customer service phone number and e-mail address, a postal address, and products that were clearly priced with no misleading information. I recommend that you do the same. Trust me. Someone at the bank or credit card company will be checking.

Fees for merchant account services vary from one financial institution to another, and one credit card to another. Typically, you can expect to pay an initial account set-up fee to the financial institution and then an ongoing transaction fee (often called the discount rate) to the credit card companies. There may be other fees, too. So read the fine print carefully!

Choosing a Payment Gateway

As I said in the previous section, merchant accounts and payment gateways work closely together. So I recommend that you get them both from the same place.

For example, when I opened my first merchant account, I did so through PSiGate, which is primarily a payment gateway. They took care of the entire application process for me, like a one-stop shop, which made things a lot easier.

Merchant accounts, payment gateways, ugh! I know it's a little overwhelming. However, most payment gateway service providers do a good job of explaining how things work and walking you through the process. After all, they want you to be able to accept credit cards and start selling stuff on your website. That's how they make money! And many payment gateways are accustomed to working with small business owners.

Here is a list of payment gateway services that cater to the needs of small business owners. Some merchant account providers (listed in the previous section) also offer payment gateway services.

Success Tip

In some cases, the payment gateway will actually collect and deposit the payment funds into your bank account. In other cases, that's done directly by the credit card company. So it's important that you find out when and by whom your funds will be deposited.

- ◆ Authorize.net (www.authorize.net)

- ◆ VeriSign PayFlow (www.verisign.com)

- ◆ First Data Global Gateway (www.firstdata.com/ecommerce)

- ◆ Plug 'n Pay (www.plugnpay.com)

In addition to being a portal between your website and the banks and credit card companies, a payment gateway service provider may provide other valuable services as well, such as the ability to accept phone orders, virtual checks, and debit card payments. Review the features of each payment gateway carefully before making your decision.

Gateways typically charge an initial set-up fee, a monthly fee, and a per-transaction fee. (If you haven't noticed already, there are a lot of suppliers that want to nibble on your sales. Welcome to the world of online business!)

Shopping for Your Shopping Cart

Once you have been approved for the various merchant accounts you may need (Visa, MasterCard, American Express, Discover, et al) and you have signed up for a payment gateway, your next step is to arrange for your website shopping cart. This is the fun part because you get to choose among a wide range of styles, features, and functionality. It's a little like decorating a room!

There are basically two types of shopping cart systems.

The first type comes in the form of software that you purchase. It's then installed on the web server that hosts your website. (More on web hosts and servers in Chapter 11.) If you're comfortable working with software in this way, then you'll find this isn't a complicated process. You can probably get your shopping cart installed and running correctly in about an hour. However, if you're not tech-savvy, then you're going to need an IT professional to do the job for you. And that, of course, will cost you a few bucks.

Warning!

If you use shopping cart software to generate the checkout pages on your website, those pages need to be hosted on a secure server. Your customers will know their transaction is secure when they see the "lock" icon on their web browser screen and the "https" prefix in the web page URL. Check if your web host offers a secure server service. And if they do, be sure to ask if any extra charges apply.

Another option, and one the majority of web-based business owners choose, is to sign up with an online shopping cart service. This is similar to using a PayPal or Google Checkout shopping cart. There is no software to install, so you can get your shopping cart up and running in just a few minutes. The only downside is that you must pay the monthly, quarterly, or annual subscription fee, which is a continuous business expense; purchasing the software is only a one-time hit to your pocketbook.

When I started my web-based business, I carefully considered both options and eventually went with an online shopping cart service: 1ShoppingCart. I didn't want to get involved in having to install and maintain software, nor could I afford at the time to purchase an expensive software package.

No two shopping cart software packages or services are the same. You need to review your options carefully to ensure you get all the features you need. Here are some important things to consider.

How do the basic checkout screens look? Do you like the basic layout, fonts, colors, and other elements? Do they fit well with the look and feel of your website?

Can you customize the checkout screens? To what extent can you change the layout, color, fonts, and fields? Is there enough flexibility to add your company name, logo, a personal message from you, and other information?

> **Success Tip**
>
> When signing up for a shopping cart service, review the payment plan carefully. Often, you can save hundreds of dollars per year by selecting an annual rather than monthly payment scheme. And in the world of web-based business, the old axiom "a penny saved is a penny earned" could not be any truer!

Can you easily add an option to accept PayPal payments? Even though you can now take major credit cards with your merchant account, some of your customers will still prefer to pay by PayPal.

Does it have sales building features? For example, is there a field on the checkout screen for accepting coupons and the ability to display suggestions of other products a customer may be interested in purchasing?

Are the checkout screens simple to follow? Look at them from a customer's perspective. Will he find the checkout screens easy to complete? Buying stuff online is still intimidating for many people. Just one confusing element on a checkout form and some customers decide not to go through with the transaction.

If you're looking at a shopping cart service, you should also consider the other features they offer in addition to the checkout screens. My shopping cart service, 1ShoppingCart, generates sales reports and maintains my customer list. It also has e-mail broadcast and autoresponder capabilities and, as if all that wasn't enough, also runs my affiliate program! So I'm getting a lot of bang for my shopping cart buck.

There are many very good shopping cart systems available. Here is a list of the most popular:

- 1ShoppingCart (www.1shoppingcart.com)
- Practice Pay Solutions (www.practicepaysolutions.com)
- 3DCart (www.3dcart.com)
- KickStartCart.com (www.kickstartcart.com)
- ShopSite (www.shopsite.com)
- Zen Cart (www.zen-cart.com)
- Fortune3 Shopping Cart (www.fortune3.com)

If you decide to go with shopping cart software rather than an online service, you pay just one price. That price can vary considerably, but the average for a good program ranges from $1,000 to $2,500.

In my opinion, going with an online shopping cart service is the best choice for the web-based business owner just starting out. Fees range from $35 to $100 per month. But you don't have to install anything and never have to update the software.

Beyond Credit Cards: Accepting Other Forms of Payment

Credit cards are by far the most popular way to pay for something on the Internet. (PayPal is a close second.) However, it's not the only way to accept payments from your website customers, nor is it always the ideal option. There are many payment alternatives you can offer in place of, or in addition to, plastic.

Checks and money orders. I'm so used to buying online with my credit card or PayPal account that I'm surprised anyone would even consider going to the trouble to write and mail a check. Yet, I consistently get requests from customers asking if they can pay this way. Some people just aren't comfortable using their credit cards online and prefer the perceived security of sending a check or money order in the mail. In fact, you can increase sales by offering your customers this payment option.

Virtual checks. In addition to paper checks, you can offer customers the convenience of a virtual check. This basically works like a bank transfer. Your customer types the information into an online form on your website; a form that often looks like a real check. Then that information is transmitted electronically to the bank where it is approved (hopefully) and deposited into your account. PayPal and some payment gateways offer virtual check services. Also take a look at www.vchecksolutions.com, www.paybycheck.com, and www.ilovechecks.com.

Online wallets. You can't pay with cash on the Internet. But you can come pretty close by using an online wallet (also known as *eCash*). Never heard of this payment method? If you live in North America, that's not surprising. Wallets have only really taken off in Europe and Asia. A wallet is an online service that securely holds your contact information, shipping details, and a quantity of cash that you deposit. Then you can simply use that wallet to buy stuff from websites that accept this form of payment. You might want to consider wallet payments if you sell overseas. Popular wallets include Yahoo! Wallet (http://wallet.yahoo.com), Wallet 365 (www.wallet365.com), and PayNova (www.paynova.com). Paypal is also a type of online wallet.

Purchase orders. If your website sells products to other businesses or other organizations, then you may want to consider accepting purchase orders. A purchase order is simply a signed authorization provided to you by a company to ship the product and send your invoice. A segment of my customers work for corporate marketing departments, so I often accept orders in this manner. However, I only do so when the company is well-established.

Offering alternatives to credit cards can significantly increase your online sales. But they can also add more administrative complexity to the payment process. So weigh the advantages and disadvantages carefully. Keep in mind that many website businesses only accept credit cards and PayPal—and still do very well.

The Least You Need to Know

- Customers expect to be able to pay for purchases on your website with a credit card or with their PayPal account.

- The easiest way to accept payments on your website is by signing up as a merchant with PayPal or Google Checkout.

- Accepting credit cards on your website requires a merchant account, payment gateway, and shopping cart.

- Consider accepting other forms of payment, such as checks, online wallets, and purchase orders.

Chapter **13**

Delivering the Goods

In This Chapter

- ◆ Creating an efficient delivery system
- ◆ Packaging and shipping merchandise
- ◆ Dealing with downloadable products

Your website just got a sale. Hurray! All your hard work in setting up your business is finally paying off. Money is beginning to roll into your bank account. But don't get too excited yet. You still haven't actually delivered the order and, until you do, the sale isn't complete.

Unlike a traditional store, a customer can't walk out of your online shop with the merchandise in hand. You have to arrange for delivery. And that can involve myriad details, from packaging and filling out waybills to dealing with couriers and tracking the shipment. In this chapter, you'll learn the basics of making deliveries go smoothly.

Creating an Order Fulfillment Plan

As I mentioned in Chapter 5, I recently received an e-mail from a customer who purchased one of my home-study courses. It's a physical product comprised of a binder of materials, a book, and a set of CDs. My customer said he was concerned that he hadn't received the course yet and wanted us to check on the delivery status. When I did, I discovered that he had placed his order just three days earlier!

Welcome to the Internet! Perhaps because instant access to information is so common on the web, online customers expect to get the merchandise they ordered quickly.

Prompt delivery is an expectation, and if you're sluggish in order fulfillment, you're going to hear about it!

If your web-based business generates revenues exclusively through advertising, affiliate products, or drop-ship arrangements with wholesalers (as discussed in Chapter 5), then you don't have to worry about order fulfillment. Move on to the next chapter!

However, if your website is going to sell products that need to be shipped, or even digital products such as e-books or software that need to be "delivered" via a download page, then an efficient order fulfillment system is crucial.

There are many examples of web-based businesses that sell products profitably but then lose money because of the time and cost of fulfilling the orders. Don't let that happen to you. You must create an order fulfillment plan to ensure that merchandise gets into the hands of your online customers quickly and cost-effectively.

Your order fulfillment plan needs to address the following issues:

◆ How will you package orders so that they arrive to customers undamaged?

◆ What packaging materials do you need to accomplish this?

◆ How much time will it take you to package and ship an order? (Be sure to include the trip to the post office!)

◆ What will it cost you to package and ship an order? This will affect your profit margin. You must include packaging materials, labor, shipping fees, and other related expenses in your calculations.

◆ How will you ship the product? Via the post office or a courier service? If you're going to use a courier, which one?

◆ Will you charge customers a shipping and handling fee to cover some or all of the costs? If so, how much?

◆ How will you handle product returns?

Even if you're just starting out and don't expect a lot of sales right away, I strongly advise you to have an order fulfillment plan in place. If you don't, you risk struggling to get your initial orders out the door—and leaving a poor impression with those crucial early customers in the process.

When I launched my home study course, I got three orders within a week. I was thrilled. Then I realized that I hadn't worked out order fulfillment in advance. As a result, I wasted a lot of time figuring out which packaging materials I needed, which courier service to use, what shipping forms I needed to fill out, and how much everything was going to cost. I lost money on those initial orders simply because I hadn't planned things in advance. Don't you make that mistake!

At the very least, you need to know how you're going to safely package your product and what packaging materials you need. (Packaging materials can be surprisingly expensive.) Also know which shipping service you're going to use and how much shipping is going to cost you.

Packaging the Goods

Remember the last time you had to package a gift for a distant friend or relative? Chances are, it took you longer than you expected. You had to find the right sized box. Then the packing tape. Then you had to stuff the box with protective material of some kind, probably crumpled newspaper. Finally, you had to label the parcel clearly and correctly.

That's okay for a holiday gift. But if you want to be successful in your web-based business, you're going to have to be a little more efficient than that! You want to be able to package your merchandise quickly and cost-effectively, and in such a way that it consistently arrives at your customer's doorstep without damage. (Damage, even a minor dent, is the number-one reason why products get returned.)

There are three ingredients in successful packaging:

- The box
- The cushioning
- The sealing

When selecting a box, don't make the mistake of getting exactly the right size for your product. The box actually needs to be a little bigger so that cushioning materials can be packed around the contents. Otherwise, an accidental drop could easily cause damage. The rule of thumb is to allow for a half-inch to an inch between the inside of the box and the product.

Success Tip

Many retail stores are required by law or policy to recycle the packaging materials from their incoming shipments. Contact some local stores and ask if you can take some of these materials off their hands. Bubble wrap, corrugated paper, protective fill, and other packaging materials can be safely used over and over again. If you can get these from local stores for free, you'll save a lot of money.

The box should be sturdy, rigid, and clean.

If you are recycling a box, make sure it's in relatively good condition with all the flaps intact and no tears. If a reused box has printing on it from another company, use a clean adhesive label to cover those markings—preferably one that contains your logo. Remember, the shipping box is the first thing a customer sees, so you don't want it to look sloppy.

When packing multiple items, experts advise you to place heavier items at the bottom. This keeps the center of balance low and reduces the chances of the box falling over during shipment.

When it comes to cushioning, you have a range of options:

◆ Newspaper. This is good cushioning material but the ink may leave stains on the product. Shipping supply stores sell blank newsprint. When using newspaper for packaging, be sure to crumple it tightly and pack it in firmly. Alternatives include tissue and Kraft paper.

◆ Bubble wrap. This is ideal when you need to wrap individual items securely. When using this material, remember to place the bubbles facing toward the product.

◆ Peanuts. Also called loose fill. When using packing peanuts, make sure it fills all the empty space within the box. If it doesn't, the protective effect goes down dramatically, sometimes to zero.

If your product is particularly fragile or delicate, consider a specialty cushioning system that uses foam or small air bags. These are more expensive options but may be worth it to ensure your product arrives undamaged.

Your goal with cushioning is to make the package drop-proof. The package should be able to fall onto a hard floor from 5 feet, or tumble down a short flight of stairs, without damage. The cushioning should also be able to protect the contents from a minor puncture, such as from a pen or the corner of another box.

Warning!

When using cushioning materials of any kind, make sure that you use just enough to fill all the empty space in the box. If you use too little, the contents may get damaged during shipping. If you use too much, the pressure from all that extra cushioning can also cause damage. The rule of thumb is to fill the empty space so that the box closes easily, without causing a bulge.

Finally, after you've placed your product in the box and cushioned it well so that it's snug and safe inside, you have to seal the box. Don't use household tape. It's not nearly tough enough for the job. You need packing tape specifically designed for shipping, which is available at most office supply stores. Make sure you seal all the box seams.

At this point you should have your product safely packaged and ready to ship to your customer. The first package will require a lot of work and experimentation. Don't worry, subsequent orders will go a lot easier and faster!

Time-Saving Tips

Packaging and shipping a product can take a lot of work. I've known many web-based business owners to complain that the hours spent on these tasks almost cancel out any profit made on the sale.

You don't want that! So consider the following tips for saving time and money on order fulfillment:

- Boxes are sold flat. To save time, have at least a few assembled in advance.

- Do all your order packaging and shipping for the day at one time rather than after each sale.

- Prepare cushioning material in advance. Have the exact amount of peanuts you need measured out or bubble wrap cut to size.

- Stock up. Have plenty of supplies available, especially tape and labels. You don't want to run out of something and have to make a special trip to the store.

- Consider arranging for a pickup service from your courier rather than having to drop off your packages. It may cost you a little more, but the time savings may be worth it. (Remember the last time you waited in line at the post office?)

◆ Shop around. Look for the best prices on packaging materials. In my experience, prices of boxes, tape, and cushioning materials fluctuate wildly from one store to the next. Look for deals.

I can't emphasize enough how important it is to be really efficient with your order fulfillment. If you're not careful, the time and costs associated with this task can really run away from you.

Shipping Made Easy

Once you've packaged your product, you have to get it shipped to the customer somehow. And because your business is online, that customer could be across town, across the country, or even overseas. Your choice of shipping service is vital.

The best place to begin? Start with your local post office. The postal services in the United States (www.usps.com/business), Canada (www.canadapost.ca), and the United Kingdom (www.royalmail.com) have a range of delivery services for small business owners. And because tax dollars support these organizations, you might as well take full advantage of the benefits.

If you're unfamiliar with shipping commercial packages, you may think of the post office as just a place to buy stamps and mail letters. However, just about every postal service website provides small business owners with a wide range of special services and online tools and features.

Sales Builder

Contact your local postal service and ask about special services for small business owners. Chances are, they can offer you a lot of free tools and information, including software, how-to seminars, manuals, packaging supplies, and special discounts. Although they have no competition for mail service, they do compete with a lot of players for package delivery. They want your business—and offer a lot of money-saving freebies and special deals to get it.

I've noticed that postal services are increasingly catering to the needs of small businesses. The United States Postal Service website even has a special section dedicated to small business shipping, offering such tools and resources as:

◆ Free shipping software

◆ Online shipment tracking and delivery confirmations

- The ability to fill out and print shipping documents online

- Address verification

- Various shipping options

- A range of convenient payment options, from PayPal to opening a business account

- Package pick-ups

- Package returns services

- Business customer support

You can even order supplies from the USPS.com site. And there is a wealth of helpful articles and other information for small business owners who ship goods to customers.

From the Mail Gal to the Courier Guy

The post office is an ideal place to start when you've just launched your web-based business and only have a few orders to ship each week. However, as your shipping volume grows, you might want to take advantage of the faster delivery options and time-saving services of a courier company.

If you intend to ship only to local customers—say, those in the Pittsburgh area—then check out the yellow pages and find a good local courier service. In my experience, many local couriers are just as reliable as the big players, such as UPS and FedEx, and are a lot less expensive. Just make sure the courier you select has experience delivering packages, not just envelopes. And be sure to check references.

Warning!

Whether you decide to use the post office or a courier company like FedEx, make sure the shipping option you choose includes the ability to track the order and confirm delivery. As part of good customer service, you'll want to be able to e-mail your customer the tracking number so he or she can check the status of delivery. You also want to ensure that your merchandise has arrived so you can prove that fact in case a customer claims it didn't.

If your customers are across the country or around the world, then you're going to want to tap into the international logistical resources of a large courier company. The big players are:

◆ UPS (www.ups.com)

◆ FedEx (www.fedex.com)

◆ Purolator Courier (www.purolator.com) (Mainly for Canada-based businesses.)

◆ TNT (www.tnt.com) (Specializes in international express shipments.)

◆ eCourier (www.ecourier.co.uk) (Mainly for businesses based in the United Kingdom.)

◆ DHL (www.dhl.com) (Focuses mainly on international shipments.)

Like the post office, most of these companies offer services specifically for small business owners. I encourage you to check out their respective websites and find out what they offer.

International Shipping

Shipping orders across town or across the country is a relatively simple process. You package the shipment, create a label or shipment waybill, and the post office or courier company does the rest.

The fun begins when your order has to cross an international border.

This hit home for me a few years ago when I ordered some educational materials from a website in the United States. I'm in Canada. The package arrived promptly just a few days later—along with an invoice from the post office for $70! That invoice was for customs fees and duties. I didn't expect this extra expense and it left me with a bad taste in my mouth. I wish that website had warned me.

So the first rule of shipping internationally is to advise customers that they may be liable for customs fees and duties. It's better to be upfront about this than to have them be hit with a surprise bill. Many web-based business owners I know have complained about high return rates—and in some cases outright refusal of the shipment—because of customs charges.

Warning!

When filling out shipping forms for international shipments, never be deceptive about what you're shipping, the purpose of the shipment, or its value just to lower or avoid customs charges. Customs agents aren't easily fooled. If your package is inspected and found to be not what you say it is, your shipment could get delayed at the border or even returned. This won't make your customer very happy. In addition, you could face additional fees from your courier company.

When shipping internationally, you have some additional forms that need to be filled out. This typically includes a special waybill plus other documents for customs purposes. Shipments between the United States and Canada, for example, require three documents: an international waybill, a Certificate of Origin, and, in some cases, a Commercial Invoice.

Is your head spinning yet? Don't worry. Most courier companies do a good job of walking you through the documents you need to prepare. And most shipping software (usually available for free from couriers such as UPS) will automatically prompt you to complete the correct documents on screen.

Your courier company can also help you determine the *landed cost* of a shipment into another country. If you're selling surfboards to Canadians from your California-based web-based business, for example, you can find out what the shipping and customs charges are going to be in advance. Then you can advise your customer or, if it makes sense to do so, cover those costs yourself.

def•i•ni•tion

The **landed cost** of a shipment is the cost of shipping plus all applicable customs duties and fees.

Who Pays What? Deciding How Much to Charge a Customer

If you've ever purchased a product online, you've no doubt come to that point in the checkout process where shipping and handling fees are discussed. Either you were told how much extra that was going to cost you, or you were given a range of progressively more expensive shipping options depending on how soon you wanted the item.

According to a study by Jupiter Research, 63 percent of online customers cited excessive shipping and handling costs as the reason they either cancelled or didn't go through with an online purchase.

Clearly, your fees must be seen as reasonable. In my experience, customers are willing to pay for much of the costs of shipping and handing, and sometimes even all of it. But if they sense that you're being excessive, or worse, making a profit from the shipping and handing charge, you're in trouble.

My advice? Try to break even. Calculate the average cost of shipping an order and then charge that amount. $7 to $25 for a domestic shipment of a small to mid-sized item is the average that customers expect to see. For international orders, $25 to $45 is the norm.

You can't always break even. I charge $39 for overseas shipping of one of my home study courses. However, the actual cost can be up to 50 percent higher. I consider that the cost of doing business with overseas customers and, basically, eat the added expense. I still make a decent profit because the course itself sells for over $500.

Be sure to clearly communicate the shipping options and costs on your checkout pages. This can be set up fairly easily in shopping cart software (see Chapter 12).

> **Sales Builder**
>
> Consider rewarding customers with free shipping if their order reaches a certain dollar value. This has been proven to get customers to buy more. Amazon.com does it all the time. You can also throw in extra shipping to reward repeat customers or as a special promotion theme: "Free Shipping. This Week Only!"

Keeping Costs Down

Shipping costs can vary widely from one courier company to the next. So it's important to watch your costs and get the best deal. Recently, I reviewed my shipping options and discovered that I was paying $3 to $5 more per order than I would be with a comparable courier company. That was a lot of money blowing out the door simply because I didn't take the time to compare costs!

Comparing prices among shipping companies is easy online. Just about every courier website has a shipping fee calculator. You simply plug in the information about your package (length, width, height, weight), along with the delivery details (your address, your customer's address), and the system will give you a list of shipping options and costs.

Success Tip _____

Many courier companies provide small business owners with free envelopes, boxes, and even cushioning material. The catch? It will have their name and logo all over it. If that isn't an issue, find out what's available and see which supplies you can get for free from your courier company. This can save your business a lot of money.

In addition to each courier company's website, there are also other online services that will automatically compare prices from multiple shipping companies for you. Here are the most popular.

- Shipping Sidekick (www.shippingsidekick.com)

- iShip Shipping Insight (www.iship.com)

- ShipGooder (www.shipgooder.com)

- ShippingAndTracking.com (www.shippingandtracking.com)

- Freightz.com (www.freightz.com)

Typically express shipping options, such as overnight delivery, are the most expensive. Standard shipping, which usually takes three to seven business days for domestic deliveries, costs much less. Most customers are fine waiting a few days to get their merchandise, provided they know it's on the way.

Outsourcing Fulfillment

At this point in the chapter one thing has probably become very clear. Packaging and shipping merchandise to your online customers is going to be a lot of work! That's fine when you're just starting your business and you only have a few orders to ship. But as your online business booms—and I have my fingers crossed for you that it will—then order fulfillment is going to take up more and more of your precious time.

The solution? Outsource.

There are many ways to get someone else to handle the nitty-gritty details of packaging and shipping for you.

The most obvious option is to hire someone to be your "shipper." (If she wants a more lofty title, you can call her your "logistics manager"!) This position doesn't necessarily need to be full-time. In fact, a local high school student looking for a part-time job for a few hours each week may be ideal. Just make sure that you have your order fulfillment procedures in place and that whomever you hire does a good job. You want products to be packaged neatly, forms filled out accurately, and shipments to be ready for the post office or courier on a timely basis.

Another option is to sign up with a product fulfillment company. This is a company that specializes in storing your merchandise and shipping orders to your customers. Depending on the company you choose, a fulfillment service can take a lot off your shoulders, handling such tasks as inventory storage and management, packaging, shipping, and even returns.

Success Tip

Selling to international customers? Then consider using a fulfillment company that is located in the country or region where a lot of your customers are located. You'll save money on customs duties and related fees because you'll be shipping your merchandise in bulk to that company's warehouse. You'll save money on shipping, too, because the orders will be delivered to customers within the country at lower domestic, rather than higher international, rates.

The fulfillment service I use for my how-to guides, audio programs, and home study courses is Speaker Fulfillment Services. They handle everything for me. In fact, once a customer places an order online, I don't lift a finger to get it delivered. The fulfillment service's system is integrated with my shopping cart program so they see the orders when they come in and ship them right away. The only disadvantage to outsourcing everything is that I don't get to pop the bubble wrap when I'm bored. Oh well.

Here is a list of popular fulfillment services for web-based business owners:

- Speaker Fulfillment Services (www.speakerfulfillmentservices.com)
- Webgistix (www.webgistix.com)
- Shipwire (www.shipwire.com)
- Moulton Fulfillment Services (www.moultonfulfillment.com)
- Rapid Fulfillment (www.rapidrulfillment.com)
- MDS Fulfillment, Inc. (www.mdsfulfillment.com)
- eFulfillment Service (www.efulfillmentservice.com)

- National Fulfillment Services (www.nfsrv.com)

- Iron Mountain (www.ironmountain.com)

- Fulfillment America (www.fulfillmentamerica.com)

- Progressive Commerce (www.prodist.com)

- ShipMyOrders.com (www.shipmyorders.com)

When selecting a fulfillment house, ask a lot of questions. You want to make sure they're reputable and do a good job of packaging and shipping your merchandise. I suggest you ask them to ship *you* something to get a sense of their speed and the appearance of the package. Most fulfillment services will agree to this.

Delivering the Invisible: Downloadable Products

A lot of web-based business owners think, "I don't have to worry too much about delivery. After all, I sell downloadable products only."

Big mistake. In fact, if your website sells such downloadable items as e-books, software, and MP3s, then an efficient delivery system is even more important. That's because customers who purchase such products often expect instant, hassle-free access. And if you can't give them that, you're going to have some frustrated customers on your hands.

When a customer purchases a downloadable product from my website, I make sure that the instructions for accessing and downloading it are loud and clear. Here is the typical scenario.

- The customer orders the downloadable product.

- Once the transaction is approved, the customer is automatically taken to a special thank you page on my website which explains how to download the product.

- The customer also receives a thank you e-mail with the same instructions repeated.

- Two weeks later, another e-mail is sent to the customer asking if they had any problems with the download and explaining how to get help.

As you can see, I take no chances in making sure that a downloadable product is "delivered" to my customer's computer.

In addition, I also provide information on my thank you pages and e-mails to help the customer with the download. You see, not all customers who purchase a downloadable product are computer savvy. You can expect some to not know how to play an MP3 sound file, or save and open a PDF. I provide simple step-by-step instructions for those novices.

Your goal is to do everything you can to make downloading and using your product as easy as possible for customers.

The Least You Need to Know

- ◆ Plan how you're going to package and ship orders—before the orders start coming in.

- ◆ Keep costs down by comparing prices and taking advantage of free shipping supplies offered by many couriers and the post office.

- ◆ Be careful when charging customers for shipping and handling. They're willing to absorb that cost, so long as it's not too excessive.

- ◆ For downloadable products, provide clear instructions on how to access the product.

Chapter 14

Tracking Success with Website Analytics

In This Chapter

- ◆ Understanding the range of information that website analytics can provide you
- ◆ Finding and installing a good website analytics program
- ◆ Using analytics to keep down costs and boost sales

How is your online advertisement doing for you? How many hits did your new product page get this week? Which search engine keywords are visitors using to find your website? Where in the world are your potential customers located? Which other websites are referring their visitors to yours?

Wouldn't it be handy to have this information? You can, with website analytics. This chapter explains how to find and use a good analytics program to increase traffic, boost conversions, and reduce your marketing costs.

What Exactly Is Website Analytics?

Say your website is humming along nicely and then, one day, for no apparent reason, you get a bunch of new sign-ups for your e-mail newsletter. Your orders spike, too. Obviously there has been a surge of traffic to your website.

That's great news! Certainly a reason to celebrate. But exactly where did all that unexpected activity, on that particular day, come from? Was it your advertising? Was it your article in a key publication? Was it the interview you gave to that blogger? Those potential customers found out about your website somehow. Something you did worked—and worked very well. If only you knew what it was, you could do more of it!

That's where *website analytics* can help.

def•i•ni•tion

A good **website analytics** program will generate reports that provide you with in-depth information about your website visitors and their behavior once on your website. This is valuable information you can use to optimize your marketing efforts and improve the effectiveness of your website pages—which, together, will increase your profits.

It can either be traditional software that needs to be installed, or in the form of an online service that you sign up for.

For example, a few months ago I placed a banner advertisement on two similar websites. I suspected I would get a comparable response, in terms of traffic generated, from each ad. Not so. According to my analytics report, the banner on the first website generated a ton of new traffic while the banner on the second got hardly any clicks at all!

Imagine if I didn't know that. I would have kept on sinking money into both advertisements, unaware that one of them wasn't working.

As you can probably guess, I'm a big fan of website analytics. For the web-based business owner, it's a must.

And because website analytics programs are so affordable and easy-to-use, there is absolutely no reason for you to be in the dark about where your potential customers are coming from and what they're doing while on your website.

You need this information to make your business profitable. Without a good website analytics program, it's like flying a plane without a window or even a dashboard! You'll crash and burn.

What Information Do Analytics Give You?

You might be surprised by how much information a website analytics program can give you about the people who visit your website and their activity once there.

There are many good website analytics programs available, but for the purposes of this section—and, indeed, most of this chapter—I'm going to use Google Analytics as an example. It's the program I use and one that is fairly representative of analytics programs in general.

Here is a list of the most common types of information that my Google Analytics program monitors for me:

◆ **Visits.** This is the total number of visits to my website, including both new and returning visitors.

◆ **Absolute unique visitors.** Here's a number to get excited about! These are my new visitors; first-timers who have never been to my website before.

◆ **Pageviews.** This is how many pages on my site were viewed by visitors.

◆ **Average time on site.** This tells me the average length of time visitors are staying on my website, a good indicator of the relevance and quality of my content.

◆ **Bounce rate.** This is the number of single-page visits where the person left my site from the same page they entered. If lots of visitors are doing that, then something's wrong. It's the equivalent of a customer walking into a retail store, taking a quick look around, then rushing out again!

◆ **Direct traffic.** This is the number of visitors who came to my site directly, by typing the website address into their web browsers.

◆ **Referring sites.** These refer to the traffic I'm getting from other websites that contain a link to mine.

◆ **Search engines.** This number is the amount of visitors who are finding my site by using a search engine, such as Google or Yahoo!. I can also see which search engine visitors are using, and what keywords they are typing in to find my site!

◆ **Top landing pages.** This analytic tells me through which website pages my visitors are entering my site. (You might be surprised that it's not always the home page.)

◆ **Top exit pages.** This reveals the last pages that visitors go to on my website before they leave.

◆ **Keywords.** This shows me which keywords visitors are using on the search engines to find my website. I can further drill down to *Paid* and *Non-Paid* keywords. *Paid* keywords are those associated with my Google Adwords campaigns (see Chapter 17).

Wow. Sure beats the old days of the Internet when the most you could do was put a hit counter on your home page!

Like most good analytics programs, Google does a great job of making the information easy to view and understand. The dashboard screen contains a lot of useful information at a glance, such as the percentage of new versus returning visitors, and a pie chart showing you where your visitors are coming from. Clicking any of the main buttons on the navigation bar drills you down to more in-depth information.

In a way, website analytics is like being the manager of a traditional retail store, watching the floor from the window of your elevated office. You can see your customers coming in, notice how long they're saying, monitor which aisles they visit, and note which products they look at most.

The Most Important Analytics You Need to Know

The amount of information you can gather from most good website analytics programs is so vast that you couldn't possibly use all that information. You'd need a staff! (In fact, many large companies have staff dedicated to analyzing these types of reports.) So as a small web-based business owner, what is the least you need to track in order to get the most out of your website analytics program?

The most important analytic you need to know concerns where your traffic is coming from. After all, you probably spend a lot of time, effort, and money on marketing your site. Wouldn't it be nice to know which of those activities are paying off and which are not?

In Internet marketing lingo, this is called *traffic sources*. Traffic sources can come from search engines, blogs, advertising, other websites, and more.

A few months ago, for example, I noticed that a lot of traffic was being referred to me from a website I had never heard of before. So I visited it and discovered that it is a popular site among my target audience and, hurray, they accept article submissions and advertising. Ultimately that website resulted in hundreds of new potential customers for my business. I doubt I would have discovered it if not for my analytics program.

def•i•ni•tion

Traffic sources are places, online and offline, where potential customers find out about your website.

Sales Builder

How do you measure the success of a web page if there is no clear call to action, such as a Buy Now button or an online form? Look at your website analytics report! If you get a high bounce rate on that page, it's because people are clicking away just seconds after visiting it. And that's not good! They're obviously not impressed with the content. On the other hand, if your bounce rate on that page is low, then that's a strong indication that your content is relevant and captivating.

In addition to traffic sources, you'll also want to know which pages on your site your visitors go to most. In analytics lingo, this is called content. Say, for example, your analytics program is telling you that plenty of people are visiting a sales page promoting a particular product but no one is buying. Then you know that traffic isn't your problem, it's the page itself. For whatever reason, it's not convincing visitors to place an order. You might need to rewrite that marketing copy!

Basically, you want to monitor enough information with your analytics program so you know how visitors are finding you, what pages they are looking at on your site, and the effectiveness of those pages.

Finding a Website Analytics Program

To get analytics reports you need a good analytics program. But before you run out and buy new software, or sign up for an online service, take a look at your web hosting plan (see Chapter 11).

Many web hosting companies offer analytics—sometimes referred to as site reports—as part of their hosting packages. In fact, you might already have analytics reports available to you and don't even know it!

The quality of analytics programs built into web hosting plans varies widely. You have to find out if the one that comes with your plan provides you with all the information you need. If it does, then there's really no reason to invest in a separate analytics software or service.

If, however, your hosting plan doesn't include the analytics reports you want, then you're going to need to find another solution. Fortunately, there are several good programs available that provide you with a wealth of analytics information and are all relatively inexpensive. Some, in fact, are free.

Here is a list of website analytics programs designed specifically for the needs of the small web-based business owner:

◆ Google Analytics (www.google.com/analytics)

◆ OneStat.com (www.onestat.com)

◆ LoadStats (www.load.com/loadstats)

◆ ShinyStat (www.shinystat.com)

◆ Opentracker (www.opentracker.net)

◆ GoStats (www.gostats.com)

◆ MetaTraffic (www.metasun.com)

◆ eWebAnalytics (www.ewebanalytics.com)

◆ nextSTAT (www.nextstat.com)

◆ Piwik (www.piwik.org)

◆ StatsAdvisor (www.statsadvisor.com)

Like any software or online service, be sure to review all the features carefully. The program needs to be able to accurately track all the information indicated earlier in this chapter and provide you with reports that are easy to interpret and use.

Warning!

Beware of free analytics programs. Many provide you with only a few basic reports and don't track all the visitor activity you need to monitor. Also avoid those cheap hit counters that are available all over the Internet. They're basically useless and some can be dangerous because of spyware lurking in the code. There are some free analytics programs that are very good. A notable example is Google Analytics.

When assessing a potential analytics software or online service, take advantage of any free trials or demos that are available. This will give you a chance to find out if the program will generate all the reports you need. You will also learn how easy, or difficult, the program is to use. At the very least, you need to be able to track the number of first-time and repeat visitors to your site during a given period, where those visitors are coming from, and which pages on your site they're going to.

Once you select a website analytics program, take the time to familiarize yourself with all the features. Most programs allow you to customize the reports so that they're automatically generated for you, which can be a real timesaver.

Getting Started with Google Analytics

A few years ago Google turned the website analytics software industry on its ear by offering a robust analytics service for websites absolutely free. All you have to do is sign up, plug the HTML code provided onto the website pages you want to track and—voilà—the system generates a wealth of information you can view online.

I use Google Analytics and have been very satisfied with the amount of information and useful reports I can access. As a result, I've never felt the need—so far—to purchase a more advanced analytics solution.

Google Analytics is free—so far. But there's no telling when they might add a premium service level that you'll have to pay for.

If you're just starting out in your web-based business, I suggest you begin with Google Analytics. It will provide you with all the information you need to monitor traffic sources, website visitor activity on your site, and much more. And it won't cost you a cent.

Success Tip

If you're running a Google Adwords campaign (see Chapter 17), then you'll be delighted to know that Google Analytics is fully integrated with that service. That means you can view the performance of your search engines ads and your website analytics within the same program.

The Sign-Up Process

Getting started with Google Analytics is really easy. To sign up, just go to Google.com/analytics and click the **Sign Up Now** link. Then enter the e-mail you'd like to use for your Google account and pick a password. (If you already have a Google account, then you don't need another one. Just use that same username and password to sign in to Google Analytics.)

When you sign in for the first time, you'll have some initial set-up to do. You'll need to fill in your website address and what time zone you're in. And you'll have to agree to the terms and conditions.

def•i•ni•tion

A **tracking code** is a few lines, or snippet, of HTML code that you need to place within the web pages you want your website analytics program to track. When someone visits a page that contains that code, information about where that person came from, and his or her activities on your site, is compiled and reports are created.

Once you've done all that, Google will provide the *tracking code* that you need to install on your website. If you have more than one website to track, you can enter them all at the set-up stage, or add them later.

Be sure to paste the tracking code provided by Google in a safe place, such as Microsoft Notepad or a similar program. The code must be saved as a text file. Some word processing programs, like Microsoft Word, alter the code when you paste it into a document. In most such programs, you should be able to use the "save as" command and then select "plain text."

Installing Google Analytics

To install the Google Analytics tracking code on your website pages, you need to go into your site's html programming and find the </body> tag for each page. Then, copy the tracking code that Google Analytics provided you after the <body> tag and before the </body> tag.

Warning!

Paste the tracking code into all the website pages you want to track, not just the home page! These will include all the general pages on your site, plus special pages such as thank you pages, download pages, and landing pages used for specific advertising and other marketing campaigns. If the code isn't on the page, the website visitor activity will not be tracked.

Feeling a little nervous? If you're uncomfortable working with the HTML code of your website yourself, your website designer can do the job for you. Depending on the amount of pages, it only takes a few minutes.

If you're using a website builder software or service of some kind, such as SiteSell.com or GoDaddy's Website Tonight, you can contact the support department. They'll safely walk you through the process of pasting the code into your website pages.

Making Sure the Darn Thing Works!

Once you've finished pasting the code on your web pages, you need to test it.

From the Google Analytics Tracking Instructions screen, click the **Continue** button. You'll see your settings so far, and the Status field at the far right of the Website Profile section will indicate if tracking has been installed.

If you get a message that says "Tracking Not Installed," don't panic. Click **Check Status.** Google will then check your site for the tracking code and let you know if it finds it or not. If it doesn't find the tracking code, then you need to try pasting it in a different area on your pages and then test it again. If the problem still persists, make sure that the tracking code is correct. It's possible that you missed part of the code while cutting and pasting. (I've made that mistake a few times!)

Google has a very good library of common questions, so search their database of helpful tips. If you still have problems, call your website designer or web builder software tech support.

Most people don't have any problems getting their Google Analytics to work. So hopefully, you'll be one of them!

Viewing and Interpreting Analytics Reports

Each website analytics program varies slightly in the way it generates reports. However, most require you to log in to a special screen. From there you typically see an overview screen with the basic information highlighted for you. Then you can click each category, for example New Visitors, to see more specific data.

Let's take a look at how to view reports in Google Analytics as an example.

To see the incredible range and depth of information that the system is tracking for you, sign into your Google Analytics account. Then click the **View Report** link next to the website you want data for. (Google Analytics lets you track more than one site.)

Google does a pretty good job of providing you with a lot of useful information at a glance. As soon as you log in you'll be greeted with an easy-to-understand dashboard screen, which will show you a graph of the daily number of visitors you've had over the past month. You'll also be able to click the main link to take a quick overview look at Visits, Pageviews, Pages/Visit, Bounce Rate, Average Time On Site, and New Visits statistics.

You can then use the navigation bar on the left to get very specific data on each category. For example, you can click the **Content** link and find out what your most popular website page is and the average time visitors spend on it.

Using the Data to Lower Costs and Increase Sales

I remember years ago, before the Internet became popular, placing an ad in a local business directory and never really knowing for sure if it worked. Was it worth the $720 I paid for the ad space? I had, at best, only a fleeting idea that it may have.

These days, on the Internet at least, you don't have to wonder if your marketing money is going down the drain. A good website analytics program can help you get the most out of your marketing efforts and budget by providing you with the information you need to quickly find out what's really working and what isn't.

Using website analytics will improve your marketing, since you'll be keeping a watchful eye on the sources of your visitors and the performance of your web pages. You'll know what content on which pages tends to draw people in, and very quickly learn what they don't like. Monitoring your keywords and traffic sources will help you target and segment your marketing, making your efforts work even harder for you.

Here are a few examples of the decisions you can make based on the information that your analytics program provides you:

♦ Low number of new visitors. Decision: increase marketing efforts to generate more traffic.

♦ Low number of repeat visitors. Decision: ramp up e-mail marketing efforts to motivate new visitors to return to the site.

♦ An unexpected keyword is being used to find your website. Decision: use that keyword on key website pages to improve search engine results.

♦ High bounce rate on a landing page. Decision: improve the marketing copy on that page.

♦ Few, if any, other websites referring traffic to you. Decision: cultivate relationships with other websites.

♦ An article or blog post on your site gets an unexpectedly high number of visitors. Decision: write more articles and blog posts like it. Consider creating a new product or service related to that topic.

♦ An ad on a website draws a lot of traffic. Decision: it's working. Keep advertising on that site!

Analytics help you make smarter decisions regarding your web-based business, so you can grow faster and more profitably. It's a no-brainer. Get a good website analytics program!

The Least You Need to Know

◆ A good website analytics program will give you insights into your visitors and their behavior while on your website.

◆ There are many website analytics programs available. Google Analytics is very good and, so far, free to use.

◆ Use analytics reports to lower costs and increase sales.

15

The Business of Running an Online Business

In This Chapter

- ◆ Understanding the basics of bookkeeping
- ◆ Completing administrative tasks more easily
- ◆ Finding administrative help

One of my early mentors in business once told me, "There are three things you need to do very well to be successfully self-employed. You need to be able to get the business, do the business, and run the business." Most web-based business owners focus primarily on the first two activities. After all, getting orders and delivering the product or service is what makes you money.

However, running the business—all that administrative nitty-gritty stuff—is important, too. Sloppy bookkeeping, stacks of undone paperwork, and disorganized files can quickly turn into a mess that costs you time and money. To get and stay profitable, you need to run a smooth operation.

Doing the Books

Before I started my online business, ForCopywritersOnly.com, I was primarily a self-employed marketing consultant. During those years, *bookkeeping* was relatively easy. I only had to manage two or three clients at any given time. I would do a project, send an invoice, and get paid. I kept copies of the invoices, checks, and bank statements in a file folder on my desk. That was my bookkeeping system!

def•i•ni•tion

> **Bookkeeping** involves keeping accurate records of your business revenues and expenses, plus all information related to taxes charged and payable. In many jurisdictions, the law requires that you maintain an accurate set of books. But even if it doesn't, good bookkeeping enables you to manage your cash flow, stay on top of expenses, and otherwise keep your business financially healthy.

Boy, was I in for a surprise when I began selling stuff on the Internet. When I opened the doors to my web-based business, selling how-to guides and home study courses, suddenly I was dealing with credit card transaction fees, shipping charges, hundreds of customer records, sales taxes, multiple product sales records, and much more. Bookkeeping suddenly became an administrative headache. Can someone please pass the Aspirin?

I can't emphasize enough how important it is to keep an accurate set of books for your business. You need these records to understand how much things are costing you, how much money you're making or losing, and what your cash flow needs are going to be in the weeks and months ahead. You can't know that for sure just by glancing at the balance of your bank account.

You also need a good set of books to keep the tax man happy. If you're ever audited and your bookkeeping is sloppy, then an auditor is going to expect that your tax returns are slipshod, too. An accurate set of books is also a requirement when applying for a bank loan—whether it's for business or personal use.

So now that I've convinced you—hopefully—that bookkeeping is important, how do you get it done?

Bookkeeping Basics

If you have little or no experience with bookkeeping for a small business, then I suggest you read a good book on the subject. *The Complete Idiot's Guide to Accounting* (Alpha, 2006) is a great place to start. *Mastering Bookkeeping* by Dr. Peter Marshall (How To Books, 2007) is another excellent guide. I also suggest books that are specific to the bookkeeping software you select (more on that in just a moment), such as *QuickBooks 2007: The Official Guide* by Kathy Ivens (The McGraw-Hill Companies, 2006).

> **Success Tip** _____
>
> To make bookkeeping easier, use just one bank account and credit card for your web-based business. The statements make it easy to complete the records you need to keep a good set of books. Some credit card companies even offer special cards for small business owners that feature detailed itemized statements for accounting purposes. Very handy! Be sure never to use your business account or credit card for personal use. That just muddies the waters and makes bookkeeping more difficult.

However, the basics you need to keep track of are the following:

- **General ledger.** This is a record of all your transactions: sales, commissions, purchases, taxes paid and collected, the works. In your web-based business, you may have dozens or even hundreds of individual transactions each month.

- **Sales report.** This is a record of all the revenues your website has generated for a particular period. Revenues could come from product sales, registrations, affiliate advertising commissions, and other sources.

- **Expense report.** This is a record of all expenses you've paid to run your business for a particular period. These can include everything from website hosting fees to credit card transaction charges to office supplies.

- **Tax report.** This is a record of the taxes associated with sales or expenses for a given period, such as sales taxes charged, paid, and owed. (Note: This is not your income tax.)

- **Income statement.** This is perhaps the most important record you need to keep. It tells you how much money you're making! An income statement is simply your sales, from your sales report, minus your expenses, from your expense report. The bottom line is your income.

Can you create all these records manually, perhaps by using a spreadsheet on your computer or bookkeeping forms purchased from an office supply store? You can. Especially if you're just starting out in your web-based business and you're not generating a lot of financial activity yet. However, as your business grows you'll want to consider buying good bookkeeping software or hiring a freelance bookkeeper.

Let's take a closer look at those two options.

Bookkeeping Software

Bookkeeping software can make the task of "doing the books" a lot faster and easier for you. Typically, all you need to do is type in the transactions as they occur and the program does the rest, automatically generating all the required bookkeeping reports.

Like most software solutions, there are basically two kinds: the kind you install on your computer, and the kind you access online by signing up and logging in. Personally, I prefer an installed program for my bookkeeping. There's something about having my financial records on my own computer rather than on some other company's database that makes me sleep better at night, even though most online services have robust data protection systems in place.

Here is a list of the most popular bookkeeping solutions available to small business owners.

- Simply Accounting (www.simplyaccounting.com)
- QuickBooks (http://quickBooks.intuit.com)
- QuickBooks Online (http://oe.quickbooks.com)
- Microsoft Office Accounting (www.microsoft.com/smallbusiness)
- Peachtree Accounting (www.peachtree.com)
- Visual Bookkeeper (www.a-systems.net)
- Less Accounting (www.lessaccounting.com)
- Clarity Accounting (www.clarityaccounting.com)
- OWL Software (www.owlsoftware.com)
- OneStep Accounting (www.enablecomputing.com)
- NolaPro (www.nolapro.com)

Although you should review all your options carefully before making a decision, I personally recommend QuickBooks. It has been my bookkeeping software for years and I have always found it easy to learn and use. It generates all the reports I need. And QuickBooks has done a great job of providing lots of other helpful resources for small business owners like us.

As I said earlier, most of these software solutions require you to input your transactions. If you don't do that, the software can't do the books for you! However, you can make it a lot easier on yourself by taking advantage of the *import feature*.

The import feature allows you to pull in transaction information from your bank account, credit card statement, shopping cart system, and other accounts. It takes a little time to set things up but, once you do, importing can save you a lot of time. My QuickBooks software is set up to import my transactions directly from those three sources and put the data in the right places within my bookkeeping records. It takes me five minutes. If I were to try to do all that manually, it would take me five hours!

def•i•ni•tion

The **import feature** in a bookkeeping software program allows you to import the financial data that exists in another database, such as your bank account.

Whatever bookkeeping software you choose, find out if it has an import feature. In my opinion, it's an absolute must.

Freelance Bookkeepers

Don't want to handle bookkeeping on your own? I don't blame you. Even with a good software system it's a tedious chore. So another alternative is to hire a bookkeeper to handle this task for you.

Many bookkeepers work with clients on a freelance basis, typically setting aside a few hours each month to do your books. You can expect to pay $35 to $55 per hour for a qualified bookkeeper.

And speaking of qualified, make sure they are! Bookkeeping is one of those professions where anyone can hang a shingle. You want to make sure that the freelance bookkeeper you select has specialized training and experience. Review their credentials. Ask for references! Don't trust your financial records to anyone who isn't qualified and reputable.

Where do you find a freelance bookkeeper? There are many virtual assistants who offer bookkeeping services. (More on virtual assistants later in the chapter in "Taking Advantage of Online Tools.") Also, let your fingers, or your computer mouse, do the walking through the online Yellow Pages (www.yellowpages.com).

Success Tip

Worried about giving a bookkeeper online access to your bank account, credit card account, or shopping cart program? Check if your online account has the option to set someone up with limited access of some sort (sometimes called a user account). This will limit the information that can be viewed by the bookkeeper and the account features that he or she can use.

In order for a bookkeeper to do her job, she needs to be able to see your business's financial records on a regular basis. This typically means giving her online access to your business bank account, credit card account, and website shopping cart transaction reports. Otherwise, you'll have to generate and provide these records to your bookkeeper manually, which takes a lot of time. (And aren't you trying to save time by hiring a bookkeeper?)

Obviously, giving a bookkeeper this kind of access requires a lot of trust. It's a little like giving the keys to your house to a maid. You want to make sure that whoever you select as a bookkeeper will keep access passwords in a secure place and maintain confidentiality. My advice? Get that assurance in writing.

Taming the Paper Dragon

Your business may be online, but you'll be amazed by the amount of paperwork that can be created. Although I make every attempt to keep records in electronic format and to automate tasks—such as bill payments—my inbox of paper grows steadily throughout the week. There are bills to pay, forms to be filled out, and stuff to file. Sometimes the paper dragon grows so quickly I feel like I have to beat it back with a stick!

Of course, there are a lot of online administrative tasks that are similar to paperwork that you have to deal with, too. Sloppy online files can cause just as many problems as the paper versions.

I define "paperwork" in two ways:

- ◆ Administrative tasks that need to get done.
- ◆ Files and other records that need to be filed.

Online or offline, it's all "paperwork" to me.

Like bookkeeping, keeping up with paperwork is important. There is nothing more frustrating than slacking off for a couple of weeks only to discover that something important has been missed or forgotten that gets you into trouble, or that an important file can't be found because it's buried in a pile of paper.

When paperwork is done in a timely manner, and files are put in the right place so that they're easy to find when you need them, you'll feel less stressed. Your business will run more smoothly without you having to worry about administrative headaches.

When it comes to administrative tasks, such as paying bills or submitting tax forms, I suggest you set aside a few hours once or twice a month for this activity. Actually put that appointment in your schedule. In my business, I schedule two hours every other week, usually on Friday afternoons from 1 P.M. to 3 P.M. for paperwork. That way it gets done.

Organizing Computer Files

I admit it. A couple of years ago my computer files were a mess. If it wasn't for the search feature in Windows, I wouldn't have been able to find anything! Then I made one simple change that made my computer files more organized and easier to find and manage. I started to use descriptive folders.

Whether you're on a Mac or a PC, you can create a folder that you can put similar computer files in. For example, as I'm writing this book all the files associated with the project are in a computer folder called *CIG Book*. Inside that folder I have other folders to further organize the information. I have a folder for completed chapters, chapters in progress, research on particular topics covered in this book, and so forth. When I open the master folder, I can easily find what I need and get started without delay. It sure beats hunting my computer for the right file!

Warning!

Regularly back up your computer files. If a fire, theft, or some other catastrophe were to destroy your computer, you need to be able to get your business up and running again quickly. And that would be very difficult to do if you lost your computer records. My favorite backup service is Carbonite.com. For just a few dollars per month, they automatically back up all my computer files. If I ever need to recover a lost file, I can do that by signing in to my Carbonite account from any computer.

For your web-based business you might have computer folders for the following administrative tasks:

◆ Bookkeeping

◆ Tax records

◆ Suppliers

◆ Marketing programs

◆ To-do lists

◆ Website host

◆ Shopping cart program

◆ Business registration

◆ Bank records

When you receive an e-mail from your merchant account provider telling you about a change in transaction fees, you can drag and drop that e-mail into your "Shopping Cart Program" folder. Then you'll always know where to find that information.

Computer folders, and folders within folders, will make your business life easier. Try it!

A Paper Filing System That Works

I wish all my files were in electronic format. However, I still have to deal with a significant amount of paper records and, chances are, you will too in your web-based business.

Before you decide how you will file paper, ask yourself, "Do I really need to?" Not every piece of paper that comes into your business or off your printer needs to be filed. I have a policy that if a similar record exists on my computer then I don't keep a duplicate paper version. I toss it in the trash bin.

For those paper records that I do need to file—receipts, tax records, contracts, etc.—I store them in a filing cabinet in my office.

I use legal-size 14" file folders, rather than the standard 12" version, because the larger size makes it easier to store all kinds of paper records and find them later on.

The most important element of my filing system is the labeling.

Most people use a descriptive label to categorize files. For example, you might label a file about Product X as simply "Product X" and then file it alphabetically. That works okay when you have only a few files to worry about. But as your business grows, and the amount of file folders stuffed in your cabinet grows along with it, finding files quickly is going to become more difficult. (*"Did I file that under N for New Product or P for Product? Or M for Merchandise!?"*)

A much better way is to file numerically. Here's how that works.

- ◆ You label your files with a numerical sequence, starting with 1, 2, 3, and so forth. So if you already have 24 files in your cabinet, the next file you make will be called "25."

- ◆ Then, on your computer, you keep a list of your files with the file numbers cross-referenced with a description of the contents.

Here's an example:

File #22 - Tax records for 2007

File #23 - Notes from web marketing seminar

File #24 - Business registration documents

Say you're looking for your business tax records for 2007. You simply open your computer file of "Files," scan it to find the file (or use the "Find" feature in Microsoft Word), notice it's file number 22, then go to your filing cabinet and pull out that file. It takes just a few seconds. Much faster than sifting through the file drawers looking for a file label that matches the description.

Making Your Business a Well-Oiled Machine

Recently I had to figure out how to use the document security features in my PDF publishing software so the e-books I create couldn't easily be copied or changed. I spent about 45 minutes on that task.

Now, next month, when I have to create a similar PDF file, will I remember how I did it weeks earlier? Maybe. Maybe not. That's why I always write down the procedures so I can do it again.

I call this "creating systems." In fact, I have a computer folder called "Systems" where I store all the instructions and procedures on how I do things in my business.

Creating a system out of an activity in your business has two benefits: first, it allows you to do that activity a lot faster the next time, without having to think about it. And second, it gives you the means to outsource that task to someone else.

In fact, a lot of administrative activities that I used to do in my web-based business are now done by others. I simply give them the step-by-step instructions for that task, which I already had stored on my computer.

If you want your business to grow, you can't be busy reinventing the wheel. You need to learn the best way to do something once, and then create a system that makes it easier for you to do again next time, or to be able to give that task to someone else to do.

Taking Advantage of Online Tools

Another way to make your business a well-oiled machine, and therefore save yourself a lot of time, is to leverage technology. There are myriad tools available on the Internet that allow you to accomplish all sorts of tasks faster and easier.

Many of these online tools are listed in Appendix B. But here are a couple of examples of two tools that work for me.

Google has a tool available for creating and sharing spreadsheets. When website visitors enroll in one of my online courses, my virtual assistant creates a Google spreadsheet containing their names and contact information. This spreadsheet exists on a secure web page in my Google account. Whenever either of us needs to view or update the spreadsheet, we simply access it online. It sure beats e-mailing the thing back and forth!

Another tool I use is TaDaList.com, a "to-do" list manager. This tool allows me to create multiple to-do lists for all my projects and other business activities in a convenient checkbox format.

These online tools are free. Check them out!

Getting Help

As your business grows, you're going to eventually need to get some help in managing all the administrative details. Otherwise, you'll drown in paperwork no matter how efficiently you've set things up to get it done.

Getting help is going to be an added expense to your business. And a lot of business owners are squeamish about making this commitment. I admit I was, too, for far more years than I care to admit. I just thought I could do it all myself. However, once I did get some administrative help, my business grew rapidly because I was able to focus more time on marketing, product development, teaching, consulting, and all the other things that more directly make me money.

When is a good time in your business growth to hire someone to handle administrative tasks?

The rule of thumb is that if you are spending more than two hours per day on activities that someone else can do cheaper, and perhaps even better, than you, then you need to take the leap. Hire the help. Your business, and your life in general, will be better as a result.

When looking for administrative help for your business, the first question you have to answer is: virtual assistant or employee?

A virtual assistant is someone who works for you on a freelance basis. They may have several other clients as well.

Typically, a virtual assistant (VA) charges by the hour, usually $25 to $50. However, there may be some tasks that a VA charges on a project or piecework basis. For example, my VA charges by the hour for most tasks but applies a per page rate for proofreading.

In my opinion, a virtual assistant is ideal because you don't have to worry about the expense and obligations of having a traditional employee. You only pay for the work you hire the VA to do for you. And if things don't work out you can easily cancel the arrangement.

Here are some great organizations that will help you find a virtual assistant:

> **Success Tip**
>
> When looking for administrative help, tap local resources. Chances are there are students or stay-at-home moms and dads in your area that would be delighted to do some part-time or occasional work for your business. Ask around. All the administrative assistance you need could be just around the block.

- ◆ International Virtual Assists Association (www.ivaa.org)

- ◆ Canadian Virtual Assistant Connection (www.cvac.ca)

- ◆ Society of Virtual Assistants (www.societyofvirtualassistants.co.uk)

There are many virtual assistants who specialize in working with web-based business owners and understand online payment systems, e-mail marketing, and so forth.

As your business grows and requires more substantial administrative help, hiring an employee, either part-time or even full-time, might make sense. You'll have more obligations as that person's employer—rather than as a VA's client—but your hourly costs will be less.

My advice? Start with a virtual assistant. Then, as your administrative needs increase, explore the possibility of hiring an employee.

The Least You Need to Know

- Don't be sloppy with your bookkeeping. It's one of the keys to a financially healthy business.

- Create systems, and take advantage of online tools, to make completing administrative tasks easier.

- Consider getting administrative help by hiring a virtual assistant or part-time employee.

Part 5

Marketing Your Site

In the early days of the Internet, you could launch a website and expect people to eventually stumble across it. Not anymore. To be successful, you need to promote your website to attract lots of potential customers to your virtual front door.

The good news is, there are many low-cost techniques you can use to spread the word to thousands or even millions of people. This part of the book gives you the basics—think of it as Web Marketing 101—and explains more than a dozen of the top traffic-generating strategies that work well for small web-based businesses.

The Scoop on Traffic Generation and Conversion

In This Chapter

- ◆ Attracting potential customers to your website and motivating them to buy
- ◆ Creating a compelling offer
- ◆ Getting customers to buy again and tell others about your website

To promote your web-based business effectively, you must understand how to attract lots of visitors to your website, and then motivate them to place orders for your products or services, or click on your affiliate advertisements. In Internet marketing lingo, these activities are commonly referred to as traffic generation and conversion. In order for your web-based business to be successful and profitable, you need to be savvy at both.

The Two Things Your Marketing Must Do

In the movie *Field of Dreams*, the main character is haunted by a voice that repeatedly says, "If you build it, they will come." Trusting that this is part of fate's plan for his life, he plows under a thriving cornfield and builds a baseball diamond. (The night lights alone must have cost him a fortune!)

Here in the real world of online marketing, that kind of wishful thinking simply doesn't work. Just because you build a great website doesn't necessarily mean people will find out about it, visit, and buy something. In fact, the chances are astronomical that your website will just sit there in cyberspace and not make you a dime.

Building a website is just the first step. You have to promote your web-based business in order to attract lots of potential customers to your virtual doorstep.

And even when you do, you've only done half the job. Getting hundreds or even thousands of visitors each month is wonderful. But you still have to convince them— through your well-organized website, compelling content, and persuasive sales copy— to click on an advertisement or place an order. If they don't do that, you won't make any money.

When you think of marketing your web-based business, there are two things you have to learn how to do very well:

◆ Generate traffic

◆ Get conversions

Traffic refers to the number of visitors who come to your site during a specific period of time. Some of these people might be new visitors, while others will be making their second, third, or perhaps twentieth visit. Think of traffic as people coming into a traditional retail store. The more people that do, the more potential sales you can make.

Traffic is often measured by the number of visitors during a specific day, week, or month. For example, there were 3,700 visitors to ForCopywritersOnly.com in July.

Conversion is the number of visitors that sign up for something on your website (such as a newsletter), or click on an affiliate link or advertisement, or buy something from you. It's like people in a retail store selecting an item and then walking up to the checkout to pay for it.

Conversion is often measured by percentage; that number is called the *conversion rate*.

def•i•ni•tion

Conversion rate is the percentage of website visitors who do the action you want them to do while on your website. There may be several such actions that you track. For example, if 28 out of 100 first-time visitors sign up for your newsletter, then the conversion rate of that action, "new visitor/newsletter sign up," is 28 percent. If 7 percent of people who visit a particular product page on your website place an order, then that percentage is the "product page/order" conversion rate.

Which is more important? Driving lots of targeted traffic to your website? Or getting high conversion rates?

The answer, of course, is both. You need to reach out to lots of potential customers and motivate them to drop by and visit your website. Once those people are on your site, however, you have to motivate them to take the actions you want them to take, which is usually clicking on affiliate ads so you can earn a commission, or placing an order for your product or service so you can make a profit.

Don't make the mistake that so many web-based business owners make and focus primarily on getting traffic. Traffic generation and conversion are the two pillars that hold your website up. If one crumbles, the whole thing comes tumbling to the ground.

Want Lots of Traffic? Think Small

A budding online entrepreneur once called me to ask how to promote her new web-based business. "I'm think of placing a few ads in the local business paper," she said. "What do you think?"

Frankly, I thought it would be a waste of money. Her website provides training and resources to human resource professionals. How many of those can she realistically expect to reach in a local general business publication? "Why not advertise instead in the newsletter of the HR Professionals Association?" I suggested. "That way you can count on almost 100 percent of the readers to be in your target market."

Even though placing an ad in that newsletter was a bit more expensive, she ended up generating a lot more visitors to her website—all HR professionals who had a high likelihood of being interested in her products and services.

By thinking small, and focusing her efforts on a smaller more targeted group of potential customers, she was able to get much better results with her marketing and more (and better) traffic to her site.

That's the key to traffic generation.

Don't attempt to promote your site to everyone. As a small business owner, you can't afford mass advertising and major publicity campaigns. Even if you could, it is probably not the best approach to marketing your business. Think small. Focus your efforts on targeted sources of potential customers, like my friend did with the HR newsletter ad.

Think about it—which marketing tactic do you think would work better for your knitting patterns website? An advertisement in a publication targeting 50,000 stay-at-home moms? Or that same ad in a targeted e-mail newsletter that is sent to 6,000 knitting enthusiasts? If you picked number two, you're right.

That's the first rule of successful traffic generation. Think small. Don't mass market. Instead, focus on those targeted pools of potential customers that you can easily reach and persuade to visit your website. You'll get much more bang for your marketing buck if you do.

Finding Your Pools of Potential Customers

In the previous section, I used the phrase "pools of potential customers." What do I mean by that? I'm referring to those places where you can easily reach out to the right kind of people and tell them about your website.

Say, for example, you want to attract coffee lovers to your website … a site that sells coffee beans and equipment. There are probably dozens of blogs that target that audience. There may be an online forum or other club online where those caffeine addicts hang out. There may even be a trade show exclusively for coffee lovers, similar to the popular wine and cheese shows. Those would all be examples of pools of potential customers.

When creating a plan for generating traffic to your site, you need to identify as many pools of potential customers as possible. These may include publications, forums, associations, blogs, radio shows, events, and more. Once you have this list, you're one step closer to persuading these people to visit your website.

Let's take a closer look at how to find these pools.

What Are Your Prospects Reading, Watching, and Listening To?

If your potential customers are knitting enthusiasts, then chances are there are many publications they read to get information on this topic. There may also be popular websites and blogs they frequent. There might even be a radio show for knitters!

To find your pools of potential customers, find out what they're reading, watching, and listening to.

How do you use this information in your marketing? You can use articles, press releases, and other publicity strategies (see Chapter 18) to get your site featured in a targeted publication or broadcast. You can also advertise in it.

Where Are Your Prospects Gathering?

Is there an annual trade show for knitters? Is there an online forum where the knitters hang out and chat? Is there a local knitting club? Find out!

The places, online and offline, where your potential customers hang out provide you with many opportunities to promote your website. For example, if there is a knitting forum, then you can participate in the discussions, answer questions, and provide helpful advice. The group will come to know you and your website very quickly.

My participation in one forum, a discussion group for corporate writers, is responsible for tens of thousands of dollars in sales for my web-based business over the past two years. And I only participate in that group 15 to 20 minutes per week.

Finding gathering places can also lead to speaking opportunities, which can also drive a lot of potential customers to your website. (See Chapter 20 for more on this.)

What Are Your Potential Customers Searching for Online?

Perhaps the ultimate pool of potential customers is the search engines.

You can use keyword tools (see Chapter 17) to find out how many people are searching for terms related to your website offerings, and then use search engine optimization (SEO) strategies, and perhaps also search engine advertising, to help those people find your website.

In addition, keywords help you understand your customers better so you can create more appealing offers that drive more traffic and increase sales.

For example, say you discover that there are more than 100,000 searches for the keywords "free knitting patterns" each month. Obviously a lot of people are actively searching for sites that have free patterns available. So here's what you do. You create a "Free Knitting Pattern of the Week" program and promote it. Potentially thousands of people will sign up—many of whom will probably purchase your more expensive patterns later on.

Top Strategies for Generating Traffic

There are dozens of marketing tactics you can use to generate traffic to your website. You should explore as many options as possible to determine which strategies are the right fit for you, given your goals, personality, and budget.

Success Tip

Fit is very important. You don't want to sink time and money into a marketing tactic that may not work well for you. For example, networking at live events can be an effective way to promote your website. But if you're uncomfortable in social business situations—if you're not an effective schmoozer—then this marketing strategy probably won't get you too far.

Here's an example. Advertising can work quite well in driving traffic to your site, if you do it right. But this is an expensive marketing strategy and doesn't always work. What if you only have a shoestring budget, sink all of it into a few ads, and end up generating a disappointingly low amount of traffic? Your business will have stopped before it got started.

Review the following top tactics for generating traffic, which are all explained in subsequent chapters in this section of the book. Then determine which ones are the best fit for you.

- ◆ Search engine marketing
- ◆ Articles
- ◆ Publicity
- ◆ Advertising
- ◆ Social media
- ◆ Direct mail
- ◆ Speaking
- ◆ Working with affiliates
- ◆ Networking
- ◆ Trade shows and other events

Most web-based business owners pick two or three marketing tactics that work well for them. It's difficult, if not impossible, for the small business owner to do them all.

Developing Your Compelling Offer

Can you imagine trying to fish with a hook but no lure? Even if you've never gone anywhere near a fishing pole before, you can probably guess that you wouldn't catch very many fish that way. As they say, you must bait your hook or you won't hook your catch.

The same is true of marketing your web-based business. You need a good lure; something that you can use as a compelling *offer* to entice a lot of potential customers to visit your website.

A big mistake that many web-based business owners make is simply promoting the existence of their website without making any specific offer. "Shop for European shoes online at _____.com." Sure, that approach can generate some interest. But people probably won't visit the site unless they are actually shopping for shoes, or at least thinking about it, at that particular moment. And how many people are doing that right now?

You'll generate a lot more traffic if you give people a reason to visit your website right away, whether they're shopping for shoes or not. And that reason is your compelling offer.

def•i•ni•tion

In marketing lingo, an **offer** refers to the deal you are communicating to potential customers in your advertisement or other promotion. It's basically a "do this and get that" proposition. For example, your offer could be "5 FREE Christmas knitting patterns when you visit _____.com." In that case, you're offering potential customers something free in exchange for dropping by your website.

For example, your marketing efforts could say, "Shop for European shoes online at _____.com and sign up for your 25 percent discount certificate." Now you've given potential customers a great reason to drop by your site. They want that discount certificate!

I've worked with many web-based business owners who experienced huge surges in traffic simply because they added a compelling offer to their advertising and other promotions. You should do the same.

There are many types of compelling offers you can come up with to promote your website. Use your imagination. Think about what potential customers may want right now, and then create an offer that gives it to them. Here are a few ideas:

- Gift basket service. Compelling offer: *Free express delivery certificate. Good for three months.*

- Coaching service. Compelling offer: *Sign up for a free one-hour coaching session.*

- Information site for freelance copywriters. Compelling offer: *Free 142-page copywriter's success kit.*

- Contact management software for real estate professionals. Compelling offer: *Free 5-week trial.*

- Website that sells premium coffee beans, supplies, and equipment. Compelling offer: *Free coffee bean taster's guide.*

- Knitting patterns website. Compelling offer: *Join our free knitting pattern of the week club.*

- Website that sells industrial pumps. Compelling offer: *Free pump purchasing checklist.*

When it comes to generating traffic, never go fishing for potential customers without first baiting your hook—with a compelling offer. And, if possible, make it a free offer.

Turning Visitors Into Customers

Say a potential customer finds out about your website somehow. Perhaps they read about you on a blog, or noticed the compelling offer you made in an advertisement, or discovered you while doing a search on Google. Now they are on your website clicking and looking around. Will they place an order for one of your products or services? Or, if your site is supported by affiliate programs, will they click on an ad?

That depends on how persuasive your website is.

Your website must motivate visitors to take the actions you want them to take. That could be to sign up for your newsletter, click on an ad or other link, or buy something. As I described earlier in this chapter, this activity is called conversion. And if your website doesn't convert, then all the time and dollars you've spent to generate traffic will have been wasted.

How do you make your website convert well? To answer that question, put yourself in the shoes of a customer. When you visit a website, what is it that makes you want to stay, explore, and buy? Is it:

- The navigation bar and other features that make it easy for you to find what you need?

- The simple, uncluttered pages that are easy to read or skim?

- A compelling offer to sign up for, such as a free newsletter or how-to guide?

- The friendly, helpful tone of the web copy?

- All the great articles, tools, blogs, forums, and other free resources?

- The product pages that fully explain everything you need to know to make a buying decision?

- The testimonials from other customers that make you feel more comfortable in placing an order?

- The ease with which you can find the address, phone number, e-mail, and other contact information in case you have questions or need support?

- The payment options that make it convenient for you to place an order?

Probably all of the above!

So, in a way, there is no big secret to getting high conversion rates. Just use your common sense! However, there are a lot of tips and tricks that can help you boost conversion rates on your website pages, which are described in detail in Chapter 21.

Don't Forget the 95 Percent Club!

There is a club that will visit your website every month. I call it the 95 percent club. They are a very interesting group of potential customers. You see, they check out your website; become interested in your products, services, or information; then leave without buying anything!

Of course, I'm using 95 percent as just an example. Your percentage of visitors in this club may be higher or lower. The point is, the overwhelming majority of first-time visitors who come to your site won't place an order right away. That doesn't mean they're not interested in what you have to offer. They just need to get to know you first.

> **Warning!**
>
> According to many studies, the majority of customers will visit a website an average of five times before deciding to make a purchase on that site or click on one of its affiliate advertisements. So providing good reasons for your website visitors to keep coming back is vital to the success of your business.

How do you make that happen?

You need to get these visitors to sign up for something, so that you can continue to communicate with them.

Most websites offer an e-mail newsletter of some kind. You can also offer free information (packaged as a tip sheet, how-to guide, or special report), a free course taught as a series of e-mails, or some other creative approach to using e-mail to communicate with the 95 percent club—like the "Free knitting pattern of the week club" example I used earlier.

Getting people who don't buy right away to sign up for something can dramatically increase your sales. It gives you an opportunity to build a relationship with them and gives them a chance to get to know you and your website better. I get the majority of my website sales from the 95 percent club.

Check out Chapter 22 for strategies on using e-mail in this way.

Cultivating Repeat Business and Word-of-Mouth

There is an old saying in the retail business. A customer will make you some money. A repeat customer will make you lots of money. A *loyal* customer, someone who buys from you again and again and tells friends and colleagues about you, will make you a fortune!

That's the attitude you must have for your web-based business. If you're looking for long-term success, and I'm guessing that you are, then you must think about marketing not just as getting traffic and conversions, but also in building a loyal base of customers for your website.

Think of your customers as a funnel, with the widest opening at the top and a narrow opening at the bottom. From top to bottom it will look like the following:

- ◆ Wide end of the funnel: Lots of website visitors come to your site for the first time. They are potential customers.

- ◆ Middle of the funnel: A percentage of those potential customers make a purchase or return to your website sometime in the future to do so. They become first-time customers.

- ◆ Middle of the funnel: A percentage of those first-time customers will return to your site to buy from you again and again. They become repeat customers.

- ◆ Bottom of the funnel: A percentage of those repeat customers continue to buy from you and also spread the word about your site to their friends and colleagues. They become loyal customers.

When marketing their websites, most business owners focus their efforts on the top of the funnel—basically on attracting visitors and motivating them to place an order. But even during the start-up phase, you need to be thinking about how you're going to move customers down the funnel to become, hopefully, loyal advocates of your website.

Imagine how successful your business would be if you had a large number of customers you could count on to buy your products and services again and again, and recommend your site to others. I know many website owners who have just such a loyal customer base, and I can tell you, they are doing very, very well!

So how do you get customers to travel down the funnel?

The secret is simple—follow up.

When first-time visitors sign up for your e-mail newsletter, follow up with them a few weeks later to ask if they are enjoying the publication. Let them know about new articles, promotions, or other information that has been added to your website.

When a customer places an order, send a follow-up e-mail a few weeks later asking how they are enjoying the product. Let them know about similar products or add-ons that they might be interested in. And don't forget to thank them, again, for their original order.

Warning!

It's a lot easier to get a customer to buy from your website again than it is to persuade someone new to make a first-time purchase. So if you're not keeping in touch with your customers, you're walking away from a lot of potential sales and profits. In fact, existing customers are your "hottest" market.

When you notice a customer buying from you repeatedly, ask if they would consider providing you with a testimonial. And if they do so, send them a handwritten thank-you card in the mail (not one of those free e-mail cards). I often enclose a $25 gift certificate from Starbucks or Barnes & Noble.

Ask "Where did you hear about us?" on your online order form. A lot of customers will answer that question. When you discover that someone was referred to your site from another customer, contact that person to thank them.

What you're doing with all this diligent follow-up is gently prodding first-time customers to become repeat customers, and repeat customers to become loyal customers. And you're doing so by not being a pest but simply by being appreciative and building the relationship.

Ultimately, all marketing—whether it's to generate traffic, get conversions, or cultivate customer loyalty—is about building relationships. The better your marketing does that, the more effective it will be.

The Least You Need to Know

- Your marketing needs to accomplish two important things: generate traffic and get conversions.

- Create a compelling offer that entices potential customers to visit your website.

- Build great customer relationships. Satisfied customers buy again and tell others.

Chapter 17

Getting Found on the Search Engines

In This Chapter

♦ How to get listed higher in the search results of Google, Yahoo!, MSN, AOL, Ask, and other major search engines

♦ Finding the right keywords for your website

♦ Buying your way in with Google AdWords and other search engine advertising programs

What do you do when you need to find something on the Internet? If you're like most people you go to Google, Yahoo!, or some other search engine and type in keywords associated with what you're looking for.

Guess what? That's what many of your potential website customers do, too! In fact, according to research by Pew Internet & American Life Project, more than 60 million U.S. adults per day use search engines. So it's important that when people are seeking the type of products, services, and information your website offers, they can easily find you in this manner. If they can't, then you're missing out on a significant amount of traffic. This chapter will help you make sure that doesn't happen!

Getting Found When People Search for You

Recently a friend of mine was looking for a wedding planning service in the Chicago area. So she typed in "wedding planning" and "Chicago" into Google and was greeted with literally hundreds of pages of search results. Of course, she didn't click on every link. In fact, she made her shortlist of potential wedding planners from the websites that were listed on just the first two or three pages.

Chances are, those wedding planners made some smart decisions regarding how their websites were structured and written. They were able to become very easy to find on Google, and probably most other search engines, too, and as a result gained a significant competitive advantage. If your website offered wedding planning services and you were listed only on page 17 on Google, then you'd be out of luck. You just lost a potential customer.

So what makes the difference between a website that gets showcased on those critical first few pages in search results and one that ends up buried on page 300? Search engine marketing.

Search engine marketing, or SEM as it's often called in the industry, refers to techniques you can use to get your site seen on the first few pages of search engine results.

How Search Engine Marketing Works

Say your website sells custom decals for bikes. You want to make sure that potential customers will easily find your site when they're looking for that type of product on Google, Yahoo!, or any other search engine.

How do you make that happen?

To answer that question, let's take a closer look at a typical search results page. If an Internet-connected computer is available to you now, do a search for any popular product using Google or Yahoo!. If you were to search for "snowboards," for example, you'd see a long list of websites listed down the left side of the search results page. Those are what is called the organic results.

Now run your eyes over to the right side of the page. Chances are, there is another list of websites that look a lot like text advertisements. That's because they are advertisements! Yahoo! calls them sponsored sites. Google refers to them as sponsored links. In the industry, these ads are referred to as paid results.

So there are two ways you can get your website listed on the first two or three pages of a search result: organic and paid.

Of course, getting your website listed high in organic results is ideal. It's essentially free advertising. And according to various studies, potential customers are four to six times more likely to click on a link in the organic results than they are an advertisement in the sponsored links section.

As you'll discover throughout this chapter, by using *search engine optimization* (SEO) tactics there is a lot you can do to influence how high your site gets listed by Google, Yahoo!, and the other search engines. However, despite your best efforts, you won't get on the first page for every common keyword or phrase your potential customers might type in. So a great strategy is to do the best you can to get listed on the first couple of pages in the organic search results for specific keywords, and then use search engine advertising to fill the gaps.

def•i•ni•tion

Search engine optimization (SEO) refers to a series of techniques for getting your web-site listed high in organic search engine results for specific keywords. It's a big subject. So if you want to move beyond the basics and learn more advanced SEO strategies for your web-based business, I suggest you pick up a copy of *The Complete Idiot's Guide to Search Engine Optimization* by Michael Miller.

Getting Your Site Listed

Okay. You want your site to rank as high as possible in the search results of all the popular search engines. But if your web-based business is new, how are these search engines going to find out about you and include you in their listings?

A few years ago, a new website would have to be manually submitted to each of the major search engines. These days, however, search engine spiders have pretty much replaced that time-consuming exercise.

A search engine spider is a tiny computer program that search engines use to scour the Internet for new or updated websites. In fact, you can expect a spider to visit your site within a few weeks after it goes live—and probably within a few days!

Warning!

Search engine spiders cannot read sound, pictures, flash animations, or online videos. So be careful when you use these elements on your website. If a video is the only information you have on a web page about, say, running a first marathon, then that page will not likely appear to people looking for that kind of information on a search engine.

A search engine spider is a text reader. It crawls through your website text and HTML code to gather information about your site so the search engine can make decisions regarding how to categorize and list you. It's vitally important that your web copy describes each web page accurately and that other elements of your site are making that easy. You're not just trying to impress website visitors about how wonderful your website products and services are, you're trying to influence the spiders as well.

Don't worry. The spiders are coming! There's nothing you need to do to invite them to visit your website. Usually, you don't need to submit any sort of request to Google or the other major search engines. However, if you want to make sure, search for your website URL on Google (for example, forcopywritersonly.com). Is your site listed? If it is, then check the description area for the word *cached*. Click on that and it will show you when the Google spider—called the GoogleBot—last visited your site and what it saw.

You can repeat this exercise for Yahoo! and Ask. Currently, MSN, AOL, and many other search engines use the search results of other search engines! For example, if your site is listed on Yahoo! it's also listed on MSN.

If, for some reason, your site doesn't appear on a particular search engine, then try manually submitting it. You can do that on Google at: www.google.com/addurl. Yahoo!'s manual submission site is: http://search.yahoo.com/info/submit.htmlfree/request.

You can't submit your website to Ask, but their spider is very good at finding websites and will probably find yours.

In addition to making sure the spiders have visited, I suggest that you also submit your site to the Open Directory Project (www.dmoz.org). This is an organization where volunteer editors—human beings, not spiders!—review your site. Many search engines supplement their database with information from DMOZ, so it's a good idea to submit your site to these folks.

The Key to Keywords

What is the most important thing you need to do in order for your website to be easily found in search engine results? Discover the *keywords* that your potential customers are using to look for the type of products, services, and information your site offers. Keywords are the key to successful search engine marketing.

def•i•ni•tion

Keywords are simply words that someone uses to describe what they hope to find when performing a web search of some kind. Keywords are often grouped together in phrases, such as "life insurance quotes," "divorce lawyer Seattle," or "size 16 dress shoes." Keywords give marketers important insights into what customers are looking for and which words to use on your site to help these customers find you.

Say your website sells used books. Which keywords would your potential customers use to find this type of product? Well, you can expect they would start their web search using words and phrases such as:

- Used books
- Rare used books
- Used book store
- Used textbooks
- Secondhand college books
- Cheap used books
- Used books online

Your potential customers might also use keywords that are less obvious. For example:

- Cheap books
- Old books
- Cheap textbooks
- Out of print books

Now what if the phrase "second hand college books" was nowhere to be found on your website? Chances are, a search engine won't display your website when someone types in that phrase. You certainly wouldn't be listed on the first page. Why? Because search engine spiders aren't human. They can't make the intuitive judgment that those who are looking for second hand college books might also be looking for used books as well. So people who are actively shopping for those products may not be able to easily find you.

How do you remedy this? You integrate that phrase into your website copy and perhaps even into the title and meta description tags. (You'll learn how to do this in the next section.)

But before you do that, you need to find out which keywords potential customers are using to find websites like yours.

Keyword Suggestion Tools

The biggest mistake that web-based business owners make is guessing which keywords potential clients will use for web searches. Usually the guesses are wrong or incomplete. For example, a friend of mine was launching a website featuring muffin recipes and associated products. He guessed right that "muffin recipes" was a popular phrase. What he didn't realize is that there were more than 30,000 searches per month on Google for "blueberry muffins"—a phrase not mentioned on his website!

So if guessing isn't the best strategy for finding the right keywords, what is? Remember that list I created for the used bookstore example in the previous section? To compile that, I used one of the many keyword selection tools available online. I simply typed in a few keywords associated with used books. (Okay, I guessed!) Then the selection tool automatically generated a list of keywords based on what people are actually using to find these types of products.

Here is a list of the most popular keyword selection tools used by web-based business owners.

- Google AdWords Keyword Tool (http://adwords.google.com/select/KeywordToolExternal)

- WordTracker Keywords (http://freekeywords.wordtracker.com)

- Keyword Discovery (http://keyworddiscovery.com/search.html)

- Web CEO (http://webceo.com/keywords.htm)

- Compete (http://searchanalytics.compete.com)

The Google tool is free. The other tools offer free basic and paid premium pricing levels. In my opinion, unless you're a serious keyword researcher you can do just fine using the free versions of these keyword selection tools. The Google tool is especially helpful because it not only suggests keywords but also provides you with monthly search volume statistics. That's how I found out that over 30,000 of my fellow blueberry muffin lovers search for that term on Google each month!

When planning your website, use these tools to create a list of the most popular keywords that your potential customers may use to find you. Then lay a trail of breadcrumbs—or muffin crumbs!—to your website. How? The most effective way is to integrate those keywords into your web copy.

Weaving Keywords Into Your Web Copy

If your website visitors are looking for "blueberry muffin recipes," doesn't it make sense to have that phrase on one of your website pages? Not only will it help get your site listed higher in search engine results, but customers who go to your website will know they have come to the right place! So integrating keywords into your web copy is not only a good search engine optimization technique, it's also a smart customer communication strategy. And that's the attitude you should take when developing your web copy using keywords.

When writing the copy yourself, or working with an editor or copywriter, make sure that the keywords fit naturally into the text. This isn't always easy. In fact, it's a real skill to integrate multiple keywords into website copy without making the text seem convoluted or nonsensical. So spend the time it takes to get it right. Remember, the copy isn't just for the search engine spiders; it's also for the customers.

Pay particular attention to headlines. Search engine spiders closely analyze these for clues as to what your website is all about. Make sure the main headline of each page, as well as all the subheads within the body copy, are descriptive—and, if possible, include the popular keywords.

> ### Sales Builder
>
> If there is a particularly popular keyword that potential customers use to find your site, then create a separate web page around that word or phrase. This will go a long way toward getting that website page ranked higher in organic search engine results when people search for that keyword.

Some SEO experts say that the first 50 to 100 words of body copy on each page are the most important because some search engine spiders only crawl that far into the text. So, as with the headers, ensure that the first paragraph or two on each page includes the appropriate keywords.

Meta Tags, Title Tags, Inbound Links, Oh My!

Integrating the right keywords strategically into your web copy is the best way to ensure that your potential customers find you on Google, Yahoo!, AOL, and the other search engines. But there are many other things you can do to climb to the top of the charts in search results.

Your ultimate goal, of course, is this: someone types a particular keyword or phrase into a search engine and your site comes up on the first few pages. According to studies, more than 85 percent of web searchers will make their decisions as to which websites to visit based on what they see on the first five pages of search results. So making it into that exclusive club is crucial.

Success Tip

An ALT tag is a special HTML code that displays an alternative text description of a picture or other image on your website. It's primarily for those computer users who are visually impaired and use audio-assisted Internet tools or for those users whose computers are not displaying the graphic for some reason. Increasingly, search engines are giving better rankings to those websites that have ALT tags. Make sure they are integrated into your website design.

Here are some other proven strategies that will help.

Inbound Links

If other people are referring their friends, prospects, and customers to your website, you must be doing something right. At least that's the attitude of the search engines. That's why inbound links play an important role in how well your website gets ranked. Search engines, especially Google, take a close look at how many other websites are linking to you.

An inbound link (also called a backward link) is simply a link on another site that directly points to your own. The more of those you have, the more impressed the search engines are with you. In fact, Google actually refers to them as "votes."

However, not all links to your website carry the same weight. For example, search engines tend to not like reciprocal links, which is the practice of trading links between two sites. They're considered to be biased. The best links are one way.

Hopefully, a lot of websites will want to provide a link to your site because your products, services, or information are so darn good! But there is a lot you can do to help this process along.

◆ Contact websites and blogs in your industry or marketplace. Ask if they would be interested in listing your website as a resource.

◆ Encourage resellers, suppliers, and other partners. Ask if they would be willing to recommend you on their websites.

◆ Contact friends and colleagues who have websites and blogs. Ask if they would please mention your website.

◆ Ensure all your press releases carry a live link to your website.

◆ Develop a helpful tool or resource on your website. People who use it may recommend it to others—in the form of a link to your site.

◆ Ensure that any article you get published includes a live link to your website.

◆ Become an active participant in online blogs and forums. Many of these sites will include a link to your website.

Cultivating inbound links to your website can take a lot of work. But if it helps you get even one page higher in search results—say from page five to page four—the effort is more than worth it.

Playing Tag with Title and Meta Tags

There are three types of tags that influence search engine rankings and the likelihood that a potential customer will click on your listing to visit your website: title tags, meta description tags, and meta keyword tags.

Let's start with the title tag because that guy is, by far, the most important.

Visit any website. Then look up, way up, to the top left corner of the web browser screen. You'll see some words that (ideally) describe the web page you're looking at. Those words—the title—are generated by the title tag embedded in the HTML code for that page.

Search engines rely on your title tag to learn what your website is all about. And so do your potential customers. Not only does the title tag display the title of your page to your website visitors, but search engines also use it to name the link to your site in search engine results.

Do a Google search for one of my websites: ForCopywritersOnly.com. The title that Google provides for the prominent underlined blue link is:

> For Copywriters Only: proven strategies for attracting more clients and better paying products.

Why did Google create the link in that way? Because that's what I put in the title tag to the front page of my website. Copywriters, my potential customers, looking to attract more clients and better-paying projects are going to see that link and know they've found a website that contains the information they need. Can you imagine what would happen instead if my title tag were simply my company name, Slaunwhite Communications?

So what you put in your title tag is important. In her special report, *Turning Clicks Into Leads with Search Engine Optimization*, my friend and SEO expert Dianna Huff provides these tips for title tags.

- Each page of your website should have its own unique title tag.

- Title tags should incorporate the keywords for which you want that specific page to rank.

- Target two or three primary keyword phrases per page.

- Keywords should be listed in the exact order you think people are using them in their searches.

Compared to a title tag, a meta description tag is considerably less important. But that doesn't mean you should ignore it. Many search engines use this tag to help describe your site in their search engines results. A meta description tag is simply a short description of your website that exists only within the HTML code. Your website visitors don't see it. I suggest it be no more than 10 words. Here's a typical example:

> *Learn copywriting, become a copywriter, free success kit.*

Of the three tags, the meta keyword tag is the least important. None of the major search engines give it any weight in determining search engine rankings. Still, just to be on the safe side, place five to seven of your most popular keywords in this tag. Hey, you never know!

Paying Your Way In with Search Engine Ads

No matter how diligently you optimize your website, you won't get on the first few pages of search engine results with every keyword on your list. However, you still can get a link to your website displayed on the first page—by paying your way in.

None of the search engines accept bribes in return for a good organic ranking. However, most offer advertising options where your ad can be displayed next to first page search results. As I said earlier in this chapter, you can see these ads as sponsored links along the right side of the page and sometimes at the top shaded in a distinct color background.

Signing up for these programs is a relatively straightforward process. Here's where you can get started:

◆ Google AdWords (http://google.adwords.com)

◆ Yahoo! Search Marketing (http://searchmarketing.yahoo.com)

◆ MSN Live Search (http://advertising.microsoft.com)

How much do these ads cost? Well, that's where things get a little complicated! Unlike print ads where you can expect to pay a flat fee, search engine ads are priced on a cost-per-click basis. That simply means that you pay a fixed fee, say $0.35, every time your advertisement appears in the search results and someone clicks it. That's simple enough to understand. Where it gets complicated is that the amount you decide to "bid" for a keyword influences where your advertisement will be placed on the page or even if it will be displayed at all.

For example, say you want to place a search engine ad so that when someone searches for "running shoes" on Google, your ad appears. Google will ask you how much you're willing to pay for each click you get. If you bid too low, your ad might not appear. If you bid too high, your ad might get displayed regularly and high up on the search pages; however, the increased expense might make the campaign unprofitable for you.

Success Tip

The competition for popular keywords can be fierce amongst search engine advertisers. So instead of fighting that losing battle, consider bidding on less popular variations of a keyword. For example, "running shoes for kids" instead of just "running shoes." Sure, there are fewer searches for that phrase. But there's also less competition. You stand a much better chance of getting your ad displayed regularly for a relatively low cost-per-click.

How Search Advertising Works

Let's take a look at how Google AdWords works, since it is the granddaddy of all the search engine advertising programs and by far the most popular.

Once you open your account, you typically go through the following steps to create an advertisement:

1. You give your campaign a name.

2. You select which language your customers speak and which countries they are located in. If you're targeting English-speaking Americans, for example, your ad will appear in English and only to Internet users in the United States.

3. You write your advertisement.

4. You input the keywords that you want to trigger the advertisements. For example, if your website sells fishing equipment and supplies then you might want the keywords "trout fish lures" to trigger your ad.

5. You select how much money you're willing to pay each time someone clicks on your ad. Google calls this your *maximum CPC bid*.

6. You input a maximum daily budget. This protects your pocketbook. Once your click costs reach this level, your ad stops running and your credit card stops being charged.

7. You save your campaign and activate it.

Of course, these are just the basics. Google AdWords and other search engine advertising programs offer a dizzying range of additional options. You can, for example, focus your campaign on a specific geographic area, such as a town or city. (Especially useful if your site sells flowers in Philadelphia!) You can also bid to have your ad placed in a specific position among the other sponsored ads—perhaps the number-one spot. Google is even experimenting with a cost-per-conversion pricing model where you pay only when someone clicks on your ad and takes some action on your website, such as signing up for your e-mail newsletter or making a purchase.

Is your head spinning yet?

If you're new to Google AdWords, I suggest you keep it simple. Start with just one advertisement for a few of your most desired keywords. Monitor the results. Learn how things work. Then build from there.

Writing a Winning Search Engine Ad

The biggest challenge in creating an effective search engine ad is size. You don't have much room. A Google AdWords ad will allow you 3 lines: a 25-character headline, 2 lines of copy that are a maximum of 35 characters each, and the URL of a web page. That's it! Not much room to tantalize a potential customer and motivate him or her to visit your website. You have to make each word count.

On my website for freelance copywriters, I'm trying to attract people who are relatively new to copywriting and want to learn more about this writing niche. So whenever anyone uses Google to find information on being a successful copywriter, I want my add to appear:

> Make Money Copywriting
>
> Free Copywriter "Success Kit"
>
> (includes 116-page Manual + 2 CDs)
>
> www.ForCopywritersOnly.com

As I said, a search engine ad has three parts: the headline, the body copy, and the URL. Let's take a look at how to write each of these effectively.

> ### Sales Builder
>
> The key to creating a successful search engine advertisement is testing. Google AdWords allows you to create two versions of your ad and have them automatically rotate so you can quickly determine, often within just a few days, which one is performing best for you. Always be testing your best ad against a new variation.

The headline is the most important element. It has to gain a web searcher's attention and motivate him to read the ad and click on it. And you have to accomplish all that using just three or four words! Google and other search engines help by making the headline a hyperlink. That means it's blue, underlined, and clickable.

Remember why a person is doing a web search to begin with. He is looking for something—an answer to a question, a solution to a problem, a fulfillment of an aspiration. So your headline should be like a hand waving in the air saying, "Hey, what you're looking for is right here!" In my case, I wanted to attract those who are looking for ways to make a good living as a copywriter. So my headline, "Make Money Copywriting," was my waving hand.

Success Tip

In addition to the amount of bucks you bid for a keyword, Google rewards you for your ad quality. The better performing your ad is—in terms of the number of clicks it gets compared to its competitors—the more it will be shown and the higher up the list it will be displayed. So make it a winner!

The next part of your search engine ad is the body copy. You only have two lines but still are working with very few words—typically less than 10. If a web searcher is reading the body copy, you've already got his attention. Your job now is to persuade him to click. How do you do that? I have found that the more effective way is to either make a compelling offer or a promise of some kind. In the example, my offer is for a free success kit of information.

The final part of the search engine ad is the link. Google doesn't make this clickable like it does the headline, so you need to spell out this link completely. Why? First of all, if a web searcher doesn't click your ad you at least want him to remember your website. Secondly, a small percentage of people will actually type in the URL rather than click on your ad! I don't know why, but it happens.

The Least You Need to Know

- There are two ways to make it easy for customers to find you on the search engines: search engine optimization and search engine advertising.

- The key to success with the search engines is keyword research. Make a list of those words and phrases that customers are using to find sites like yours.

- Inbound links and title tags also play an important role in getting seen on the search engines.

- Advertising programs, like Google AdWords, can be a cost-effective way of driving traffic to your website because you only pay when your ad is clicked.

Chapter 18

Spreading the Word with Online Articles and Publicity

In This Chapter

◆ Building a media list of online publications that are popular amongst your target audience

◆ Options for getting your articles created and published on popular websites and in e-mail newsletters and blogs

◆ Generating publicity so that you get featured or quoted in online publication stories and articles

The number-one reason why people use the Internet is to find information, which is often in the form of an article of some kind. For example, if you're looking for tips on selecting the best running shoes and type "running shoes shopping tips" into a search engine, you're going to find a multitude of articles and blog posts on that subject.

Being the author of an article published online, or getting quoted or mentioned in one, can drive dozens or even hundreds of targeted visitors to your web-based business. And the best part is, you don't necessarily have to be a writer or public relations wiz to make that happen. This chapter will show you how.

Building a Media List

Your first step in getting publicity and spreading articles about your website all over the Internet is to build a *media list*.

A media list is simply a list of online publications that would be ideal for your web-based business to be mentioned in. These are websites, e-mail newsletters, and blogs whose readership represents potential customers for your products and services. These days, they may also include podcasts and videocasts. The more targeted the better.

For example, say your website sells quilting supplies and related how-to information. I'm sure you'd love to get a blurb in People Magazine Online or USATODAY.com. But the chances of that happening are pretty slim. (If it does, congratulations!) Your best opportunities to place articles and get publicity are with smaller, niche publications that target your specific audience. These will include popular blogs, e-mail newsletters, and informational websites for quilters.

Sales Builder

Don't just focus on big publications. Oftentimes, an e-mail newsletter, blog, or e-zine with just a few thousand readers can be an ideal candidate for your media list. Why? Smaller publications are often very specialized in a specific topic area; therefore, the readership can be remarkably loyal. In addition, it's often easier to break into a smaller publication with your press releases and articles than it is a larger one.

Put yourself in the shoes of your target customer. What online publications does he or she read that are specific to the type of products and services you sell? Find those and you'll have found your ideal media list.

Here are some resources that can help you with that search:

- Google Blog Search (blogsearch.google.com)
- Podcast Blaster (www.podcastblaster.com)
- Podcast Alley (www.podcastalley.com)
- MagPortal.com (www.magportal.com)
- New List (www.new-list.com)
- StumbleUpon (www.stumbleupon.com)

And don't forget to include major print publications in your area. Most popular magazines and trade publications have online versions, often with articles, blogs, and other features that are distinct from the print edition.

Your goal should be to find at least 10 online publications that are read by your target audience.

That's not always easy. Some of the smaller e-mail newsletters and blogs may not be listed anywhere. Here's a tip. When I began my first web-based business, I did an informal survey of potential customers I knew and asked them what they were reading. Even though I knew the market very well—or thought I did—I was surprised to learn about publications I've never heard of before.

Placing Your Articles

Contributing articles to popular websites, e-mail newsletters, and blogs is such an effective Internet marketing strategy that there's even a special name for it: *article marketing*.

Article marketing is the process of developing and distributing articles that are related to your website's products and services. The idea is when people read your article, they are also going to find out about your website, by way of the byline or the "About the Author" *resource box* section, and visit it.

Here's a typical example of how this works.

I have a product on my website—a handbook called *Cracking the Case Study Market*. It's aimed at freelance writers who want to make money writing case studies and success stories for companies. Using article marketing as a strategy to drive prospects to my website, I wrote an article called *6 Reasons Why Case Studies Are a Terrific Market for Writers*. Then I managed to get that article published at FreelanceWriting. com.

def•i•ni•tion

A **resource box** is a small block of text, usually placed at the end of an article, that contains information about the author. In a resource box, you are usually able to include a short promotional blurb about your website, along with a link to your website.

As you can imagine, that site gets a lot of traffic from people looking for information on freelance writing. A portion of those visitors found and read my article and, with a simple click of the link in the article resource box, were immediately taken to my website to learn more about the product. And, happily, several placed an order.

Getting Resourceful with the Resource Box

Your resource box is your payment for contributing the article. It's like a free advertisement. However, most online publications have strict guidelines as to how long your resource box can be and what you can say in it.

Here's a typical example:

> Steve Slaunwhite helps freelance professionals get the projects they want, from the clients they want, at the prices they want. To learn more about his popular Fast Track to Great Clients program, visit: www.fasttracktogreatclients.com.

Most publications allow you to include a resource box with your article. However, there are a few websites, e-mail newsletters, and blogs that are very restrictive, sometimes only giving you a byline and little else. However, if it's a popular publication with a high readership, then even that modest mention can be enough to drive a lot of traffic your way.

Planning Articles and Brainstorming Topics

The key ingredient to successful article marketing is, of course, an article. Without one of those, you're not going to get too far!

What are the characteristics of a good article?

Obviously, your article topic needs to be associated closely with the products, services, or information you provide on your website. No sense developing a piece about cooking the perfect BBQ steak if your website is about vegetarian living! Meat eaters will rarely fork out dough for a good tofu stir-fry recipe!

As a rule, articles on the Internet tend to be shorter than their print counterparts. You might find stories in print magazines running up to 2,000 words. That's almost unheard of in an e-mail newsletter or website publication, where the average article length hovers around the 500-word mark. Blog posts tend to be even shorter, averaging 200 to 350 words.

How long should your article be? To make it suitable for most venues on the Internet, I suggest you aim for about 500 words. That's about two pages, double-spaced. If a particular publisher or editor prefers it to be more concise and shorter, or more in-depth and longer, you can easily revise it to fit their requirements.

Sales Builder

Is your topic already well covered on the Internet? Then focus on a narrow subtopic. For example, if your website specializes in coffee reviews, there are probably a gazillion articles online about how to keep coffee beans fresh. One more by you won't make much of an impact. But what about a piece on keeping coffee beans fresh while traveling? That's a variation that would definitely attract the attention of die-hard java drinkers who wouldn't dare leave home without their beans, grinder, and portable filters.

Generating Topic Ideas

Coming up with topic ideas can often be the most challenging aspect of creating articles. Here are some brainstorming tips that can help:

- Make a list. This is the easiest type of article to write, and often very popular with publishers and readers. Example: *6 Timesaving Tips for Building Your Deck.*

- Tell a customer success story. People enjoy reading real-world accounts of customers using a product or service. Example: *How Jill and Her Family Ski Prestigious Resorts at Pauper Prices.*

- Solve a problem. People are always looking for solutions, especially on the Internet. Example: *How to Get Great Clients in a Crummy Economy.*

- Put in your two cents. Provide your expert opinion or insight into a current hot topic. Example: *Stretch Before Running? The Surprising Answer ....*

- Interview an expert or celebrity. Interviewing someone who is well known to your target audience can make for a well-read article, and drive lots of traffic to your site. Example: *Steve Slaunwhite Reveals His 5 Secrets to a Sizzling Website Sales Page.*

- Explain how-to projects. What is the best way to do something? Your instructions can make a great article. Example: *How to Post Your Podcast on iTunes.*

- Write a review. Provide your candid opinion on a product or service. Example: *Review of ACME Coffee's New Spirit-of-the-Orient Blend.*

When developing article ideas, the biggest mistake that web-based business owners make is to mimic the topics that they are already seeing in their industry or niche market. For your piece to get noticed, it must be fresh and enticing. If your article is just like all the others, it will get lost in the crowd.

Getting Your Articles Written

If you have a knack for writing, or if you're on a tight budget, or both, then you should consider writing the article yourself. It will take you a little time, but you'll save money.

However, if you've never written an article for publication before, the process may intimidate you. You're not alone. Even experienced writers, me included, get the jitters. After all, once an article is published somewhere on the Internet, it's available for the world to see. People are going to read it. Judge it. They may even post a comment about it online. Yikes!

Relax. As long as you focus on providing good information and presenting it well, it's difficult to go wrong.

Success Tip _____

When writing your article, keep the tone conversational. You're not composing a grade 10 essay on Shakespeare. What you want to end up with is a piece that is informative and readable. Think about the articles you enjoy reading most on the Internet. Doesn't it seem like the authors are having a conversation with you? That's the style you want to achieve. Let them hear your voice!

When you sit down to write an article, begin by jotting down four or five key points you want to make. For example, if you're planning to create a list-style article, "5 Ways to Fly First-Class at an Economy Price," then write down those five ways. Once you've done that, you're halfway there. You now know what you want to say. Your next step is simply to say it.

Some web-based business owners find it helpful to talk their way through an article, as if they've just been asked a question and are simply answering it. If this strategy seems like a good fit for you, use a tape recorder and "speak" your article. Then have it transcribed. Many of my clients use this technique and are often surprised at how little editing is required to turn the transcription into a finished piece.

Working With Writers and Editors

If you need some help in getting your articles created, there are lots of freelance writers and editors available who can help.

A good editor can transform your rough draft into a polished piece ready for publication. He or she can also make sure it flows well and is error-free.

The cost of hiring a freelance editor depends on the work your article requires. If it's a reasonably good draft and just needs a polish, you can expect to pay less. If your article is a mess and requires a substantial revision, you're going to have to fork out more dough.

Editors typically charge by the hour, with fees ranging from $35 to $65 per hour, although some may charge fixed fees for certain services. For example, the freelance editor I use charges $5 per page for a simple proofreading to check for errors.

Where do you find a good editor? The following associations have search engines and referral services that will help match your needs to the right professional:

> **Warning!**
>
> Unfortunately, it's all too easy for someone to hang a shingle and call himself or herself an editor or writer. So be careful who you select. Ask for portfolio samples and client testimonials. And don't be swayed by bargain-basement rates often charged by amateurs. Trust me, it's worth the few extra bucks to hire a qualified professional.

- The Editors' Association of Canada. (www.editors.ca)

- Editorial Freelancers Association— U.S. (www.the-efa.org)

- Society for Editors and Proofreaders—UK (www.sfep.org.uk)

Although editors are often also good scribes, if you want to completely farm out your article project, a freelance writer is what you need.

A freelance writer will interview you about the article topic, study the background materials you provide, and craft the article for you. The writer is acting as your ghost-writer so you remain the credited author.

How do you find a good freelance writer? See Chapter 10 for a list of resources.

Getting Your Article Published

Okay, you've written an article, either on your own or with the help of a freelance editor or writer. Now what?

Ideally, you want to get it published in an e-mail newsletter, information website, or blog that is popular amongst your target audience. Look at your media list and select two or three publications that you suspect would be a good fit between your article topic and their audience. Then contact the editor or publisher and ask if they would consider reviewing your piece.

Sounds simple, doesn't it? Simple, yes, but not always easy.

Your first step is to find out who to contact at a particular online publication and how. For smaller e-mail newsletters and blogs, that's usually the website owner, and you can usually reach that person with an e-mail or phone call.

For larger publications, go to the website and look for a link called Write For Us or something similar. That page will explain how to submit an article and provide you with other important information, such as word count requirements, desired topics, and more.

After you have followed the instructions and submitted your article, most publications will get back to you in a few days with either a yea or nay. If they don't do so within a couple of weeks, follow up by phone or e-mail.

Pitching an Article Idea

Sometimes publishers and editors of larger publications prefer you to pitch them on your article idea first, before you send the whole thing. This saves them the trouble of reading the entire piece, and also gives them the opportunity to provide you with some ideas or direction.

When pitching an article idea, keep the call or e-mail short. Explain your topic, one or two interesting points you're going to cover, and why the publication's readers will be interested in reading the piece. Ultimately, publishers and editors want articles that will generate a high readership, so the last point is perhaps the most crucial.

It may take a few days before the publisher or editor gets back to you. This is normal. After about a week, send a follow-up e-mail or, better still, pick up the phone and ask if she had a chance to consider your idea. The editor might have forgotten your original call or e-mail (these are busy folks) so be prepared to verbally pitch your article idea again.

If you get turned down, ask permission to get back to them with another article proposal. Be persistent. Eventually your efforts will pay off.

Submitting to Article Directory Websites

One of my articles, "9 More Writing Tips for Successful E-mail Marketing," has been published on over 40 websites, plus dozens of e-mail newsletters, blogs, and even a couple of print publications. It has driven hundreds of people to my website.

How did I make that happen?

For this particular article, I didn't directly approach a single publisher or website owner. All I did was submit my article to an *article directory*. The entire process took less than five minutes!

Here's how an article directory works:

Say your website features products and information of interest to cat owners. Ideally, you want your cat care articles published in as many places as possible—information websites, e-newsletters, blogs—where cat owners (your target market) will read them. So you submit your articles to Ezine Articles.

What happens next? Ideally, publishers using Ezine Articles to look for pet-related articles will find one of yours and want to use it for their website, newsletter, or blog. When they do, they simply follow the reprint instructions provided.

def•i•ni•tion

An **article directory** makes articles on a broad range of topics available to publishers and website owners who need them for their websites, e-mail newsletters, blogs, and other publications. It's essentially a matchmaking service, helping publishers find the articles they need, and authors (that's you) get their articles published.

Publishers who want to reprint articles submitted to EzineArticles.com and other article directories must follow certain rules. Typically, they have to credit you as the author, are not allowed to alter the article in any way, and provide a resource box that contains a link back to your website.

In most cases, article directories are free to both authors and publishers, although many charge fees for additional "premium" services. Here is a list of the most popular of these sites:

- ◆ Ezine Articles (www.ezinearticles.com)
- ◆ GoArticles.com (www.goarticles.com)
- ◆ SearchWarp.com (www.searchwarp.com)

- EasyArticles.com (www.easyarticles.com)

- Amazines (www.amazines.com)

- Articlesbase (www.articlesbase.com)

- JustArticles.net (www.justarticles.net)

- U Publish (www.upublish.info)

- A1 Articles (www.a1articles.com)

- Article Dashboard (www.articledashboard.com)

If a website, newsletter, or blog has picked up your article, and it's a publication you want to get more of your articles into, contact that publisher or editor directly. A thank-you card works well!

How do you find out if your article was published? Typically, you receive a monthly report via e-mail from the article directory website.

Practically Perfect Press Releases

Do you ever get jealous when a competing website owner gets quoted in a popular e-mail newsletter or featured in a well-known blog? Or worse, when a competing website product or service gets a seemingly free plug in a major online publication?

How did this happen?

Very likely, it happened because the website owner actively sought publicity through the use of effectively written and distributed press releases.

The press release may be older than the combustion engine. (It really is!) But it is still the easiest and most effective way to get the attention of publishers and editors, and get your website and its products talked about and written about in the media.

A press release—also called a media release or news release—is one or two pages long and is written like a news or magazine story. It typically contains facts, quotations, and other information that editors can pull out and use in their own articles. In some cases, a press release may be reprinted *as is* without changing a word. This is common practice among the more modest online publications, such as e-mail newsletters.

Success Tip

Consider adding a "Press Room" link on your website. When publishers, editors, and journalists want to learn more about you, your website will often be the first place they'll look. Your press room can contain an archive of press releases, background information on your products and services, biographies of you and your staff, and anything else you think the media might want to know.

Here is an example of a press release sent by my friend and fellow web-based business owner, Ed Gandia.

Gandia Communications Inc.

Contact: Ed Gandia

Phone: 770-419-3342; e-mail: ed@TheProfitableFreelancer.com

2028 Drogheda Lane

Marietta, GA 30066

For immediate release

New Report Helps Freelancers Put an End to Low-Paying Work

Successful Freelancer Reveals His 7 Secrets to Landing More Lucrative Freelance Projects in a Free Report

Marietta, GA (PRWEB) May 14, 2008—Gandia Communications Inc., a publisher of information products to help freelancers launch, grow, and run profitable freelance businesses, today announced the release of a new report titled 7 *Steps to Landing More Lucrative Freelance Projects.* Freelancers can receive a complimentary copy of this report by subscribing to the company's free biweekly newsletter, *The Profitable Freelancer,* at www.TheProfitableFreelancer.com.

This detailed 16-page report is based on the real-world experience of the company's president, Ed Gandia. As a successful 11-year sales professional, Gandia built a number of profitable sales territories and businesses prior to becoming a freelance copywriter. By applying many of the same principles to his nascent freelance business, he grossed more than $163,000 in his first full year as a full-time freelancer.

"Over the course of 27 months, I experimented with dozens of different strategies to build a successful freelance business," said Gandia. "Fortunately, I took good notes of what worked and what didn't. This report summarizes the seven key ingredients I found to be essential to landing profitable freelance projects—regardless of whether you're a copywriter, designer, illustrator, photographer, speechwriter, or PR specialist."

Normally retailing for $19, the report is available at no cost for a limited time to freelancers who subscribe to Gandia's free biweekly newsletter, *The Profitable Freelancer*, a publication dedicated to helping both aspiring and working freelancers launch, run, and grow a profitable freelance business. To subscribe, visit www.TheProfitableFreelancer.com.

About Gandia Communications Inc.

Gandia Communications Inc. is a publisher of information products to help freelancers launch, grow, and run profitable freelance businesses. To learn more, visit www.CopywritingActionPlan.com.

Ed's press release follows the industry-accepted format:

- An attention-grabbing headline.

- The dateline—placed at the beginning of the first paragraph.

- The first paragraph, or lead, that acts as a summary of the story.

- Body copy that expands on the story and provides plenty of interesting facts and quotations (which, hopefully, an editor will want to use).

- A section that tells the editor about the person or company who sent the release, and how to contact them if more information is required.

Don't improvise. You should follow this format closely in all your press releases.

Making It Newsy

A press release is news, or at least it should be. So any news about your website and its products and services that might interest your target publications is worthy of creating and distributing a press release. You can send out a press release when:

- You launch a new product or service.

- Your product or service gets a favorable review by a well-known expert, publication, or organization.

- You win an award.

- You have an opinion on a hot industry topic. (The more contrarian, the better!)

- You have a happy customer who is willing to share his or her story with the world.

- You are speaking at a major industry event.

- You hit an important milestone, such as years in business or becoming number one in your niche market.

- You are a success story and you want to be an inspiration for others.

- You discovered a new way to do something and you want to share it with others.

The keyword is *newsworthy*. Your press release must say something new and of interest to the readers of a target publication. Otherwise, there really is no reason for the editor to use the information.

And be careful not to come across as too promotional. Of course, you're issuing a press release in the hopes of getting publicity for your website and its products and services. But if you come off like a Ginsu knife salesperson, editors will be turned off. Worse, they may be reluctant to review any future press releases from you. And you don't want that!

Getting Your Release Released

A few years ago, press releases were sent to media contacts by mail or fax. These days it's done almost entirely online. However, before you blast an e-mail press release to every website, newsletter, and blog on your media list, make sure you review the publication's submission guidelines. The major publications, especially, have specific contacts and e-mail addresses you must use when submitting a press release.

I suggest you send your press release in two ways. First, make the extra effort to submit your release individually to each publication on your media list. These are your target publications and you want to give them your personal attention. Second, use a *media release company* to send your release to the hundreds or even thousands of other publications that match the topic or audience of your release.

def•i•ni•tion

A **media release company** is a service that maintains a large database of media contacts and distributes your press release on your behalf. You can usually select which types of publications and broadcasts to target. Although there are some free services available, the best media release companies charge $250 to $1,500 per release.

There are several media release companies online that you can use. Here are the most popular amongst web-based business owners:

◆ PRWeb (www.prweb.com)

◆ 1888 Press Release (www.1888pressrelease.com)

◆ 24-7 Press Release (www.24-7pressrelease.com)

◆ PRLog (www.prlog.org)

◆ PR.com (www.pr.com)

◆ i-Newswire (www.i-newswire.com)

◆ PressMethod.com (www.pressmethod.com)

◆ Press Release 365 (www.pressrelease365.com)

Most of these companies operate primarily online. So you can access the service, submit your release, make a payment, and send your press release directly from the website.

The Art of Getting Interviewed and Quoted

A couple of years ago, I discovered that *The Writer*, a prestigious magazine for freelancers, was going to do a story about copywriting. Since I had a website on that topic, I contacted the editor and explained that I had a lot of useful information to share on that topic. She put me in touch with the writer assigned to the piece. And, long story short, I was interviewed.

Several months later, I had actually forgotten all about it. Until one day, while browsing at my local bookstore, I noticed *The Writer* on the magazine stand with copywriting as the cover story. I grabbed a copy, anxiously flipped through the pages, and there I was—a picture of yours truly along with the story featuring several quotes from me.

I purchased every copy on the rack!

My simple effort of contacting the editor and offering help and information got me featured in a major article in a high-circulation publication in my niche.

How do you make this happen for your web-based business?

In addition to press releases, there are several ways to get interviewed by editors, writers, and publishers of magazines, newsletters, and blogs:

Review the editorial calendar. An editorial calendar is a list of topics a publication is planning to cover in upcoming editions. You can usually find this on the publication's website. If there is an upcoming topic on your area of interest or expertise, contact the editor and ask if you can be a source.

Get listed in a media source directory. There are a number of directories that editors and journalists use to find sources for their stories. The most popular are www.expertclick.com, www.sources.com, and www.medialine.com. You usually have to pay a fee to get listed in these directories, but if your website depends on lots of publicity to build traffic and sales, the investment will likely be worth it.

Suggest topic ideas. For e-mail newsletters and blogs, try contacting the owner directly and making topic suggestions. I recently contacted a popular blogger and asked if she would be interested in interviewing me on the topic of tele-teaching. She said yes and the blog post appeared just two weeks later. (Things can happen fast on the Internet!)

Getting quoted in blog posts and articles takes some effort. You need to be proactive. But considering that just one mention in a popular online publication can drive hundreds of potential buyers to your site, it's worth the work!

The Least You Need to Know

- Create a media list of popular websites, e-mail newsletters, blogs, and podcasts that your target audience reads.

- Develop articles and submit them to key publications and article submission sites.

- Use press releases to get the word out about newsworthy developments in your business.

- Take action to get interviewed and quoted in publication articles and stories written by others.

19

Advertising Online, Offline, and On Air

In This Chapter

- ◆ Using advertising to build your web-based business
- ◆ Finding the best places to advertise
- ◆ Creating successful ads

Advertising is tricky. When the stars align, and you have the right advertisement in the right place at the right time, you can drive a lot of traffic to your website cost-effectively. However, if your ad isn't written well or designed effectively, or if it's placed in a publication that few potential customers read, then you're going to have an expensive dud on your hands. And you can't afford too many of those!

This chapter gives you the basics of creating and placing winning advertisements that drive lots of potential customers to your website.

Should You Advertise?

Your website is up and running. It looks fantastic. You're ready to take orders and ship products. You couldn't be more excited. Now all you have to do is advertise your business and a flood of potential customers will be banging down your virtual front door. Right?

I suspect you know it's not that simple.

Advertising can be very effective in driving targeted traffic to your web-based business. However, it can also be a costly waste of time and money.

I have worked with small business owners who have used advertising very successfully. And I have known just as many others who have lamented at the hundreds and even thousands of dollars spent on ads that generated barely a trickle of website traffic.

Advertising doesn't work for all web-based businesses. How do you determine whether or not it will work for you?

Think for a moment how advertising works. A potential customer notices your ad in a publication she's reading. She becomes interested in what your website has to offer. Then she decides to visit your site.

Notice the three important things that are happening in that scenario:

- There is a publication that your target audience reads regularly.

- The publication accepts advertising.

- The advertising is cost-effective enough so that the revenues generated by the traffic to your site far exceed the costs.

Let's take a look at the first criteria. Is there a publication that your target customers regularly read?

Say your website sells beer recipes, books, and supplies for home brewers. Many of these enthusiasts might be faithful readers of The Home Brewers Blog every week. (Of course, many might read *The Wall Street Journal*, too, but that publication doesn't target your market specifically and will cost you a fortune to advertise in.)

Now the second criteria. Does The Home Brewers Blog accept advertising? Some blogs do, others don't. That's easily determined by simply visiting the blog and seeing if there are any ads displayed, or by contacting the blogger directly.

Success Tip _____

If a website or blog doesn't appear to accept advertising, don't give up just yet. Contact the owner and ask if they would consider posting your advertisement. Many smaller, targeted websites and blogs are looking for ways to generate more income and will be open to the idea. And if your ad is the first, and perhaps the only, one on that site, it has a much greater chance of getting noticed and clicked.

Finally, the third criteria. You need to determine if the cost of the ad is worth it. If it costs $500 per month to place your ad on the blog and it only generates a couple of dozen visitors to your site, then—as Internet marketers say—that's very expensive traffic! Remember, you can expect only a small percentage of those visitors to eventually become customers. Will those precious few purchase enough from your site to pay for the ad? Probably not.

On the other hand, if a $500 ad generates hundreds of new visitors to your site—potential customers who sign up for your newsletter in droves and place orders—then that may be the best 500 bucks you've ever spent!

How do you determine, in advance, if the cost of placing an ad is worth it? You can't. However, you can make a pretty good guess based on the number of people who read the publication. If, for example, The Home Brewers Blog gets 1,000 visitors per day, then if just 1 percent clicks your ad, you'll generate 300 visitors per month. Not bad. On the other hand, if the blog only gets 50 hits a month, you'll be lucky if your ad gets even a single click.

So take a close look at those three criteria before you decide to try advertising. Then, start small. Place one ad at a time. Watch what's working and what isn't. Then build on your successes.

Make Every Ad a Direct-Response Ad

Imagine two advertisements for a website that lists reputable plumbing contractors in your area. The first ad simply states:

> _When you need a plumber, visit _____.com for a list of qualified contractors in your area._

The second ad, by contrast, says:

> *FREE Guide: 7 Ways to Spot Leaks BEFORE They Happen. Get your copy at*
> *_____.com.*

Which advertisement do you suspect would generate the most visits to the website?

If your gut is saying the second one, you're right. In fact, the second type of ad will often get at least twice the response than the first one. And sometimes a lot more.

This illustrates the two types of advertising that businesses do:

- Awareness advertising
- Direct-response advertising

An awareness advertisement is one that is designed to simply make people aware of your website. It's saying, "Here I am. If you need what I sell, drop by for a visit." The hope is that the reader will remember your website and, the next time they need what you offer, visit it. (Keep your fingers crossed!)

Unfortunately, awareness ads suffer from a serious Achilles' heel. You must advertise often enough for customers to become aware of you. If they don't, they'll only visit your site when they see your ad at exactly the same moment they need what you sell!

"But what about Coca-Cola and Apple computers?" you might be thinking. "Virtually all of their ads are awareness." True. But they are already well-known brands and invest millions in advertising campaigns. You, as a small business owner, don't have that budget. So your advertisement needs to do more than just build awareness—it also needs to get the reader to act now.

That's where the second type of advertising, direct response, comes in.

A direct response ad is simply one that makes an offer of some kind … an offer compelling enough to get the reader to visit your website right away, rather than waiting until they have a need for your product or service.

An awareness ad is like a person waving his hand and saying, "I'm here if you need me." A direct-response ad is like that same person adding, "… and I have something special to give you right now." That something special is your compelling offer.

So make sure every ad you place is a direct-response ad, in that it contains a compelling offer of some kind. You can find out more about creating a compelling offer in Chapter 16.

Finding Advertising Opportunities

The biggest mistake I see web-based business owners making is placing ads in publications that are too general.

One particular entrepreneur I worked with a few years ago had a website that sold knitting supplies. She complained that her advertisements in a local community newspaper weren't working. No wonder! Even though the newspaper had thousands of readers, how many actual knitting enthusiasts would see the ad? Probably very few. I advised her to instead place ads in knitting-oriented magazines and websites. She took my advice and began to get a lot more traffic.

Don't place your ad in general publications that contain only a small percentage of your potential customers in their readership. Put your ads in highly targeted publications that are read specifically by your prospects. If your website promotes business seminars for electrical contractors, advertise in an electrical contractor magazine. If your site features information on parenting, place a banner ad on a popular parenting blog.

You have many choices when it comes to advertising venues. Here are the ones that, in my opinion, represent the best opportunity for small web-based business owners.

Success Tip

Many publications offer special deals for time-to-time advertisers. Magazines, for example, will often provide you with a discount in exchange for the option of placing your ad anywhere it will fit. Online publications also announce specials from time to time. Let the publisher know that you are interested in discounts and other specials—ask to be notified when these are available.

- ◆ Trade, professional, and special interest magazines
- ◆ Newsletters of associations and groups that your potential customers belong to
- ◆ Trade show and conference materials
- ◆ Websites and blogs
- ◆ E-mail newsletters
- ◆ Search engines such as Google
- ◆ Radio shows

How do you find these advertising venues? Ask your customers. If you have an e-mail newsletter already, do a survey and ask subscribers which websites, blogs, magazines, and newsletters they read, as well as which radio shows they listen to.

If your website isn't up yet, do some research online.

Once you've decided on a publication to place your advertisement in, how do you make that arrangement?

Visit the publication's website and look for a link called "Advertising" or something close to it. This section will typically provide you with all the information you need to schedule an ad placement, including artwork requirements, pricing, and other details you need to know.

Feel free to contact the publisher for any additional questions you might have. And don't be afraid to ask beginner questions. Most publications are used to dealing with small business owners who are advertising for the first time and are more than willing to guide you through the process. After all, they want to sell the ad space!

Getting Clicks with Online Ads

If you're new to advertising your business, I strongly suggest you start with *online advertising*. It's simpler, less expensive, easier to track, and often much more effective than its print counterpart.

def•i•ni•tion

An **online advertisement** is any advertisement that appears on the Internet or in an e-mail message. The most popular formats are search engine ads, banners, and text-based ads. However, online video and Internet radio advertisements are becoming increasingly popular as well.

A print advertisement requires a reader to jump over an additional hurdle to get to your site. He has to note your website address and then remember to go there the next time he's at his computer. Let's face it: that might not happen!

Online advertisements, by contrast, don't have that hurdle. When a potential customer sees an online ad, he simply clicks it and—voilà—he is taken immediately to your site. This characteristic alone gives online ads a huge advantage over their printed counterparts. But it gets even better.

Because online ads are clickable, they can easily be tracked. So you'll be able to determine precisely how many website visitors it's generating for you. With a print advertisement, tracking is more difficult—sometimes impossible.

And, of course, online advertisements are less expensive to create because they don't require printing.

There are three types of online ads used most often by small web-based businesses: search engine ads, banners, and text-based e-zine ads. Search engine marketing is covered in detail in Chapter 17. Let's take a look at how to create successful campaigns using the other two types.

Standing Out with Effective Banners

In many ways, a banner advertisement is the online equivalent of a billboard. However, many major online advertisers are using banners with special effects, animations, and even online video. In fact, as online video becomes easier to play on computers with slow Internet connections, some banners are looking more like television commercials than billboards.

For the small web-based business owner, however, the billboard analogy is the best place to start. You want to create a simple yet effective banner that drives traffic to your website. After you have developed one that works well for you, you can always experiment with more expensive special effects later on.

Example of a banner advertisement.
(Courtesy of Pete Savage)

Because of the relatively small size, a banner typically contains only a few words of copy. So you have to make every word count!

Warning!

If you plan to hire a freelance writer to create your banner ad, make sure he or she has a good track record in this medium. Review portfolio samples and ask how successful those banners were in terms of clicks generated. Not every freelancer knows how to craft a successful banner. See Chapter 10 for tips on how to find one who does.

Writing a banner requires you to craft a compelling headline and, if there is still room available, one or two lines of copy.

Once you have your banner written, you'll need to work with a web designer to create the artwork. Make sure the design and layout help to clearly communicate the message. For example, a banner ad for a travel website might show a family throwing a Frisbee on the beach. Also, make sure that the text stands out and is easy to see. Don't expect people to squint to read your banner. They won't.

Making It Easy with E-Zine Ads

I'm a big fan of text-based e-zine advertisements (advertisements placed within an e-mail newsletter) because they're relatively easy to create and inexpensive to place. In addition, e-zines are often very well-targeted publications.

If you subscribe to any e-mail newsletters, you probably have noticed this type of advertising. Perhaps you've even clicked and responded to some of the offers made.

Although banners can be placed in e-zines, the most common format is the text-based ad. By that I mean the ad is primarily text with little or no artwork of any kind. Typically, it is comprised of a headline, a paragraph or two of text, and a link to the advertiser's (that's you) website.

In my web-based business, I find that I often get much better results from e-zine ads than I do from banners. But that's just my experience. Yours may be different. That's why testing different advertising approaches to find out which one works best for your business is so important.

Here is an example of a text-based e-zine advertisement:

Want More Copywriting Clients?

Get Your FREE "Copywriter's Success Kit"

If you want a successful copywriting career, you need to know: how to write effective copy, how to attract great clients, and how to price your services.

The "Copywriter's Success Kit" shows you how to do all three!

Comprised of a 79-page manual and two 1-hour audio programs, it's packed with practical tips and strategies that get your copywriting business off the ground or, if you're already a copywriter, take your business to the next level of success.

Want your free copy? Get it now at:

www.forcopywritersonly.com/successkit.html

As with banners, effective copywriting is key. Remember, the person seeing the ad is primarily interested in the content of the newsletter. So your offer, and how well you present it, will need to be compelling enough to get them to click away from their reading and to your website.

Packing a Punch with Print Ads

As I said in the previous section, if you're new to advertising I strongly advise you to start with online ads. Print advertisements—in newspapers, magazines, newsletters and other publications—are more expensive and difficult to track.

But if there is a print publication that focuses specifically on your target audience, and you can place an ad in it cost-effectively, then by all means give it a try. It may be a real traffic-booster for you.

As with online ads, get it written first—before you hire a graphic designer. The copy is the most important ingredient of a successful advertisement.

When creating your print ad, there are two things that you want to have jump off the page:

1. Your compelling offer

2. Your website address

If the reader doesn't notice and remember both of those, your print ad will fail.

When you have a mock-up of your ad created, be your own worst critic. Imagine the

> **Warning!**
>
> Print publications often have strict guidelines concerning advertising content, size, allowable colors, and more. When considering advertising in a specific publication, be sure to request a copy of the required ad specifications. This will save you a lot of time and headaches when it comes to creating your ad.

advertisement is on a page cluttered with articles and other ads all competing for the reader's attention. Then ask yourself: "Would I notice, read, and respond to this ad?" If your answer is no, go back to the drawing board.

Example of a print ad.
(Courtesy of
ForGraphicDesignersOnly.com)

Freelance Graphic Designers

Do you want more clients?

Do you want higher fees?

More of the work you want?

This free subscription will help.

FREE profitable business-building resource subscription.

ForGraphicDesignersOnly.com

Radio and Other Broadcast Advertising

Major web-based businesses—the big guys—like eHarmony.com, Travelocity.com, and FreeCreditReport.com have generated hundreds of thousands of visitors to their websites through television commercials. However, this advertising medium is out of reach for most web-based business owners.

However, you can still take advantage of broadcast advertising in another way that is much more cost-effective. Radio.

Compared to other broadcast media, radio commercials are inexpensive to create, so the cost of radio spots is within the budget of most small web-based businesses.

Even Google is getting into the act. They recently launched a new service called AudioAds, which is part of their larger Google Adwords program. They'll assist you in getting the ad created and then broadcast it to their participating network of over 1,600 radio stations across the United States. For more information, visit www.google.com/adwords/audioads.

Radio spots are sold in time units, usually 10-, 15-, 20-, or 30-second and sometimes 1-minute spots. When you buy advertising time on a radio station, you get a number of spots to be placed at specific times in their schedule. For example, you might buy 25 10-second spots to be run on weekend afternoons.

Like any advertising you do, the more targeted the better. Try to get your advertising spots scheduled for those radio shows that are popular with your target market. For example, if your website sells Broadway show tunes sheet music, then it makes sense to get your radio commercial on a show that caters to show tunes fanatics (like me!). The audience will be smaller—much smaller than prime time spots like weekday mornings—but you'll reach more of your potential customers who will (hopefully) visit your website.

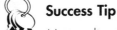

Success Tip

Most radio stations do a good job of helping small business owners create effective radio commercials. In fact, many stations will produce a simple one for you for free, provided you agree to buy a minimum number of spots. Contact the radio stations that target your market and ask to speak to someone about advertising.

How do you get started with radio ads? The best way to begin is with a simple commercial that consists only of a single narrator. This is the most inexpensive type of ad to script and produce.

Most radio stations have a roster of radio commercial narrators—called voiceover talent—available. In addition, check out these online resources.

- ◆ Voice123 (www.voice123.com)
- ◆ Voices.com (www.voices.com)
- ◆ My Voice Over Guy (www.myvoiceoverguy.com)
- ◆ SunSpots Productions (http://sunspotsproductions.com
- ◆ VoiceOver LA (www.volatalent.com)
- ◆ The Just Voices Agency (www.justvoicesagency.com)

When it comes to writing your radio commercial, try to find a freelance copywriter with experience in radio advertising. The radio station can also set you up with their in-house writer. If you decide to go it alone and craft your own commercial, following are some tips that will help.

◆ Make sure your web address is easy to spell and remember. Keep in mind that a radio listener may not be able to write anything down, especially if he or she is in a car.

◆ Keep it simple. Don't try to communicate too many ideas within just a 15-second time slot. Deliver one clear, compelling message, then your website address.

◆ If possible, mention your website address twice. Do so at the beginning of the radio commercial, then again at the end. This is one piece of information you don't want listeners to forget!

Once you have your radio commercial written, read it out loud to someone who hasn't heard it yet. Ask them to be brutally honest with you. Did they understand what you were saying? Were they motivated to visit your site? Did they clearly understand the web address?

Then, when you're confident you've got a winner, put that baby on the air!

The Least You Need to Know

◆ Print, online, and radio advertising are effective advertising strategies for small web-based business owners.

◆ Make your advertisement about your compelling offer, not your website.

◆ Always track the success of your advertisements so you learn what works and what doesn't.

Chapter 20

Other Proven Ways to Market Your Business

In This Chapter

- ◆ Promoting your business
- ◆ Getting the most out of your promotional strategies
- ◆ Generating high-quality traffic to your website

In the previous chapters, we discussed search engine marketing, articles, publicity, advertising, and affiliates as ways to generate traffic to your website. These are the top strategies and work very well for a wide range of web-based businesses. However, there are other marketing techniques—online and offline—that you should also consider.

The new kids in town, social media sites, are proving to be very effective, as are the old workhorses of marketing: direct mail, trade shows, networking, and speaking. This chapter provides you with a basic overview of each.

Getting in Touch with Direct Mail

Direct mail is perhaps the world's oldest marketing method. There is evidence that letters were used hundreds of years ago to get in touch with potential customers and persuade them to use a particular merchant or make a purchase.

In this age of online marketing, you might think that direct mail isn't that effective anymore. Think again. Direct mail works well these days specifically because so many companies are running online campaigns. An old-fashioned direct mail piece faces less competition, and therefore has a better chance of gaining the attention and interest of the customer.

Direct mail can take several different forms. The most common are:

◆ A letter inside an envelope. There might be other contents, too, such as a brochure.

◆ A postcard.

◆ A self-mailer. This is a piece that is folded in such a way that it can be mailed without requiring an envelope.

◆ A flyer.

Direct mail is still one of the best ways to directly contact a prospective customer.

Should You Use Direct Mail?

Can you use direct mail to actually sell products offered on your website? You can. However, you're essentially setting up a separate mail order business that works in conjunction with your web-based operations. That's a big undertaking, and I would advise you to build your success online before you enter the riskier world of mail order.

The best way to use direct mail is to generate traffic, not orders.

What you want to do is mail something to potential customers to encourage them to visit your website. Then your website can take over the task of building relationships with those visitors and turning them into customers. It's a lot easier to persuade someone to visit a website than it is to get them to buy something based on what they've received in the mail.

> ### Sales Builder
>
> Want to be more successful with your direct mail marketing? The post office can help. The national postal services in the United States, Canada, and many other countries offer a wealth of free resources for small business owners, such as direct mail seminars, how-to guides, and even special discounts. Check out the website of your postal service to learn more.

Before you think seriously about a direct mail campaign, you need to understand that only a small percentage of people who receive your mailer will respond to it. In fact, that number will likely be less than 5 percent. (In marketing lingo, we call that the response rate.) If you sell low-priced items, then the cost of creating and mailing 1,000 postcards to get 50 new visitors might not be worth it. However, if you sell high-value products—such as expensive subscriptions or equipment—then one sale could pay for the cost of the mailing many times over!

Getting Started with Direct Mail

So how do you use direct mail to generate lots of traffic to your website?

There are three elements of a successful direct mail piece:

- The mailing list
- The compelling offer
- The copy and design of your direct mail piece

The mailing list refers to the people who are going to receive your mailing. I have a lot of experience creating direct mail, both for my own business and for major clients, and I can confidently report that you'll get a much higher response rate if your list is well targeted.

If you're selling custom embroidered running shoes, for example, then "exercise enthusiasts" would be a targeted list. "Runners" would be a better list because it's more targeted. "Runners who have purchased shoes online"—an even better list! See what I mean?

How do you find such lists?

Success Tip _____

Your best list is always your house list. That's the list of customers who have already purchased something from you online. Perhaps they haven't visited your website for a while? A direct mail letter with a savings coupon attached could encourage them to visit again and buy!

The easiest way to find a new list is to work with a *list broker*. You can find one by searching www.yellowpages.com

def•i•ni•tion _____

A **list broker** represents magazine publishers, trade show organizers, popular online merchants, and others who have lists available. You just tell the broker what type of list you're looking for and he or she will let you know what's available.

How much does it cost? Mailing list fees can vary considerably, from 50 cents to up to $5 per name and even higher depending on the quality of the list. The good news is you don't have to pay the broker a commission. The list owner takes care of that.

The next step to direct mail success is the compelling offer. (Remember that from Chapter 16?) It's not enough just to announce the existence of your website to your mailing list. You won't get too many visitors that way. You need to also make a compelling offer to entice them to go to your website right away.

That could be in the form of a free giveaway of some kind, a special discount, or other motivating incentive.

The final component to a winning direct mail campaign is the copy and design. Your letter, postcard, or other type of direct mail piece needs to gain attention and motivate the reader to drop what they're doing, visit your website, and take advantage of your compelling offer.

Direct mail copy and design is not for amateurs. I suggest you find a professional—at the very least, an experienced copywriter—who has experience and a track record of success in this area. (See Chapter 10 for tips on finding good freelancers.)

"But I'm just going to send out a simple letter," I hear someone saying. "Can't I write that myself?" You can. Many of the basics of web copywriting as explained in Chapter 10 are also applicable to printed marketing communications like direct mail.

However, if your budget allows, seriously consider hiring a professional copywriter who knows all the tips and tricks of writing an effective direct mail letter. Sure, you'll spend a few hundred dollars—but you'll likely get a much higher response to your mailing in return.

Warning! _____

Don't blow your entire marketing budget on a major direct mail campaign. That's too risky. Instead, start small. Try a simple one-page letter or a postcard mailer to a small, targeted list of potential customers. See how that works for you. If you find that you're generating a lot of traffic as a result, you can safely test larger lists.

Speaking for Profits

Last month I volunteered to do a 45-minute talk at a writers' conference on the topic of getting lucrative corporate projects. There were approximately 75 people in the audience. By the time I shut off the PowerPoint projector, more than 60 participants had signed a sheet to receive my website's e-mail newsletter. It gets better. When I returned to the office, three new customers had placed orders on my website for the how-to guides and home study courses I sell.

Speaking is an extremely effective strategy for promoting your website, especially if you target a well-defined niche market that gathers together in some way at association meetings, conferences, workshops, summits, and other events.

How does speaking work as a marketing strategy for promoting your website?

Your first step is to create a short presentation that potential customers would be interested in. For example, if your website features information and resources on nutrition for kids, then you could create a simple presentation called "Six Healthy Eating Tips for Kids Who Love Sweets."

Then you need to find meetings, conferences, and other events that your potential customers are likely to attend. It's conceivable, for example, that _Today's Parent_ magazine might sponsor an event like Today's Parent Expo—an ideal venue for your presentation.

Success Tip _____

Build a file of conferences, meetings, and other events that your potential customers are likely to attend. That way you can stay on top of potential speaking opportunities. Organizers of these events typically include major publications, membership associations, seminar and conference producers, and special interest groups.

Next, you do some research to find the person responsible for event planning. The best place to start is to check the event's website. If that doesn't work, pick up the phone and ask to speak to the person responsible for booking speakers.

Once you get in touch with a meeting planner, you'll find that most are eager to talk to you. At smaller organizations, such as local chapters of professional associations, the meeting planner is a volunteer. They want to fill the event schedule with great speakers and topics with as little hassle as possible. So they're going to be open to hearing your pitch.

def•i•ni•tion

A **one sheet** is a description of your presentation topic that you send to event planners and others who book speakers.

I suggest you prepare a one-page overview of your presentation in advance so you can e-mail it to the event planner immediately once they indicate an interest. Your *one sheet*, as it's called in the event planning industry, should include the title of your presentation, an overview of the topic, and a bullet list explaining what audience members will learn.

Success Tip

Place a "Need a Speaker?" link on your website. This will let people know that you're available to speak at events. In the "Need a Speaker" section of your site, list your speaking topics, a brief description of each, and how to contact you. If you have some available, also include a few testimonials from satisfied audience members and event planners.

There are many different types of presentations you can do. Here's the rundown:

- **Traditional presentation.** You speak in front of a live group; it usually lasts 30 to 60 minutes, although this can vary.

- **Panel presentation.** This is a presentation you do jointly with other speakers. In most panels that I've been involved in, there have been three or four speakers. Each does a short presentation, usually just 5 or 10 minutes. Then there is a question and answer session with the audience.

- **Webinar.** This is a presentation that you give online. It's much like a live seminar where the audience can hear your presentation and see your slides and other visuals. However, it's all done via computer. The audience could be scattered all over the world.

- **Teleclass.** This is a seminar conducted on a teleconference line. The audience members call in to a special number and key in an access code to attend. I've done dozens of teleclasses for several organizations. It's a very popular format.

Does speaking make you nervous? Join the club! Most web-based business owners feel the same way.

If you're apprehensive about doing a 45-minute talk all on your own in front of a live audience, here are a couple of ideas for sticking your toe in the water. First, try to get an invitation to speak on a panel. That way, your presentation will be short and you won't be all alone on stage. Second, consider joining Toastmasters International (www.toastmasters.org). It's a self-help organization that helps people learn to speak effectively before groups. Many professional speakers learned their craft at Toastmasters.

I'll never forget the first time I spoke in front of a group to promote my web-based business. The presentation went fine. But on the drive home I realized that I had actually done little to promote my business. I didn't pass around a sign-up sheet for my newsletter. I didn't even invite audience members to visit my site!

Don't waste a speaking opportunity like I did. You want to provide a valuable presentation to the group. But never forget that it's all part of promoting your web-based business.

Here are some tips on doing just that:

- Place your website address at the header or footer of each slide.

- Pass around a sign-up sheet for your e-mail newsletter.

- Place an invitation to visit your website on the last slide of your presentation. This slide remains on screen as you answer questions, giving audience members lots of time to make note of it.

- For small audiences, pass out handouts of the presentation with your website address on it. For larger audiences, place the handout on all the seats before they arrive.

- Give away a product from your website to an audience member during your presentation. You can ask a question and the person who answers it wins.

- Get the contact information of people who come up to you after the presentation. These are your hottest prospects. Send them an e-mail or thank-you card when you get back to the office.

Speaking is one of those marketing tactics that works better the better you get. Keep at it. Constantly improve your presentation skills. Hone ways to get more audience members to sign up for your e-mails and visit your website.

Exhibiting at Trade and Consumer Shows

Trade and consumer shows date back to medieval times. Yet they are more popular today than any other time in history, which is amazing when you consider how "old school" this marketing strategy is.

Today there are trade and consumer shows for every conceivable type of business and interest, from wedding shows to carpentry shows to sports memorabilia shows to wine and cheese shows. *Tradeshow Week* (www.tradeshowweek.com), the publication for that industry, lists more than 8,000 annual trade shows in North America alone. And there are thousands of other smaller specialty shows.

The basics of using trade shows to promote your web-based business are relatively straightforward:

- ◆ You select a trade show that you want to participate in as an exhibitor.

- ◆ You contact the trade show organizer to rent an exhibit booth.

- ◆ You arrive the day before the show to set up your booth, which typically includes a display table and signage.

- ◆ You work the show by meeting people who stop by your exhibit and you talk to them about your website and what it offers.

Sounds simple, doesn't it? And for the most part it is. However, each of those four steps requires a lot of work.

Finding a potential trade show to participate in is the easiest step. There are plenty of directories and online resources you can access to search for trade or consumer shows that your potential customers attend. Check out www.tsnn.com, www.biztradeshows. com, or http://directory.tradeshowweek.com/directory.

Once you find a show, it's a little like placing an advertisement in the Yellow Pages. The event organizer is going to try to sell you on a lot of upgrades such as more floor space, a prime location, a premium listing in the show directory, and so forth. My advice? If you're new to trade show exhibiting, start with the basics: a standard booth and nothing more. Exhibiting at trade shows is time-consuming and expensive. You want to start simply and try a couple of shows first to see how it's working for you.

Sales Builder

At your exhibit booth, have a draw for something valuable—such as a product from your website. On the contest sign-up form, be sure to ask permission to send your e-mail newsletter. That way, you'll leave the show with potentially hundreds of new subscribers that you can follow up with and, hopefully, turn into new customers.

Trade show organizers will rent you the space only, and sometimes also table and chairs. It's up to you to dress up your booth with signage, product samples, and other decorations that will gain the attention of passersby and encourage them to visit.

Your final step, of course, is to work the show.

If you learn just one thing from this section, I hope it's this: get some help! Trade shows are grueling. Many shows, especially consumer shows, run 12 hours a day—and most show guidelines require that your booth be manned continuously. If you plan on taking any bathroom breaks, you need someone to fill in for you. Hire a temporary assistant or a high school student to assist you. (And here's a bonus tip: wear comfortable shoes! Twelve hours on your feet in dress shoes or heels is not fun.)

Here are some additional tips for successful exhibiting:

- ◆ Spread the word and invite people to visit you at the show. Post a notice on your website. E-mail your subscriber list. Blog about it.

- ◆ Showcase your website products at your exhibit booth.

- ◆ Trade show attendees collect things. You'll see them carrying bags stuffed with flyers, brochures, free gifts, and other goodies. So have something available that visitors can take away with them.

- ◆ When talking to visitors, ask them to tell their friends about your website. Most will be glad to.

- ◆ If it's a consumer show (rather than a business or trade event), offer something free for kids. Balloons work well! They're inexpensive but draw in the family crowds.

- ◆ Don't eat in your booth. People will not want to interrupt your meal.

- ◆ Stand in front of the exhibit booth table, not behind it.

- ◆ If permissible by the show organizers, sell products at your booth. Sales during the show can potentially cover all the costs. The additional traffic to your website is a bonus.

As I said earlier, trade shows are expensive. It's not uncommon for an exhibitor, even with a modest-sized booth, to invest thousands of dollars for just a two- or three-day show. Is it worth it? The only way to know for sure is to test it. Try a local show in your area. See if it generates enough traffic to your site to justify the time and expense.

Meeting Potential Customers at Networking Events

Are there meetings, shows, conferences, and other events where your potential customers gather? If so, then attending these events and networking can be a great way to make people aware of your web-based business.

For example, say your website sells coaching programs, teleclasses, and how-to guides on the topic of work-life balance for female executives. You could attend monthly meetings of the local Women Executives League and schmooze with people who could become customers of your website and spread the word to their friends and colleagues about it.

Networking can be very effective. However, it is also time-consuming. You have to dress appropriately, travel to the meeting, meet people, chat, and perhaps even volunteer at the event to give yourself a higher profile. It's a lot of work. However, many web-based business owners—especially those who sell high-value products and programs—swear by this technique.

It's a myth that networking is only for those who are naturally sociable and can effectively "work the room." The fact is, anyone can attend a meeting, conference or any other event, meet a few people, and talk about their business. You don't have to be a shark. Just be yourself. Say hello to the people you run into and when you're asked, "So, what do you do?" answer by giving them a brief blurb about your business.

Success Tip

Arrive early at a networking event, especially if it's your first time there. This will give you an opportunity to quickly meet a few people and get comfortable with the surroundings before the natural cliques develop. If you arrive early enough, offer to set up chairs or help in some other way. In just a few moments, you'll be considered part of the group!

Here's an example of what I say:

I operate a website called ForCopywritersOnly.com. Basically, it helps freelance copywriters get the projects they want from the clients they want at the prices they want. It does that through a series of how-to guides, home-study courses, and coaching programs. How about you? What do you do?

Pretty simple, isn't it? Even I can comfortably handle an interaction like that. And I'm definitely on the shy side when it comes to new social situations.

Look for any opportunity to say hello to someone new. Introduce yourself to everyone at the table or in your row. If you notice someone standing alone, walk up and introduce yourself.

And always have business cards available that you can exchange. (Make sure your website address is on them!)

Leveraging the Online "Water Coolers"

When I started my own business over 15 years ago, networking was still done primarily at live events, such as meetings and conferences. Not anymore. These days it's possible to meet in networking situations with dozens of potential customers or clients every week by utilizing the *online water coolers*—and without ever having to put on a suit!

def•i•ni•tion

What's an **online water cooler?** That's Internet slang for forums, blogs, and discussion boards where you can post questions and comments and interact with others. It comes from office culture, where people really do hang out and talk at the water cooler! No matter how narrow your target market is, chances are there is an online water cooler that is popular amongst your target audience.

For example, WhitePaperSource is a forum that brings together those who have an interest in white paper marketing—everyone from writers and designers to consultants and marketing managers. I've met dozens of people on that forum who have either become customers of my site, ForCopywritersOnly.com, or have helped my business in other ways.

If you're new to online water coolers, here's my suggestion: find two or three blogs, forums, or discussion boards that your potential clients are active in. Familiarize yourself with the topics and guidelines. Then start participating. You'll not only meet potential clients but add new colleagues and friends to your network as well.

Following is a recipe for generating traffic to your website by networking at forums, blogs, discussion boards, and other online water coolers.

Step 1: Identify up to three discussion boards, forums, or blogs that your potential customers are active on.

Step 2: Plan to post on each site at least once per week.

Step 3: You'll need a signature line. This is a short blurb—typically 10 to 15 words—that describes a bit more about you and your website. It's very much like a business card.

Don't be too promotional. Here's an example:

Jane Smith,

Owner of NeatKnitting.net

Join our free Knitting Pattern of the Week club at www.NeatKnitting.net/club

Most forums will automatically insert your signature when you post. For others, you'll have to do so manually.

Step 4: Position yourself as a helper; a source of great ideas and advice. This is very easy to do. Simply answer questions posted on the site that relate to your website's products, services, or information.

Step 5: Avoid controversial topics, especially those that involve politics or religion. Stick to business.

Step 6: Always welcome newcomers to the forum with a personal e-mail. Everyone remembers the first person who welcomed him or her to a new group.

It only takes a half hour or so each week to network with your potential clients on blogs, forums, and discussion boards. I schedule an hour each Friday afternoon and always see a boost in website traffic on that day.

Getting Sociable on Social Media Sites

Have you "linked in" yet? How many followers do you have on Twitter? Can I be a friend on your Facebook page? If those questions seem a little strange to you, you're not alone. Even those who have some experience with social media sites have a difficult time keeping up with the latest *Web 2.0* trends.

Social media sites are simply websites where people can meet and interact in a variety of interesting ways. As a small business owner, you can use social media to gain the attention of those potential customers who enjoy these sites and are active in them.

def•i•ni•tion

Web 2.0 refers to special websites that are focused on building communities where people can share information and interact in some way. For example, on YouTube, people can share their favorite videos. On LinkedIn, business professionals can meet and connect with other professionals. As a web-based business owner, you can take advantage of social media websites to attract more website visitors and customers.

A friend of mine who has a very successful web-based business recently used social media sites to help promote a new series of online seminars. In addition to all the usual ways of marketing such events—e-mailing, advertising, working with affiliates, etc.—he also created Facebook and Twitter pages. He says many sign-ups came directly as a result of those social media sites.

The advantage of using social media sites to reach potential customers is also their disadvantage: interactivity. You have to be active on them on a fairly regular basis—at least weekly—in order to get any results. And that takes time.

My opinion? I think social media sites are here to stay and I believe they are an effective marketing technique for the web-based business owner. You can't beat the costs—you can set up special pages on, and participate in, most social media sites for free.

Here is a list of popular social media websites:

Reddit (www.reddit.com). A source for what is new and popular online. Users upload stories and articles to drive traffic to their website or blog.

Digg (www.digg.com). Users submit content from the web and the member community discusses and votes on their favorites.

Delicious (www.delicious.com). A site where users share their favorite online bookmarks with the rest of the community.

StumbleUpon (www.stumbleupon.com). Users are provided with a toolbar to search websites that are tailored to their specific interests. The community rates the sites and shares their discoveries with other members.

Technorati (www.technorati.com). Members register their blogs with this network to increase readership and exposure.

Squidoo (www.squidoo.com). Users share their knowledge with others by creating individual web pages on a variety of topics. Bio pages include links to blogs, websites, and other online signposts.

LinkedIn (www.linkedin.com). A popular networking site where professionals and business associates can exchange ideas, information, and opportunities.

Facebook (www.facebook.com). While primarily a social networking site, professionals can also advertise, promote events, and create a business presence with interactive Facebook pages.

YouTube (www.youtube.com). A very popular site where users, including businesses, can upload their videos and commercials, and let their clients know about what they do each day.

Ryze (www.ryze.com). A business networking site where members create a free networking-oriented home page and can send messages to other members. They can also join other networks related to their industry.

Fast Pitch! (www.fastpitchnetworking.com). Fast Pitch! is designed as a one-stop shop for business professionals to network and market their businesses.

Twitter (www.twitter.com). A purely text-based medium, users post short messages on their pages to alert friends, clients, and associated businesses about what they are doing.

Naymz (www.naymz.com). A professional networking platform that allows people to find and discover new connections, opportunities, ideas, and information based on their backgrounds and reputations.

Biznik (www.biznik.com). With a growing membership worldwide, this is a community for people who are building businesses to connect globally online and also meet face-to-face with other professionals within their local areas.

As with traditional and online networking, I suggest you schedule an hour each week for social networking. Give it a try. You might find that it not only attracts lots of potential customers directly to your site, but also gets people talking and spreading the word about your website.

Social media sites are all about building a community of people that could eventually become customers of your website. So focus on meeting people and building relationships rather than doing any hard-core promotion on these sites. My friend Ed Gandia got over 800 "followers" on his Twitter page in just a few weeks, many of whom were potential customers for his products and services. To get similar results from an advertising campaign would have cost him a small fortune.

The Least You Need to Know

◆ Old-fashioned marketing tactics such as direct mail, networking, speaking, and trade shows can still be very effective.

◆ Find and participate in the online water coolers and social media websites that your potential customers are active in.

◆ As with any marketing strategy, start small. Notice what's working and what isn't. Then build on your successes.

Part 6

Converting Clicks Into Customers

It's not enough to merely drive a lot of traffic to your website. Like a boxer in a championship match, you need the winning one-two punch—a combination of both traffic and conversions. That means creating a great experience for your website visitors so they take the actions you want them to take. Those actions could be to sign up for your newsletter, click on your affiliate ads, or place an order. This part of the book shows you how.

Chapter 21

Proven Tactics for Boosting Conversion Rates

In This Chapter

- ◆ Maximizing conversion rates
- ◆ Giving website visitors an optimal buying experience
- ◆ Using proven strategies to boost sales

While it's important to drive a lot of traffic to your website, you also need to get a lot of conversions. As discussed in Chapter 16, conversion refers to the process of persuading a website visitor to take the action you want him or her to take. That may be to sign up for your newsletter, take advantage of a free offer, click on an affiliate advertisement, or place an order online.

Boosting the conversion rates on your website pages is, by far, the quickest and most cost-effective way to generate more revenues. By implementing just a few key changes, you can dramatically increase clicks and sales— virtually overnight!

Conversions Are Just as Important as Traffic

Several months ago a website owner called asking for my help. He had a great web-based business offering products that, in my opinion, were excellent. The problem was he wasn't generating nearly as many orders as he thought he should be getting.

"What I plan to do," he said, "is to drive more traffic to my site using a combination of Google Adwords, advertisements in targeted e-zines and blogs, and publicity. That way I'll get more sales."

Those were all great ideas. However, those marketing tactics were going to cost him a lot of time and money. "Before you do all that," I recommended, "why don't we explore some ways of converting more of the website visitors you're already getting into customers?"

> ### Sales Builder
>
> Your greatest opportunity to increase sales is to improve your website pages, especially the marketing copy, to increase conversion rates. The greater the percentage of website visitors that can be persuaded to place orders, the more revenues you will generate. Even a minor increase in the conversion rate on a key product page can quickly increase sales.

He agreed to give it a try. We worked together on one of his product landing pages, making improvements in how the marketing copy was structured and written. We also made some changes to the e-mail series—the autoresponders—associated with that page.

Once these changes were implemented, the landing page conversion rate (the amount of people who visited the page and placed an order) went up 180 percent. That meant that nearly three times as many people were placing orders.

His sales of that product almost tripled! And all we did was make some simple changes.

This is a common scenario among web-based businesses. You can spend a lot of money to generate traffic to your site, but if you can't convert a significant percentage of those into paying customers, you won't make much money.

That doesn't mean your website needs to be packed with sales hype, like a carnival-barking snake oil salesman. That rarely, if ever, works. But your website does need to communicate like a good salesperson; the kind who is helpful, informative, and honest while guiding the website visitor through the process of learning about your offerings and making a buying decision.

How you write the web copy (see Chapter 10), structure the text, and organize the information all comes into play to maximize conversion rates.

There are other proven tips and tricks for boosting website clicks and sales as well, which are also covered in this chapter.

Help Them Find What They Need

Ever get frustrated in a retail store because you couldn't find what you were looking for? Remember that feeling? You certainly don't want your website visitors to feel that way, do you?

When visitors arrive at your website, they are on a mission. They've come to find information, look for a solution, take advantage of a special offer, shop for a specific kind of product, or any number of other quests. If they can't easily find what they need, they'll quickly click away—and may never return.

Recently, I responded to an Internet banner ad offering a free special report. I was interested in the topic, so I clicked. On the landing page I was taken to, I expected to find an online form or some other instructions on how to get the report. But it wasn't there! I searched around and eventually found the information I needed on a different web page. But that was way too much work. Most website visitors would have simply given up.

How do you make it easier for website visitors to find what they need? Here are some proven strategies:

> **Warning!**
>
> Many studies in Internet marketing have shown that first-time visitors will give your website about eight seconds to prove that the content is relevant to their needs. That isn't very much time! So your web page content has to make it very clear to them that they are, indeed, at the right place and will easily find what they're looking for.

- ◆ Use descriptive headers. You've probably seen plenty of clever headlines produced by Madison Avenue ad agencies. But they don't work so well on websites. To help visitors more easily find what they need, use simple headers that clearly describe what the page is all about. Headers include the main page headline and all the subheads within the body copy. (See Chapter 10 for more headline writing tips.)

- ◆ Tell them they're at the right place. If your website sells used books, then say so in the web page copy. *"If you're looking for used books, in great condition, with FREE delivery on purchases over $49—you've come to the right place!"*

◆ Make all links intuitive. The most popular place where people look to find information on a website is the navigation bar. Make sure the links are descriptive and identify clearly what those sections of the site are all about. Don't worry if you have lots of links. That actually makes things easier to find for the website visitor. And it's okay to have sub-links to a main link, or even two or three links pointing to the same page. Whatever works!

◆ Be repetitive. Don't worry about repeating similar information on multiple pages. It's perfectly okay to explain your shipping policy on your shipping page and then again on one of the checkout screens. Put applicable information anywhere a website visitor would expect to find it.

◆ Don't send everyone to your home page. There may be other pages on your site that make more sense to send potential customers to. For example, when I advertise my home study copywriting course, I send those who respond to that product page, not to my home page. After all, that's the information those website visitors are looking for.

◆ Place important information "above the fold." This refers to the information that is visible on a web page without the visitor having to scroll down. Internet marketing studies show that website visitors will pay much more attention to what is above the fold than what is below it. So position your most important text in that area.

◆ Make the web copy scanable. Eye path studies, where they track people's eye movements as they read a web page, reveal that website visitors are three times more likely to scan online content than comparable printed information. So it's important to make your text scanable. Use bullet lists, bolded text, alternate text colors (ideal for subheads), and short paragraphs. If a website visitor can't get the gist of the message by quickly running their eyes down the web page, then your text is not scanable enough.

Sometimes we're so close to our own website business, and know the products, services, and information so well, that we lose perspective and can't easily see our website the way others do. Ask a friend to put himself into the shoes of a potential customer and review your website. Give him a list of things to find, like a scavenger hunt. The feedback will help you identify ways to make shopping on your site easier for your website visitors.

Guide Them Through the Shopping Process

In most kinds of marketing communications, the customer doesn't have to think about how the shopping process works. A television commercial plays from beginning to end and then tells you what to do. ("Eat KFC!") A brochure guides readers through a front panel, the inside panels, and then a back panel. Even most retail stores are fairly intuitive, with shoppers coming in the front door, finding what they need in clearly labeled and organized aisles, and then proceeding to the checkout. It's a no-brainer.

On a website, however, things are not so clear for the visitor. The home page may have a dizzying clutter of links and other information. Where do you go first? And according to statistics, more than 20 percent of first-time visitors to a site will arrive on an inside page, not the home page. Will they be able to find their way around?

The very nature of a website makes it easy for a website visitor to get lost or distracted, or confused about what he or she needs to do next.

Success Tip

Use text links strategically to guide customers through your website. The most effective text links are simple and intuitive for the website visitor, such as "Learn more …," "Find out how …," and "Next Step: Get a Free Estimate …." You might be tempted to get creative with text links and put them in an unexpected color or format. Don't. Keep your links in blue text and underlined. People know that blue underlined text is clickable.

That's why it's important that your website structure, links, and web copy guide the website visitor through the buying process. Think about each page and ask yourself, "When a customer lands here, what is the next step I want him or her to take?" That next step could be to visit another page, sign up for your newsletter, click on an affiliate link, or place an order.

Here are some examples:

♦ A visitor reads an article on the website about how to quote on freelance writing jobs. Next step? "Learn more about the how-to guide: *Pricing Your Writing Services.*"

♦ A visitor clicks on the Contact Us page. Next step? "Contact us for a prompt same-day quotation."

♦ A visitor reads a product description page. Next step? "Read what buyers are saying about this product."

- A visitor reviews a web page highlighting the advantages of a new industrial pump. Next step? "Click here to download a PDF containing the technical specifications."

- A visitor goes to a web page promoting a new seminar. Next step? "Register today. This program is filling up fast!"

- A first-time visitor arrives at the home page. Next step? "Click here to learn how online coaching works."

I suggest you put a next step suggestion of some kind on every page of your website. Many customers will prefer to explore your site on their own, but some will want to be guided. Be that guide.

Answer Their Questions—Before They Ask!

If your website visitor has a question about a product or service on your website, there is no one to ask. He or she is all alone. So you want to make sure that your website clearly explains everything that a potential customer needs to know to make a buying decision. Otherwise, that person will be very reluctant to place an order.

I know what you're thinking. "The website visitor is not alone. Our toll-free number is clearly listed on every page. Plus we have a customer service online form they can fill out."

Those are excellent features. But the truth is, very few people will use them. Website visitors expect to find all the information they need to know about your product or service on your website. If they can't, they'll simply click away.

Think about it this way. Have you ever spoken to a salesperson that wasn't able to quickly answer your questions or provide you with the information you needed? Did you buy from that person? Probably not.

Your website is your salesperson. So you must make sure that it answers all the questions a website visitor might have about your offerings.

Pretend you're a customer and brainstorm a list of questions you might have before buying one of your products or services. I did this exercise recently for one of my products, a $700 home study course online. Here's what I came up with:

- Who created the course?

- What are his credentials?

- How much does it cost?

- What do other buyers say about the course?

- How do I place an order?

- What course materials do I actually receive?

- How long does it take to complete the course?

- Do you have a payment plan?

- How are the course materials delivered?

- What exactly will I learn when I take the course?

- Is there a money-back guarantee if I'm not satisfied?

If your website leaves just one question unanswered, your conversion rates may not be as high as they could be.

When customers are confused about something, or have unanswered questions, their default answer is a no. Too many of those and your site won't be selling much!

Make Special Offers

There is a reason why your weekend newspaper is stuffed with flyers announcing sale after sale after sale. Making special offers is a proven way to increase revenues. That's why you should consider this technique for your own website.

For example, on my website I make a special offer to those who subscribed to my e-mail newsletter and have received a few issues. At the six-week "anniversary" of their subscription, I send them an e-mail with a gift: a discount certificate for one of my courses.

I won't tell you the actual numbers, but a significant number of people who receive that e-mail take advantage of the offer and purchase the course.

I ran another promotion last year where I bundled 10 of my audio programs together and offered them for a special price during a three-day sale. I generated thousands of dollars in sales within hours of announcing that special to my e-mail newsletter subscriber list.

> **Warning!**
>
> Be careful not to make too many discount offers too often. Your customers might get so used to seeing them that they'll wait until the next "sale" before buying anything from your website! If that happens, your sale price becomes your de facto regular price and you've just lost a chunk of your profit margin. By all means offer special discounts from time to time, but do so sparingly.

Of course, special offers don't necessarily have to be in the form of a sale. Here are some other ways to use this technique to boost revenues:

♦ Offer free delivery for purchases that exceed a certain dollar amount. (Amazon. com uses this technique very successfully.)

♦ Give a discount when purchasing multiple items.

♦ Throw in something extra, such as an accessory. "A free bag of premium coffee beans with every order of the ACME Home Brewer."

♦ Provide a discount when an order goes over a particular amount.

♦ Offer convenient payment terms. I use this technique with my home study courses by allowing customers to pay in installments.

Obviously, you want the majority of your sales to come from customers who pay the full price for your products and services and are happy to do so. However, offering a special deal once in a while is an effective way to get those who are still on the fence about buying from you to finally pull out their credit cards and place an order.

Free (and Almost Free) Trial Offers

Another form of special offer is the free trial. This is common for many types of products that are difficult to learn about without first taking them for a test drive.

For example, one of my clients, IXACT CONTACT, provides an excellent online contact management system for real estate professionals. But simply describing all the great features of that product and explaining how it works is not enough to convince most people to sign up. So they offer a free five-week trial.

Sales Builder

When determining the length of a free trial, use an unexpected period such as 5 weeks instead of the typical 30 days. Why? Because everyone uses that time frame, so your offer gets lost in the crowd of other free trial offers. However, if you say 5 weeks, or 45 days, or another atypical period of time, it stands out and gets noticed. I've tested this technique with many web-based business owners. It works.

Those who try a product for a particular period of time are likely to decide to buy it. In fact, I've seen some free trial offers with an over 90 percent conversion rate. In addition, people who are reluctant to make a purchase right away are more likely to sign up for a free trial. So this technique can dramatically increase your sales.

A trial doesn't always have to be free. A fellow website owner I know offers his website visitors an opportunity to "try" his how-to manual for 30 days for just $7 plus shipping. After the 30-day mark, the customer can return the manual and get charged nothing, or keep the materials and have their credit card billed for the full purchase price of $295.

Won't some unscrupulous customers simply photocopy the manual and then send the original back for a refund? That's the risk of making this type of free trial offer. But if the increased sales outnumber the losses, it's worth it.

Exit Offers

There is a significant number of your customers who will read your product sales page, hesitate, and then decide not to place an order at that moment. They're on the fence. And they may never get off. How do you turn these almost-customers into dollars for you? Try an exit offer.

An exit offer is simply a special offer you make to those who decide not to push the Buy Now button. You simply place a link below that button that says something like, "Click here only if you have decided NOT to buy now."

That link takes the customer to another page that makes a special offer, usually a discount or a free extra.

For example, a successful marketing coach I know makes exit offers to those who decide not to purchase one of his how-to guides. The guides are in binder format—a physical product that needs to be packaged and shipped. On his exit offer page, he offers a compelling alternative to those still on the fence: an online version of the guide they want at a much lower price. Web-based business owners I've spoken with say they're getting an increase of 10 to 20 percent in conversion rates by using this technique.

Up-Selling and Cross-Selling

Buy any book from Amazon.com and what do you see on the very first checkout page? "Customers who purchased this product also bought …." Amazon sure knows how to *cross-sell!*

Cross-selling refers to offering customers who have already placed an order, or are in the process of doing so, other complimentary products. If a customer buys a travel guide to Australia, it makes sense that he might also be interested in a hiking map of the Outback.

Effective cross-selling can increase your sales per order significantly. It takes advantage of the fact that the customer already has his wallet out and is in "buying mode."

def•i•ni•tion

Cross-selling is offering customers complimentary products to the items they have just ordered or are about to order.

Sales Builder

The products you offer as a cross-sell don't necessarily need to be your own. You can increase your profits per order by recommending related affiliate products. You can do this on the final thank you screen after the transaction is completed, or in a subsequent e-mail. See Chapter 6 to learn how affiliate programs work.

How do you cross-sell? There are many spots in the checkout process where you can place a cross-sell offer:

◆ On a special web page before the main checkout screen. The customer clicks on **Buy Now** and, before being taken to the checkout screen, is presented with an offer. "Would you like to add _____ to your order?"

◆ On the checkout screen itself. The shopping cart program I use, 1shoppingcart.com, has a feature that lets you display cross-sell products on the checkout screen. All the customer has to do is click the checkbox next to the product and it's automatically added to the order.

◆ On the thank you page after the order is placed. This works well if you're offering an affiliate product as your cross-sell offer because these usually cannot be promoted on your checkout pages.

◆ In the thank you e-mail after the order is placed. Again, great for affiliate products. Thank you e-mails are the ideal place to test cross-sell offers because they require very little effort to create.

A variation on the cross-sell technique is the *up-sell*. This involves offering the customer a premium version of the product or service he has decided to buy. It's like an automobile salesperson offering you a sunroof for just an extra $500.

Perhaps the easiest way to present an up-sell offer is right on the main product sales page. You simply offer two or three versions of the same product, such as Basic and Premium.

Here's an example.

def•i•ni•tion

Up-selling is offering the customer a premium or upgraded version of the product they are interested in purchasing.

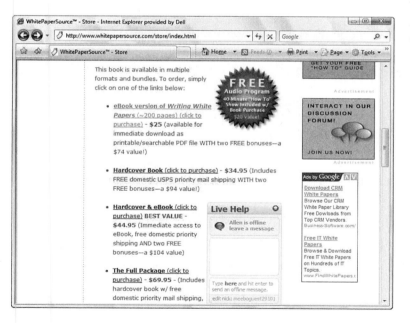

Example of an up-sell made on a product sales page.

You can also make up-sell offers on a special page that appears before the main checkout page, or on the checkout page itself.

A friend of mine uses up-sell and cross-sell techniques in a very daring way. When he sees an order come in while he's at the computer, he immediately picks up the phone and calls the customer to make an up-sell offer. "Hi. John Smith here. I noticed you just purchased Product X. I have a complementary Product Y available at a 20 percent discount. Would you like me to add that to your order?" According to my friend, a surprising number of customers are delighted he called and accept his offer!

Success Tip

If your website sells a service or an information product of some kind, such as an e-book, seminar, or consulting program, then customers are often willing to pay extra for access to an expert. For example, if you sell an e-book on growing roses in colder climates, consider offering a 30-minute coaching session as an up-sell. Some people who purchase the e-book will also appreciate an opportunity to get answers and guidance directly from the author.

The point of up-selling and cross-selling isn't to squeeze every dollar you can out of a customer. It's to offer other products and extras that customers may already be interested in, if only someone would present those options to them.

Look at your product line and think about the types of products that naturally go together, or products that you can create premium versions of. Then try a few up-sell and cross-sell offers. You might be pleasantly surprised with how much additional sales you can generate in this way.

Closing the Deal with Effective Landing Pages

If you visited my website, ForCopywritersOnly.com, and clicked on a link to learn more about one of my how-to guides, courses, or coaching programs, you'd be taken to a page that explains that product in detail and attempts to persuade you to place an order. That's a landing page (also known as a sales page or product page).

You should have a separate landing page for each special offer you make and product or service you sell.

When people visit a landing page, they are already interested, at least to some degree, in that particular offer, product, or service. The job of the landing page is to convert that interest into a click or sale.

Your landing page needs be informative and persuasive because this may be your only chance to convince a customer to take the action you want him or her to take. (No pressure!)

In Chapter 10, there is an excellent formula called *the motivating sequence* you can use to write persuasive web copy of any kind. Here are some additional tips specific to landing pages.

♦ Keep the layout simple. Ideally stick to one main column of text and, at most, one sidebar column.

♦ Be careful with images. An image on a web page is proven to draw the eye of the website visitor. That's okay if the image helps communicate what you're trying to say. But if it doesn't, it's just a distraction. And distractions are what you don't need on a landing page.

♦ Stick to one topic. Don't introduce other products or information on a landing page. The sole topic of the landing page should be the product or offer you're trying to sell. Nothing else.

♦ Don't place ads on a landing page. If your website is supported in part by affiliate advertising, don't place these on the landing page. Customers might be tempted to click the ad instead of buying your product. (In Internet marketing, we call that "click and bye!")

♦ Simplify the navigation links. Navigation bar links are tempting. They encourage website visitors to click and explore. But when a potential customer is on a landing page, you only want him or her to focus on one link: the link to buying the product. So, if possible, reduce the navigation links on your landing page to just a link back to your home page.

♦ Provide enough information. I covered this earlier in the chapter but it's worth mentioning again here. Be sure to provide all the information a customer needs to make a buying decision. If that means that your copy runs three for four screens in length, so be it. Trust me, customers won't mind.

♦ Put a Buy Now button above the fold. "Buy Now," "Register today," "Download your free e-book"—whatever your action link is called, make sure at least one is visible on the screen without the customer having to scroll to find it. Some may arrive on your landing page wanting to buy right away, and you don't want them having to hunt for the button.

♦ Use multiple Buy Now links. If your landing page is longer than a screen, put a Buy Now link near the top and at the bottom. If it's a very long screen, also consider placing one somewhere in the middle. Always make your action link easy to find on the landing page.

Here's an example of a landing page that follows all these strategies:

Landing page example. (Courtesy of HeartOfBusiness.com)

Always be tweaking your landing pages. As I mentioned earlier in this chapter, just a few minor improvements can have a dramatic increase in sales.

Top Internet marketers are constantly testing landing pages. They try new headlines, new offers, and new sections of body copy. They even test such minute details as font colors.

The easiest way for you to test a landing page is to create a duplicate. Split up your ads, e-mails, and other marketing efforts so that traffic is driven to each page. Then track which page is performing best. The winner might surprise you!

The Least You Need to Know

◆ Increasing conversion rates on your website is often the faster, and more cost-effective, way to boost sales.

◆ Look for ways to help visitors find what they need and get answers to all their questions.

◆ Use up-sell and cross-sell techniques, as well as effective landing pages, to build sales.

Chapter 22

Building Relationships with E-mail

In This Chapter

♦ How to use e-mail to convert website visitors into customers, and customers into repeat buyers

♦ The rundown on e-mail newsletters, promotions, and other types of e-mail communications

♦ The basics of setting up an e-mail broadcast service and creating effective e-mail campaigns

One of the most important ingredients to web-based business success is to build great relationships with the people who visit your site, and the customers who buy from you. How do you do that? The easy and most cost-effective way is with e-mail.

In this chapter, you'll learn how to use e-mail in a variety of strategic ways to stay in touch with website visitors, motivate customers to buy from you again and again, and keep your website front of mind with your target audience.

The Nuts and Bolts of E-mail Marketing

There are two basic steps to effective e-mail marketing. The first is to get website visitors to subscribe or otherwise *opt-in* to receiving e-mails from you. The second step is to communicate with those prospects via e-mail to convert them into buyers and, ideally, long-term loyal customers.

Chances are, you've been on the receiving end of this process many times.

def•i•ni•tion

In e-mail marketing, **opt-in** refers to when a website visitor has provided you with permission to send him or her your newsletter or other form of e-mail communications. In the United States, as well as many other jurisdictions, getting an opt-in from a website visitor before you send him or her marketing e-mails is not just industry best practice, it's the law.

A few months ago, for example, I subscribed to an e-mail newsletter at a website that specializes in news and information of interest to runners. Now, every two weeks I receive tips on how to run better, news about running events in my area, and of course, recommendations on running-related products. The newsletter is so well-written, entertaining, and useful that I find myself returning to the website again and again.

Guess what? I've also clicked on several of the advertisements on the website and made some purchases.

That's a classic case of how to use e-mail wisely to convert website visitors into customers, and nurture those customers until they become repeat buyers and spread the word about the site to their friends and colleagues.

If that runners' website didn't communicate with me regularly via e-mail, would I have returned so many times and clicked on its advertisements? Probably not. I was initially interested in their website when I first visited it. But it was their valuable newsletter and other e-mails that *kept* me interested.

E-mail marketing is important because rarely will prospects buy from you the first time they visit your website. And if you don't stay in touch with them, they may very well forget about your site and never return—or remember your site, but not be able to easily find it again.

As a web-based business owner, e-mail marketing is your number-one tool for converting website visitors into customers.

Getting Started with an E-mail Marketing Service Provider

If you're just starting your web-based business, don't be tempted to use a personal e-mail service, such as Outlook or Gmail, for your e-mail newsletter and other e-mail marketing communications, even if your list is small. These services just aren't designed for this purpose and your e-mail marketing program will rapidly become difficult to manage as your list grows. In addition, most personal e-mail accounts do not allow mass broadcasting of e-mails for marketing purposes—a rule that, if violated, can result in your account being suspended.

These days, there are many affordable *e-mail marketing service providers* that will take care of broadcasting your e-mail messages to your opt-in list, as well as handling a host of other tasks such as generating sign-up forms for your website and managing your list.

def•i•ni•tion

An **e-mail marketing service provider** broadcasts your e-mail message to your opt-in list on your behalf. Although the e-mail is sent from their computer servers to your prospects and customers, the message appears to come directly from you. These providers will often also store your subscriber database and provide you with a myriad of other related services as well.

How do you select an e-mail marketing service provider that's right for your business? Here is a list of criteria you should consider:

- ◆ Do they have a strict policy of compliance with all spam laws and other best practices of permission-based e-mail marketing? (You want to make sure you're dealing with a reputable company.)

- ◆ Are they proactive in building solid relationships with Yahoo!, Gmail, and other major e-mail service providers, so your e-mails get through to your subscribers rather than being mistaken for spam? (E-mail deliverability is a big issue these days.)

- ◆ Do they provide a wide range of list management services, such as automatic handling of unsubscribes, list import and export, search, etc.?

- ◆ Do they provide you with a means of signing people up on your website, and automatically adding those new contacts to your contact database? (Most e-mail marketing service providers have ready-made forms that you can customize and use on your website.)

◆ Do they offer templates that make it easy for you to create great-looking e-mail newsletters, special announcements, and other communications?

◆ Do they provide live online or phone support should you need it? (Avoid services that give you only an e-mail address or online form when you need help.)

◆ Do they provide you with useful reports that show you how well your e-mail campaigns are doing? (Are people opening your e-mails? Are they clicking on the links?)

◆ Do they automatically handle e-mails that bounce and are otherwise undeliverable?

Another tip is to check their customer list and testimonials to see if other companies like yours use the service. This is a good indication of whether the e-mail marketing service provider is suited to your particular type of web-based business.

The most popular e-mail marketing services used by small web-based businesses include:

◆ Constant Contact (www.constantcontact.com)

◆ AWeber Communications (www.aweber.com)

◆ Campaigner (www.campaigner.com)

◆ GetResponse (www.getresponse.com)

◆ iContact (www.icontact.com)

◆ VerticalResponse (www.verticalresponse.com)

◆ Benchmark Email (www.benchmarkemail.com)

◆ Emma (www.myemma.com)

◆ Bronto (www.bronto.com)

◆ Boomerang (www.boomerang.com)

I recommend that you take the time to review each of these services and select the one that is the best fit for your needs and budget.

And speaking of budget, the fees charged by e-mail marketing service providers vary widely. Most base their prices on the size of your list. The service I use, for example, charges $25 for 0 to 2,500 contacts; $50 per month for 2,500 to 5,000, and so forth. There are other services, however, that charge a fixed fee per 1,000 e-mails sent, regardless of the list size. So be sure to review the fee structure closely.

Signing up for an e-mail marketing service is a fairly straightforward process. Typically, you fill out an online form, provide your payment information, and receive (or choose) a username and password. Then, when you're ready, you log in to the system to set up your e-mail preferences, upload or input your contact names, and so forth.

Warning!

Carefully read the instructions for uploading an existing list to an e-mail marketing service provider. All the reputable services have strict rules—and wisely so—regarding using opt-in lists only and may even require that an e-mail be sent to everyone on your list asking them to re-subscribe.

Getting Newsy with Newsletters

E-mail newsletters—also referred to as e-newsletters, e-zines, or just zines—are, by far, the most common form of e-mail communication used by web-based business owners. And for good reason! The newsletter format is very versatile and can convey just about any type of information you want prospects and customers to receive. In addition, people who subscribe to a newsletter expect to receive it regularly. So they're not going to complain about you contacting them so much. (Well, at least in theory!) With a newsletter, you stay on the radar screens of prospects so that when they think about your kind of products and services, they also think of you.

The cornerstone of an effective e-mail newsletter is great content. The news and information you convey to your subscribers must be valuable. If it isn't, people will simply unsubscribe and, as a result, may never visit your website again. Ouch!

Sales Builder

Subscribe to competitor e-mail newsletters. This will help you monitor the articles, news, special offers, and other information that similar web-based businesses are sending to their prospects and customers. Look at what they're doing well, and not so well, and use that "competitive intelligence" to make your own e-mail newsletter even better.

There is a delicate balance that you have to achieve when creating your e-mail newsletter. If you just have great content—articles, news, etc.—but make no mention of your website products and services, then your newsletter isn't going to generate many orders. However, if you're too promotional and cram your newsletter with one sales pitch after another, then your readers are going to abandon ship (unsubscribe) like it's the Titanic!

Depending on your products and services, and your target audience, the ideal balance will be approximately 80/20. That's 80 percent good, solid content in the form of articles, news, and other valuable information and 20 percent promotional copy, such as product specials and offers.

Here is an excellent example of a newsletter.

Example of an e-mail newsletter.

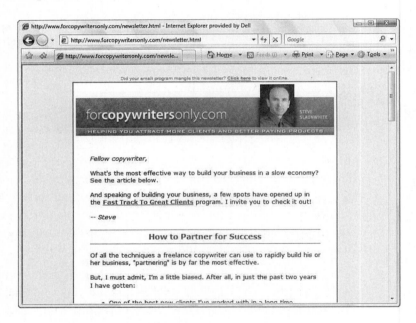

How often should you send your newsletter? The consensus in the Internet marketing community is at least once per month. Any less frequently than that and your subscribers might forget you! If your target audience is particularly hungry for the type of information your newsletter provides, or if they are avid readers of your topic, then publishing bi-weekly or even weekly may be more advantageous. I publish my newsletter every two weeks, and subscribers have told me that this frequency is ideal for them.

Easy Does It with E-mail Design

The design for e-mail newsletters and other types of e-mail marketing communications can vary widely, from a simple plain text message that is little more than a neatly done presentation of the text to a colorful, professionally designed piece that rivals anything you'd see in a glossy magazine.

Unfortunately, there's more to e-mail design than simply creating a great-looking layout. *E-mail rendering* plays a huge role in how your e-mail will be designed. You have to make sure the text and images in your e-mail newsletter display correctly in most of the popular e-mail services—Outlook, Gmail, Yahoo!, and AOL, for example. I say "most" because rarely does an e-mail look exactly the same in all these programs.

E-mail design is a specialty all to itself. So if you're not a professional designer, you have a couple of options:

Hire a freelance designer or design firm to create a custom template for you. Make sure they have experience in e-mail newsletter design and understand how to create a template that will render correctly. Expect to pay in the $500 range for a professional design.

Use a ready-made template. Most e-mail marketing service providers offer their subscribers a wide range of ready-made templates—free. All you have to do to create a new newsletter issue is fill in the text! This is by far the fastest and most cost-effective way to launch your newsletter.

def•i•ni•tion

E-mail rendering refers to how an e-mail looks in your subscriber's e-mail service. Because not all services interpret the underlying code exactly the same way, your e-mail may look different depending on which type of e-mail account your subscriber has. That's why it's important to test your e-mail newsletter's appearance in the popular e-mail services that your target audience uses.

By the way, if you use a ready-made template, you can always hire a freelance designer to add some custom touches for you, such as a logo.

Whether you do it yourself, hire a designer, or use a template, the consensus among Internet marketers is to keep the design simple. Don't add any unnecessary images. Keep the layout to just one or two columns. Make the focus of your newsletter the great articles, news, and offers. At the end of the day, subscribers will be attracted to the great content of your newsletter, not the great design.

Beyond Newsletters: Other E-mail Marketing Strategies

Newsletters are the most common form of e-mail marketing communications. But there are many other ways to stay in touch with prospects and customers via e-mail that you should consider. In fact, depending on your website's products and services, you might decide not to publish a newsletter at all, and use one of the following formats instead.

For example, a friend of mine has a website that offers an online course on knitting. Instead of a newsletter, she decided to develop a limited series of e-mails that teach a particular knitting technique. This is her way of giving website visitors a sampling of her fuller online course. The idea is, people will be impressed by the mini-e-mail course and buy the bigger one. And it's an idea that has been working very well for her.

A few years ago, I was hired to write e-mails for RadioShack.com. Like its brick-and-mortar cousin, the online store is a mecca for electronics shoppers. So instead of a newsletter, the company sent a list of weekly specials by e-mail. RadioShack customers didn't want articles, they wanted deals. So the virtual flyer format was a smart move.

Take a look at the alternatives to e-mail newsletters that follow and see which ones may be appropriate for your website and target audience.

By the way, there's no reason why you can't have a regular e-mail newsletter and also send supplementary e-mails in the following formats. In fact, mixing things up is a good idea.

Virtual Flyers

My Saturday newspaper is stuffed with flyers, coupons, and other advertisements each week. My wife goes through these looking for deals before she does her shopping. Are your website customers also looking for deals? If so, then the virtual flyer e-mail can potentially be an excellent sales builder for you.

A virtual flyer e-mail is similar to printed flyers you receive in the mail or on your doorstep. Typically, it contains a list of featured products available from your website that are usually, but not always, being offered at a discount.

Say you have a website that sells coffee beans and related accessories. You could have a virtual flyer e-mail that features a "Bean of the Week" for 20 percent off.

Success Tip _____

Most website shopping cart systems enable you to create coupons that you can offer to your prospects and customers. These are usually in the form of a special code that the customer types into a coupon field on the checkout page to apply the discount. You can create a coupon as a percentage or fixed-price discount, and set up an expiration date.

E-Mail Series

While an e-mail newsletter is an ongoing publication, an e-mail series has a limited run.

If your website sells golfing equipment, for example, you could have an e-mail series called "Improve Your Swing in Just 6 Weeks." Website visitors who sign up would receive an e-mail each week containing a golf swing lesson they could practice and perfect until the next lesson. At the end of the six-week period, the e-mail series ends—ideally with a special offer to make a purchase.

E-mail series work well on single-product websites where website visitors are not likely to buy on their first visit. The e-mail series gives them a taste of the product, and keeps their interest, until they are ready to buy.

Solo Promo

This type of e-mail is the virtual equivalent to an advertisement or sales letter. Unlike a newsletter, flyer, or e-mail series, the entire purpose of this type of e-mail is to promote a specific offer and get the order!

Say you're promoting a special event on your website, such as a teleclass or webinar. On the day before the event, you could send out a "Last chance to register …" e-mail to bring in more sign-ups. That's a *solo promo* e-mail in action.

Solo promos also work well for special discount offers, new product launches, seminars and other events where there is a deadline, and more. In fact, you can probably think of many good reasons to send a solo promo.

But be careful. Although solo promo e-mails are proven to generate sales, they also irritate your subscribers—especially if you send too many.

My e-mail newsletter is published every two weeks, and I can usually send one solo promo per month without much problem. However, if I send two per month, I start to see a sharp increase in unsubscribes.

Follow-Up Autoresponders

An autoresponder is an e-mail that is scheduled to be sent automatically after a website visitor has signed up for your newsletter or made a purchase. You've received autoresponders yourself, perhaps without realizing it. When you buy something online and receive a "Thank you" e-mail a few minutes later, that's an autoresponder.

The neat thing about autoresponders is that you can set them up to be sent precisely when you want prospects or customers to receive them. Subscribers to my copywriting course, for example, receive an e-mail 30 days after they subscribe, asking for their candid opinion of the newsletter. I call it my "How am I doing?" e-mail, and it works very well in building relationships with my readers.

I have another autoresponder that is sent 60 days after someone has subscribed to my newsletter that offers a $100 discount—good for three days—for any one of my home study courses. I get a lot of orders from that autoresponder!

Success Tip

Autoresponders are available through most shopping cart services and some e-mail marketing service providers. So if you want to use autoresponders extensively in your marketing, be sure to check that your shopping cart or e-mail service has this feature.

Autoresponders are very flexible. You can set them up to be automatically sent days, weeks, or even months after a particular event, such as someone subscribing, purchasing a particular product, making a second purchase, and more. Get creative! I recently received an e-mail asking me to re-order the printer cartridge I purchased online, which was obviously an autoresponder that was scheduled to be sent nine weeks after my last order—just when my current cartridge would be running out!

Boosting Sign-Ups with Effective Online Forms

Ask any successful website entrepreneur what their most valuable business asset is and 90 percent will give you the same answer: "my list." Your list is all those website visitors who have signed up to receive your e-mail newsletter or other e-mails. They are your best prospects and customers and will likely generate the majority of your online sales. So building your list is not just important—it's essential!

Where do you start? Step one is your sign-up form. You must have the means of creating a form, placing it on your website, and having clients who sign up get automatically added to your list database.

Most e-mail marketing service providers have features that make it easy to create such forms and post them on your website. The service I use, AWeber Communications, walks me through the set-up process and then provides me with the HTML code I need for my website sign-up form.

Here is an example of a typical website sign-up form for an e-mail newsletter.

Sales Builder

Internet marketing experts suggest that you place a sign-up form on every page of your website, not just the front page. You never know for sure on which page your visitors are going to enter your site—It's not always the front page!—and you want to make sure they have an opportunity to opt-in.

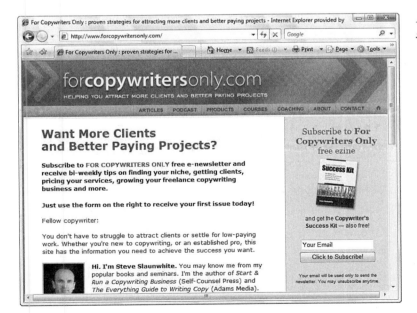

Example of e-mail newsletter sign-up form.

Notice that I only ask for an e-mail address. This works for me, as I'm only interested in following up with subscribers via e-mail. However, you might consider adding more fields, such as full name, company name, address and phone number, especially if you want to communicate with your prospects by mail or phone.

Pop-Ups, -Downs, -Overs, and -Unders

In addition to a form placed on a web page, you can also have your sign-up form appear like magic. You can have it pop up automatically when someone visits a page, fade a minute or so later, pop down when they attempt to leave—the options are almost endless.

In general, website visitors hate pop-ups. They're annoying. Most web browsers even include features that stop them—like an e-mail program that stops spam. However, a pop-up can increase the percentage of website visitors who sign up for your newsletter or other e-mail communications. So it's worth at least considering.

Warning!

If you decide to use a pop-up, make sure it is set up so that it does not appear again to repeat visitors. You don't want those who have already visited your website and signed up for your e-mail newsletter to be constantly greeted with this type of in-your-face advertisement.

There are many software packages and services available that can generate pop-ups for you. First, see if your current e-mail marketing service provider or shopping cart service offers pop-ups. If they don't, check out these options:

- Instant PopOver (www.instantpopover.com)
- Advanced DHTML Popup (www.dpopup.com)
- Ace PopUp Generator (www.cgiscript.net/site_software.htm)

Don't go pop-up crazy. It will make your website look like a hyped-up, carnival barking sales site that online shoppers will go out of their way to avoid.

Putting the Squeeze on Squeeze Pages

An effective sign-up box is a great way to motivate website visitors to opt-in to your e-mail newsletter or other e-mail communications. However, it does have one significant drawback. A sign-up box competes with all the other information on the web page. And when a visitor is confronted with multiple choices—product descriptions, links, offers—they may get distracted and not sign up.

That's where a squeeze page comes in.

A squeeze page is a web page that is entirely dedicated to persuading your website visitor to sign up for your e-mail newsletter or other e-mails. It's like taking the sign-up box and stretching it until it fits the entire screen. Usually, there is no other information or links—nothing that may distract the visitor from signing up.

Here's a typical example:

Example of e-mail newsletter sign-up form.

Squeeze pages are proven to convert more visitors into subscribers. So it makes sense to get one created for your website. When you advertise or otherwise promote your website, consider sending people to your squeeze page rather than your website front page. Or, better still, test both approaches and see which one generates the best results for you.

Encouraging More Sign-Ups with a Free Bonus

In the early days of the Internet, an e-mail newsletter was a novelty. It was relatively easy to get website visitors to subscribe.

Not anymore. Today there are a gazillion e-mail newsletters all competing for the attention of your target audience. So in addition to offering great articles, news, and other information to motivate visitors to subscribe, it's also a good idea to offer an extra incentive. That could be a free report, product sample, tip sheet—any giveaway that is related to your website and that would be enticing to your potential customers.

Traditional print newsletters and magazines do this all the time. A cooking magazine, for example, will send you a letter offering you a chance to subscribe at a discounted rate, and if you "Act now, you'll also receive this recipe shopping software absolutely free!"

Study your potential customers. Think about your products and services and how they relate to their problems and ambitions. Then come up with a free giveaway that will give your website visitors that extra nudge to subscribe to your e-mails.

Tracking Your E-mail Marketing Success

You send out an e-mail—and nothing happens. No sales are generated from your website. Is it time to sulk in the corner of your office with a pint of Häagen-Dazs? Maybe not. A lot of positive things may very well have happened. People may have read your newsletter, passed it on to others, and clicked on the links to products and other pages on your website—all activities that can eventually lead to sales. So it may have been a great day after all!

How do you know for sure?

You need to make sure that key activities in your e-mail newsletter and other e-mail campaigns can be tracked. There are two particular activities that you need to pay close attention to:

- ◆ **Open rate.** This is the number of people who have received and opened your e-mail message.

- ◆ **Clickthroughs.** This is the number of people who have clicked on links embedded within your e-mail message.

Most e-mail marketing service providers will offer you reports that provide you with this information.

Your open rate is an indication of how well read your newsletter and other e-mails are. If your open rate is 20 percent, for example, that means 20 percent of recipients have at least clicked on your message in their inbox. That doesn't necessarily mean they read your message. But they at least opened it!

Your clickthroughs are an indication of how many people are visiting your website after receiving your e-mail. If you're promoting a special discount on a new product, for example, the clickthrough rate will tell you how well that promotion is working. With that information, you can make any necessary changes, such as improving the marketing copy.

Keep an eye on your e-mail statistics. They can help you tweak your e-mail newsletter and other e-mail communications so that you get better and better results.

The Least You Need to Know

◆ Use e-mail strategically to convert website visitors into buyers.

◆ Create an effective sign-up form to motivate your website visitors to opt-in to your e-mails.

◆ Consider publishing a regular e-mail newsletter and make good use of other e-mail marketing communication formats.

◆ Keep track of open rate and clickthrough statistics so you can continually improve your e-mail campaigns.

23

Increasing Sales by Working With Affiliates

In This Chapter

- ◆ How an affiliate program can increase your sales
- ◆ The basics of setting up and managing your affiliate program
- ◆ How to find the best affiliates to promote your website products and services

Imagine having a worldwide army of salespeople enthusiastically promoting your website products. They work hard for you, spreading the word about your offerings on their own websites as well as pitching your products in their newsletters and blogs. The best part is, you don't have to pay them a salary or even hire them as employees. You simply reward them with a percentage of the money they make for you. Straight commission.

Sound too good to be true? Actually, this model is commonplace among web-based business owners. It's called an *affiliate program* and it can substantially increase your website revenues and profits.

In fact, these days it's very difficult, if not impossible, to build a successful web-based business without one. And frankly, you'd be foolish to ignore the additional exposure and sales that just a handful of loyal affiliates can generate for you.

In this chapter, we take a closer look at affiliate programs and learn how to set one up.

What Is an Affiliate Program?

Before you can understand what an affiliate program is, you first need to know the definition of *affiliate*.

In the world of online business, an affiliate is someone who agrees to promote your website products for a fee or commission. Although some specialize in advertising the affiliate products they represent on search engines and other online venues, most affiliates own a website, e-mail newsletter, blog, or other online property from which they can tout your website offerings.

Here's a typical example.

When I created my pricing manual for writers called, unoriginally, *Pricing Your Writing Services*, I sent a copy to my friend Nick. He publishes a popular e-mail newsletter for online copywriters—an ideal market for my new product. Nick reviewed the manual, raved about it, and offered to be an affiliate. That meant I would pay him a commission for every sale he made.

Over the following weeks, Nick published a review of the manual on his website and mentioned it regularly in his newsletter. Dozens of sales were generated as a result. At the end of the month, I cheerfully wrote him a check for his commission.

Now that you know what an affiliate is, what's an *affiliate program?* That's simply a program that you set up for recruiting affiliates, tracking their sales, paying the commissions they earn, and managing the entire process.

> **Sales Builder**
>
> The best affiliates are those who own a popular website, online newsletter, or blog with a huge audience, a large segment of which are potential customers for your products. For example, if your website sells gourmet coffee beans, then you'll want to reach the java-loving readers of a site like CoffeeDetective.com.

How an Affiliate Program Works

If you were to take a bird's-eye view of a typical affiliate program, it would look something like this:

◆ A potential affiliate visits your website and discovers that it offers a product he would like to sell on his own site.

◆ He clicks on your **Become an Affiliate** link and signs up for your program.

◆ Now you have a new affiliate! You provide him with the information he needs and an affiliate link to the product he wants to promote for you. (More on affiliate links in the next section.)

◆ Your new affiliate adds your product to the "Recommended Resources" section of his website.

◆ Here's where it gets exciting. Over the coming weeks, people visit his website, see your product listed, click, and get taken to your website product page to place an order.

◆ Behind the scenes, your affiliate system tracks this activity and credits your affiliate with the sales that are made.

◆ At regular intervals, you pay the affiliate his well-earned commission. You've made money. He has made money. It's win-win all the way.

Of course, there are variations to this scenario. You may have contacted the affiliate to sign him up rather than the other way around, or the affiliate may have a blog instead of a website. But that is essentially what an affiliate program looks like.

Getting Started

To launch a successful affiliate program, there are three things you need to know:

1. How are you going to track sales and manage your affiliate program?

2. What commission rate are you going to pay your affiliates?

3. Where are you going to find affiliates?

The rest of this chapter will help you answer those questions.

Setting up an affiliate program is a little like planning a dinner party: you prepare the room, send out the invitations, get the food ready, and greet your guests at the door. Once the party gets started, you're going to have a good time!

Selecting Your Affiliate Software or Service

When I first started my affiliate program years ago, I admit it was a clumsy effort. My first affiliate was a colleague who agreed to pitch my product in his blog. I used a separate product number to track his sales and did everything else manually, from counting the orders to providing him with a sales report to calculating his commission.

It was a lot of work.

Fortunately, these days, there are plenty of software products and online services available that will handle most of the administrative drudgery for you. There's no reason to duct tape a program together like I did!

Ideally, you want a solution that automates affiliate program management as much as possible. The affiliate service I use today handles all of the following tasks for me. It automatically:

❑ Creates an affiliate sign-up link for my website.

❑ Sends an e-mail "welcome letter" to new affiliates, and provides them with information on how the program works.

❑ Creates an online affiliate resource center where affiliates can review my products and access a range of tools such as artwork for ads, e-mail templates, and more.

❑ Generates the appropriate *affiliate links* so that affiliates can be credited for the sales they make.

❑ Tracks all affiliate sales and provides me with a range of useful reports.

❑ Allows affiliates to log in and see a record of their clicks and sales.

❑ Alerts me when it's time to pay my affiliates their commissions.

I suggest you use this as a checklist. Make sure that the solution you ultimately select for your affiliate management does all of these items, at the very least. There are so many nitty-gritty details to managing an affiliate program that it is just too time-consuming—and ultimately unprofitable—to try to handle them all manually.

def•i•ni•tion

An **affiliate link** is a hyperlink that contains a special tracking code specific to each affiliate. When a buyer clicks on this link, your affiliate management system credits the appropriate affiliate with the sale. An affiliate link usually takes the form of a weird-looking website URL, such as www.forcopywritersonly.com/454rf, or a snippet of HTML code that the affiliate cuts and pastes into the HTML code of his website, blog, or e-mail newsletter.

There are basically three types of affiliate management solutions you can use.

Traditional Software

There are many good affiliate software products available. The best way to find them is to simply type "affiliate software" into your favorite search engine.

Affiliate software installs on your computer and communicates with your website server and shopping cart system to track sales and generate reports.

The disadvantage of affiliate software is that you have to install it. And we all know that installation of any software doesn't always go smoothly. You also need to be diligent and regularly download updates and new versions. And that can be a hassle.

What's the advantage? Well, you own it! Once you purchase an affiliate software package, that's it. No further payments. All the other options discussed in this section require some sort of monthly, quarterly, or annual fee.

That being said, the majority of web-based business owners I know prefer using a hosted software solution for their affiliate programs, which is a techie way of saying that the software is provided as an online service.

Online Services

Don't like the idea of installing software? Then sign up for an online, or hosted, software service for affiliate program management.

Technically, an online service is software. But instead of being installed on your computer, the program resides on the software company's website. You simply subscribe to the service, get a username and password, log in to set things up and, voilà, your affiliate program is ready to go.

Did you notice I said "subscribe"? Yes, you have to pay a regular fee for this type of affiliate management system and that fee can be hefty—upward of $100 per month. The advantage is that you don't install software and maintain it.

Shopping Cart Systems

One of the most popular options among web-based business owners just starting out is to select a shopping cart system that includes an affiliate management module. This makes a lot of sense because your affiliate program has to work with your shopping cart system anyway. Why not get them both in the same package and avoid any compatibility issues?

These days, virtually all major shopping cart systems include an affiliate program plug-in of some kind. (Although you often have to pay extra for it.) But just because it has some affiliate management tools doesn't mean they will meet all your requirements. Review the features carefully and make sure you're getting everything you need.

Deciding How Much to Pay Affiliates

In some ways, affiliates are like salespeople. You have to pay them enough to keep them motivated and selling for you.

How much is enough?

Be careful. You may be tempted to provide your affiliates with just a small cut. After all, you did all the work creating your product line and building your website. Why should they get more than, say, 5 percent or so? I can understand how you might feel. The reality is, however, you won't attract very many affiliates—especially the top sellers—unless you offer an attractive commission rate.

Keep in mind that many affiliates have worked hard building their own successful websites, e-mail newsletters, or blogs. They may have a large audience of readers or subscribers that has taken them years to cultivate. If you want an affiliate to recommend or advertise your product to all those potential buyers, you're going to have to make it financially worth his or her while.

When setting your commission rate, you'll need to pick a percentage that appeals to affiliates while still making it profitable for you. A good formula is to subtract your product cost (including shipping) from your selling price, take a look at what you have left over, then consider offering affiliates up to 25 percent of the remainder.

For example, if your website sells specialty coffee beans for $15 per bag and your product cost is $5, then you have $10 to work with. You could probably offer a 15 percent affiliate commission, or about $2.25 per bag, and still have plenty of profit left over to keep your banker happy.

If your website sells downloadable products, such as e-books or software, then you don't have to worry about manufacturing or shipping costs. You're selling electrons! You can offer a more tantalizing commission, say 25 percent.

Flat-Rate Commissions

In some cases, it might make sense to offer a flat-rate commission rather than a percentage. That simply means that you pay a specific dollar amount for a sale. In our coffee example, you could offer a flat-rate commission of $2 and promote your affiliate program with the slogan: *Earn 2 bucks per bag!*

Tier One and Tier Two

Here's where it gets a little more complicated! You can offer affiliates tier one and tier two commissions, which may motivate them to recommend not only your products but your website as well.

Here's how it works.

Say your website sells custom embroidered socks. Your affiliate, a blogger with a site called Crazy About Socks, recommends your product to her readers. With me so far? Now, what if a buyer she sends to you places an order for socks—and also for one of your embroidered sweaters?

In a simple affiliate program, your affiliate will only earn money on the sock sales. But with a tier one/tier two program, she would earn full commission for the socks (tier one) and a smaller commission on the sweater (tier two)—even though she didn't specifically refer the buyer to your sweater products.

A tier one/tier two affiliate program provides an affiliate with a further incentive to promote your products. They make more money. However, it is more complex for you to manage. If you decide to go this route, make sure the affiliate software or service you select supports tier two commissions.

Finding the Right Affiliates

Now that you have your affiliate program set up, all you need to do is find a large network of eager affiliates who will promote your products on their websites and in their blogs and e-mail newsletters. Right? Then the sales will just roll in while you're sipping margaritas on a beach in the Caribbean.

Well, it's not quite that easy.

While it is true that a robust affiliate network can help you grow your web-based business, it can take a lot of time and effort to attract the right affiliates and build those relationships.

Warning!

Don't make the mistake of assuming that all you need to do to attract affiliates is put a "Become an Affiliate" link on your website. Sure, you'll get a few people signing up that way. But if you want the best affiliates—those who can potentially generate a lot of sales for you—then you're going to have to actively seek out and recruit them.

It's important to have a plan in place for identifying the right affiliates and attracting them to your program. Here are some ideas for doing just that:

◆ Place a link to your affiliate program on every page of your website, not just your home page. Potential affiliates often visit sites looking for opportunities to promote products. Make it easy for them to click and find out about your program.

◆ Tap your network. If you're starting a web-based business, then chances are you have some friends and colleagues who are online as well. Perhaps they have websites, e-mail newsletters, blogs, and podcasts that reach your potential customers? If so, contact them and ask if they would like to join your program. Because these people know you, you are likely to get a positive response.

◆ Find the popular sites. Take a close look at your target audience. What websites do they visit? What e-mail newsletters do they subscribe to? What blog and discussion forums do they frequent? Find out who runs these online properties. They will be ideal candidates for your affiliate program.

◆ Collaborate with your competitors. This might seem strange to you, but your competitors can become your best affiliates. After all, they target the same type of customers you do and, like you, want to make more money from their websites. If you have a product that fills a gap in their product line, they may be more than willing to promote it as an affiliate. Several of my competitors are affiliates of my products, as I am of theirs.

◆ Ask your customers. One of the most overlooked sources of potential affiliates is a web-based business's own customers. Think about it. Who better to promote your product than those who have purchased and endorse it? Having an Internet presence these days is so commonplace that chances are many of your customers have their own websites or blogs. Send them an e-mail describing your affiliate program and inviting them to sign up.

◆ Get active in affiliate marketing communities. Although there is no recognized national association for affiliate marketing—yet—many smaller groups have sprung up. For example, the Rocky Mountain Affiliate Marketing Association caters to website merchants (that's you) and affiliates in Utah. If there is an affiliate organization in your area or industry, join it. It's a great way to promote your program and meet potential affiliates.

◆ List your program in an affiliate program directory. There are a multitude of directories on the Internet where you can list details of your affiliate program—usually for free. See Chapter 5 for a complete list.

Perhaps the best way to find affiliates is to keep your eyes open for opportunities. A few years ago, I was a speaker at a writers' conference in New York. After my presentation, a woman came up and asked if she could interview me for her website. I soon learned that her site was popular among *mom-preneurs* (moms who are also home-based business owners). A light went on in my head. Could mom-preneurs be a good target market for my online courses and e-books for copywriters? I invited the woman to be an affiliate and she agreed. She went on to promote many of my products and did very well. I'm glad I met her!

Approaching a Prospective Affiliate

As I said earlier, unless your website products are hugely popular, don't expect the best affiliates to come knocking on your door. You're going to have to make the first move.

How do you do that?

Say you've launched a website that sells training programs for serious bodybuilders. In your market, there is a hugely popular blog that is visited by thousands of brawny readers every day—all potential customers for your products. Obviously, that blogger is an ideal candidate for your affiliate program. You definitely want him selling for you!

So you send him the following e-mail:

> *Hi John,*
>
> *My name is Debra Smith and I operate a website called _____. We specialize in selling training guides and programs specifically for the female bodybuilder.*
>
> *Your blog is very popular among my target audience. In fact, I'm an avid reader myself!*
>
> *Would you be interested in reviewing one or two of our products with the aim of becoming an affiliate? We have an excellent program. Commissions are paid monthly and range from 30-45%.*
>
> *We're proud of the quality of our training guides and programs and I'm confident that you'll be equally impressed.*
>
> *I look forward to hearing from you!*
>
> *Debra*

Chances are, the owner of the blog is going to respond positively to your message. You've done it right by respecting that he cares about the quality of products he recommends to his readers and by offering him a generous commission.

What will likely happen next is that the blogger will reply to your e-mail, or call you, with questions about your affiliate program. Expect him to visit your website and check you out. He may also take you up on your offer to send him a product sample to review. If that happens, ship it right away along with a friendly note. Then follow up in a couple of weeks.

It may take weeks or even months to court a potential affiliate who has a popular website, e-mail newsletter, or blog. Don't give up. When you do get one of these *power affiliates* on your side, they can give your website sales a giant boost.

def•i•ni•tion

> **Power affiliate** is a term used in online marketing to describe an affiliate who has a track record of generating a lot of sales for the affiliate programs he or she participates in. Usually, a power affiliate owns a website or blog with a lot of traffic, or an e-mail newsletter with thousands of subscribers.

Keeping Affiliates Happy ... and Selling!

You've signed up a few great affiliates. You're done! Now you can relax, knowing that these guys are going to continuously promote your products and generate a steady flow of sales for your web-based business.

If something tells you that's not quite true, you're right. In order to build a loyal base of affiliates, you have to nurture those relationships. Don't make the mistake of taking these people for granted. If you do, you'll risk losing their interest—and their sales.

My rule of thumb is that you should treat affiliates as you would your very best customers. Stay in touch. Show your appreciation for their efforts. Say "thank you" when they promote your product in their e-mail newsletter or blog. It's worth the effort. In my experience, it's much easier to *keep* an affiliate than it is to get a new one.

Here are some ideas for building loyal affiliate relationships.

- Create an affiliate resource center. Set up a special page or section on your website containing helpful information for your affiliates. This could include selling tips, e-mail message templates, artwork for ads—any resource that makes it easier for them to promote your products.

- Send a thank-you card or note. I suggest you do this by mail rather than e-mail. A card or note received in the mail is so rare these days that it makes a special impact. Recently, an affiliate phoned me specifically to thank me for the thank-you card I mailed her. She said it was the first she had received in years! For the mere cost of a postage stamp, I made a significant impression.

- Pay well. A lot of web-based business owners get stingy when they set their affiliate commissions. Recently, I came across a program that offered 5 percent on a $9 product—a measly 45 cents!—hardly enough to get an affiliate enthusiastic about selling it.

- Pay promptly. Few things annoy an affiliate more than a merchant dragging his or her feet to pay commissions. When it comes time to pay your affiliates, do so promptly.

- Give them a call. Move the relationship beyond e-mail. Pick up the phone and say hello every once in a while. In my experience, the best affiliates are those you get to know well in person or on the phone.

◆ Respond quickly to support inquiries. Just as customers do, affiliates demand good service. They may call or e-mail you with a question about your program, a request for a product sample, or a problem with an affiliate link. When that happens, get back to them quickly, ideally within one business day.

◆ Offer to represent their products. Often affiliates are also website owners with their own affiliate programs. If they have products that complement your product line, sign up as an affiliate. If you scratch their backs, they'll be more likely to scratch yours.

◆ Run a contest. A friend of mine, a fellow web-based business owner, recently ran a contest among his affiliates. He offered an iPod to the top seller of the month. The promotion created a lot of excitement—and sales. Several affiliates made an extra effort to promote his product in their newsletters and blogs. Running a contest can obviously work very well. Try it.

You can probably think of many other ways to make your affiliates delighted with your program and products. The best affiliates are those that stay with you long term, learn your products inside and out, and understand how best to promote your offerings to their particular audiences.

Top-selling affiliates are gold. Keep them happy!

The Least You Need to Know

◆ A network of affiliates can increase your website sales significantly.

◆ Don't stick an affiliate program together with matchsticks and glue. Find a good affiliate software program or online service.

◆ The best affiliates are those who have a popular website or blog that targets your potential customers.

◆ Treat your affiliates as you would your very best customers. Never take them for granted.

24

Customer Service with a (Virtual) Smile

In This Chapter

- ◆ Keeping customers satisfied, so they buy more and tell others
- ◆ How to handle refunds, returns, complaints, and requests for help
- ◆ Techniques and ideas for automating customer service to save time and money

There's an old saying in the retail business. A happy customer will tell 3 of her friends about her experience, while an unhappy customer will tell 10! The same holds true on the Internet—but with one important difference. A customer who is dissatisfied with your website or products won't complain to just 10 people. She'll tell 10,000!

The Internet provides numerous opportunities for dissatisfied customers to tell their story to the world, everything from blogs to e-mails to friends to online customer review forums. As a consequence, your level of customer service will dramatically impact your sales. So don't treat customer service as an administrative necessity. Treat it instead as a sales-building opportunity. This chapter will show you how.

Putting It in Writing

It is standard—and smart!—business practice for web-based businesses to have a page on their website that explains their customer service policy. You need to convey information such as:

- How to get help

- How to contact you or your customer service department

- What the refund policy is and how product returns are handled

- Where on the website to find other important customer service information

I can't emphasize enough how important it is to have set customer service policies and make those clearly stated and easy to find on your website and in your other customer communications. You'll prevent a lot of potential problems that way.

A few years ago, when I launched my first physical product (a how-to manual), a customer decided to return it. She not only demanded a refund of the purchase price and the shipping fee she paid, but also wanted me to arrange and pay for the return shipping of the item. Since my written refund policy wasn't clear on those points, I had to comply.

When it comes to effective customer service policies, clarity is king. It needs to be written in plain English. Avoid the fine print legalese that only a supreme court judge can decipher. It must be written like a persuasive marketing message. You *want* your customer to read and understand it.

Consider the following example:

> *It is the policy of SecondReaderBooks.net to advise purchasers of their rights and duties under the terms of our product returns policies. In the circumstance of buyer dissatisfaction with the product purchased, he or she may, at his or her discretion, return ship the said merchandise to the SecondReaderBooks authorized returns address for a refund of purchase, less appropriated original shipping and handling fees at time of original purchase ….*

Huh? That is, of course, an invented example. But check out a few online stores and you're bound to find similar policy statements that are so muddled the average customer doesn't have a hope of understanding it. (Unless, of course, she's a lawyer.)

Here's a more effective version of that policy:

> *When you purchase a used book from SecondReaderBooks.net, you can be assured that it will arrive in the exact condition it was advertised. Should this not be the case, simply return the book to us within 30 days, at the return address below, for a full refund of your purchase price. Sorry, we cannot refund shipping charges. Your refund will be issued within 7 business days of us receiving back your product.*

Isn't that better? Customers will have no problem understanding that customer service policy.

Helping Customers Reach You

A few months ago, I purchased a special runner's shirt from a website. When it arrived, it looked great. Exactly what I wanted. I couldn't wait to wear it during my next jog. There was only one problem. It was the wrong size!

As a website business owner myself, I understand that product fulfillment and delivery isn't always perfect. So I thought, "No problem. I'll just contact this online store and request a replacement." That's when things got complicated. When I visited the site, I realized that the only contact method they offered was an online form. No phone number. Not even an e-mail address! Worse, as I checked into the site further, I realized that there were no instructions on how to return merchandise for exchange or refund.

I was starting to feel very uncomfortable with this website! Now, as it turned out, I did submit the online form and the company did get back to me soon thereafter promising to replace the shirt. However, the damage was done. The difficulty in getting in touch with this company has made me reluctant to shop there again.

Success Tip

According to numerous surveys and studies, the number-one reason why customers complain about an online business is the perceived difficulty in reaching someone who can help them. So you can gain a competitive advantage simply by making it as easy as possible for your customers to get the assistance they need when they need it.

The first rule of customer service is to be accessible. You want customers who have questions about, or problems with, their purchase to be able to contact you easily. If they experience difficulties finding something as fundamental as a phone number or e-mail address on your website, then you're going to have a lot of frustrated customers on your hands. And when they do finally reach you, they're going to be grumpy!

Your Contact Us page is the best place to start. It should be a link that is easy to find on your website, and contain all the important information a customer requires to get help, find answers, and if necessary, contact you.

Don't underestimate the importance of clear and complete contact information. There have been many websites that I have been hesitant to buy from simply because key contact information—such as a business address or e-mail—is missing. I wonder, "Why are they hiding?" And I'm sure I'm not the only website visitor who asks that question.

Keeping Customers in the Loop

A certain segment of your customers are going to have questions about their purchase. There is no avoiding that. Welcome to the world of selling stuff online!

However, you can keep the number of calls and e-mails to a minimum if you antici-pate what questions or concerns customers are likely to have and then address those on your website, in your e-mails, and in your other customer communications.

For example, say your website sells backyard playground equipment. Each product is shipped in a large box with instructions on how to assemble it. Now, it's conceivable that some customers will misplace parts or claim they never received them. If you sim-ply wait for a customer to contact you, he might be frustrated at that point. In addi-tion, handling customer calls is time-consuming and expensive.

So here's what you do. You include a message on your website, in your "Thank you for your purchase" e-mail, and in a letter that is included with the product. For example:

> *Lost or missing parts? Don't worry. Just contact us at 1-800-555-1212 or e-mail parts@playgrounddreams.net. Tell us which part you need and we'll courier it to you right away.*

Not only will a blurb like that dramatically reduce phone calls from angry custom-ers, it will also decrease product returns. In addition, addressing a potential problem or concern up front makes the customer feel more assured that he has made the right decision in buying from your site. He knows you stand behind your products and are committed to making customers happy. He's more likely to buy again.

Sales Builder

Customers who are happy with the after-sales service are more likely to spread the word to their friends about your website than those who are just happy with the product they purchased. That means that the quality of after-sales service is just as important to building your web-based business—and perhaps even more so—as the quality of your products.

Put yourself in the shoes of your typical customer. Write down the questions or issues that you anticipate a customer might have. Then provide those answers, in advance, in your customer communications.

This is exactly what I do for my website products. For example, for a home-study course I created that is comprised of a binder of materials and a set of CDs, I anticipated that my customers might have the following questions.

♦ "I've lost my password to the course information web page. How do I retrieve it?"

♦ "The CDs skip or won't play. What do I do?"

♦ "The home study course has arrived damaged. How do I get a replacement?"

♦ "If I don't understand some aspect of the course, can I get help? If so, how?"

♦ "This course is not what I'm looking for. How do I return it for a refund?"

♦ "How long does it take to complete the course?"

Once I predicted the most common customer service issues that might arise with my course, I included clear answers in my thank-you e-mail and in the letter sent with the course. As a result, I get very few calls or e-mails asking for help and get less than 1 percent product returns.

When a Customer Complains

This may seem strange at first, but a customer who contacts you to complain about a product purchase is actually a great opportunity to get repeat business, a testimonial, and even good word-of-mouth from that person!

Years ago, not long after I set up my first web-based business, the day that every Internet entrepreneur dreads finally arrived. A customer e-mailed me asking for a refund. He had purchased one of my handbooks and was obviously upset. Here's what he wrote:

> *Sir, I am completely and utterly unsatisfied with the handbook I purchased from your site yesterday. I couldn't find a single tip in its 47 pages that I didn't already know. It's lightweight fluff that isn't worth a dollar let alone the 29 bucks I paid for it. I demand my money back immediately. Rest assured, I have already deleted this PDF off my computer.*

Ouch. That hurt! If it weren't for the fact that I had previously received dozens of e-mails from customers raving about that particular handbook, I would have been reaching for the Advil! Instead, I empathized with him. It's a sad state of customer service on the Internet when people feel they have to be loud and aggressive just to get the refund they have every right to receive.

So I replied with the following:

> *Mr. _____ . Thank you for giving the handbook a try. I'm sorry it wasn't exactly what you were looking for. But hey, that's why I offer a no-hassle money-back guarantee! Your full refund will be issued today. I sure hope this doesn't discourage you from purchasing other products from ForCopywritersOnly.com. If you have any questions, or need further assistance with this, don't hesitate to contact me personally at ….*

The next day I received a glowing testimonial from that customer! And he went on to purchase several other products and programs from my website.

Handling Complaints Professionally

It pays to handle customer complaints and other types of customer service calls and e-mails professionally. Here are some guidelines.

- Be prompt. Reply to customer service e-mails and voice-mail messages as soon as possible—preferably the same day.

- Don't take it personally. If a customer is angry, he's angry at the situation, not at you.

- Allow the customer to vent. So long as the customer is not being abusive, allow him to let off a little steam. Telling him to calm down will likely have the opposite effect.

- ◆ Apologize. Often, what customers want to hear most is that you're sorry the product or service didn't meet with their expectations.

- ◆ Make a promise. Tell them how you are going to help solve the issue. That may include giving a refund, arranging for return shipment, sending a replacement, providing instructions, etc.

- ◆ Keep your promises. Do what you say you're going to do. If you promised the customer that you'll call him back by 3:00 P.M. with an update, make sure you do just that!

- ◆ Follow up. Contact the customer a few days afterward to make sure he's satisfied with what was done and that there are no further issues.

This may seem like a lot of points to cover in a customer service process. However, it actually saves you time. When you deal with a customer service issue promptly and thoroughly, it doesn't linger or fester. Unresolved issues, by contrast, tend to get worse and worse and take up more and more of your time.

Dealing With Unreasonable Requests

Sometimes a dissatisfied customer will ask you for something you just cannot provide. Say, for example, a customer purchases an embroidered towel from your website and then, six months later, asks for a refund. (This happens!) If your refund policy is 30 days, then you can't very well accept a return of a product that is probably used and not saleable. You just have to say no.

Here's an example of what you could say to such a customer in an e-mail:

> *Thank you for purchasing the embroidered towel on [insert date]. Sorry, but we cannot accept items back for refund after such a long period of time. However, I do invite you to shop for other products on our website, which are all covered by our no-hassle 30-day money-back guarantee.*

This statement is firm, but friendly. It emphasizes that the current refund policy is a good one. If the customer still balks and demands that you comply with his request, stand firm. Remember, you sold the goods under fair terms and there's no reason why you have to agree to a customer request that is unreasonable.

> **Success Tip** _____
>
> Make sure your refund and product returns policies are clearly explained in all your customer communications. Spell it all out in easy-to-understand terms on your website, in your "Thank you for your purchase" e-mails, and in the letter or other materials included with the product shipment.

Fortunately, this kind of situation rarely happens. But when it does, remember: you can please most of your customers, but not all.

Helping Customers Help Themselves

Recently, I had a problem with my e-mail newsletter. So I visited the website of my e-mail marketing service provider (see Chapter 22) to contact their customer service. While I was on the site, however, I noticed that they had a Frequently Asked Questions (FAQ) section. In less than a minute, I was able to find the answer to my problem in that FAQ—without having to contact a human being.

Helping customers help themselves, with such tools as FAQs and other systems, can lower the amount of customer service calls and e-mails you receive significantly.

Making It Easy with FAQ Pages

Perhaps the easiest format to help customers get the answers they need is to put a Q&A or Frequently Asked Questions section on your website. This could be as simple as a dozen or so commonly asked questions listed on a single web page, to a more complex system complete with a search feature and a database of hundreds of answers categorized by topic.

> **Warning!** _____
>
> An FAQ page doesn't eliminate all customer inquiries. Despite there being a clear and easy-to-find answer to a question within an FAQ, you'll still get some customers who want to get hold of someone personally. So be prepared for that. However, the more complete and organized your FAQ is, the fewer customer inquiries you will receive.

Even if your FAQ is short, I suggest you organize it into sections that make it easier for customers to find the answers they need. If your website sells customized gift baskets, your FAQ might include such categories as: Deliveries, Making Last Minute Changes, Damaged Goods, Cancelling an Order, and so forth.

Handling a Heavier Load with FAQ Software

If you anticipate a lot of repetitive customer service questions, then consider a more robust FAQ system or software. Once installed on your website, these systems intuitively answer questions that your customers type into an online form. It's kind of like having a smart robot in charge of your website's customer service department. Questions that the system can't answer are directed to you to deal with personally.

There are many such systems available:

- QueryBot (www.querybot.com)
- FAQ Lite (www.scriptmate.com/products/smfaql)
- Omnistar Kbase (www.omnistarkbase.com)
- Interspire Knowledge Manager (www.interspire.com/knowledgemanager)
- FAQ Manager Professional (www.faq-manager-pro.com)
- KbLance (www.kblance.com)
- Universal FAQ Manager (www.universalfaqmanager.com)

Be careful. These systems can sometimes seem more like a barrier rather than a service to an online customer. Make sure that the system you select supports you being able to customize and humanize it so that customers always trust they can get the help they need.

Dealing With Refunds and Returns

It's going to happen. Despite how wonderful your product is and how responsive your customer service is, if you have a money-back guarantee—and even if you don't!—some customers are going to ask for a refund. It's just part of doing business online.

Assuming that the refund request is within your guarantee period and meets any other conditions of sale, your first step is to communicate with the customer.

I suggest you do this as promptly as possible—ideally the same day. Customers are often worried about getting hassled when asking for a refund. Your customer might be concerned that you'll interrogate him as to why he doesn't like the product, or treat him rudely as punishment for returning the product. (Some companies actually do this!) Don't *you* do that. You want your customers to have a satisfying experience dealing with your web-based business, whether they are asking a question, buying a product, or returning an item.

Here's a typical example of a refund request response:

> *Thank you for trying the MomsWithTots.net membership site. We're sorry to hear that the information and services provided didn't meet your expectations. Your registration fee will be refunded to you right away.*

> *If you paid by check or money order, a refund check will be mailed to you within the next 2 weeks. If you paid by credit card or PayPal, a credit will be issued to that account within the next 3 business days.*

> *If your refund doesn't arrive as stated above, please contact us at _____.*

> *We update the content and services on MomsWithTots.com frequently, so please check back again. We'd love to have you back as a member.*

Once your customer has received approval of their request, your next step is, of course, to refund their money. You can do this with most shopping cart systems (see Chapter 11), which makes it easy. In the shopping cart system that I use, I simply log in, find the transaction, and press the Refund button. PayPal and Google Checkout have a similar procedure in place.

Success Tip

It can be a hassle to issue a refund to a customer who has paid by check. You have to write it, print a cover letter to go with it, and then mail it. So instead, ask the customer for permission to issue the credit to his PayPal account. Tell him it's the fastest way. (It is.) This will save you from having to deal with checks, postage, and trips to the post office.

If the product sold is a physical good, rather than a download, subscription, or registration, then your final step in the refund process is to get it back. This can make things complicated because it involves the customer repackaging the item and shipping it. Here are some tips for making that process easier for you and the customer:

◆ In the product documentation, request that the customer hold on to the shipping box and other materials in case the product needs to be returned for some reason.

◆ In the event of a refund request, ask the customer to return the product in the same shipping box that it came in. This will help ensure it arrives back to you undamaged.

◆ Advise the customer to package the item carefully as it must be returned in saleable condition in order to qualify for a refund.

◆ Clearly provide a full postal address for returns, especially if that's different from your main business address.

◆ Provide the customer with any reference number or information you want him to put on the package.

◆ When the returned item is received by you, check that all is okay and then notify the customer.

Who pays for the return shipping? It's customary for most companies to require the customer to cover the costs of mailing or shipping the product back for refund. In my opinion, this is fair. After all, the customer got the chance to try your product risk-free for a period of time. The only exception to this policy should be those circumstances when *you* made the error, such as shipping a blue sweatshirt when the customer ordered red.

Customer Service Timesaving Tips

When you're just starting out in your web-based business, customer service is relatively easy to manage. After all, you have only a few customers. You may only get one or two calls or e-mails a week. And you can easily handle those without too much difficulty.

However, as your business grows, handling customer service inquiries is going to take up more and more of your time … time that may be better spent on other aspects of your business. That's when you need to find ways to deal with customer calls and e-mails more efficiently. Otherwise, you'll be the customer service manager for your business instead of the CEO!

Creating Scripts and Templates

The easiest way to make customer service more efficient is to create model letters and scripts based on the most common questions and other inquiries customers tend to ask you. That way, you don't have to compose a new response every time.

Success Tip

As your web-based business grows, hiring someone to handle customer service for you will save you a lot of time. Consider a virtual assistant. These are professionals who freelance their administrative support services to small business owners and other professionals. And the best part is, you pay only for the services they provide. You can find a virtual assistant at www. ivaa.org or www.nvas.org.

For example, I sometimes get requests from customers who want to know how a teleclass works. (That's a class that is conducted on a teleconference line rather than in a live classroom.) Rather than compose a special e-mail each time, I have a template already prepared that explains everything. I simply copy and paste that into the e-mail and press send. The whole process takes just a few seconds and saves me a lot of time.

If you plan to have a staff member or virtual assistant handle customer service for you, it's especially important that you have prepared responses to the inquiries you anticipate getting from website visitors and customers.

Support Ticket Systems

Another way to save time spent on managing customer service is to sign up for a support ticket system. These systems are affordable for most web-based businesses and can make managing customer service tasks a lot easier; however, there are some significant drawbacks.

A support ticket system is a system that turns a page on your website into a virtual customer service receptionist. The customer types her question, complaint, or inquiry into the online form, along with her name and contact information, and presses submit. That ticket is sent to you for handling. The customer is given a ticket reference number ... and waits for your response.

Support ticket systems can keep your customer service organized and ensure that no customer inquiry falls through the cracks. A ticket remains "open" until it's resolved. The system also maintains a historical database of customer service events that may be useful for you to track.

Here is a list of the most popular systems:

◆ osTicket (www.osticket.com)

◆ Helperoo (www.helperoo.com)

◆ Helpdesk Pilot (www.helpdeskpilot.com)

- eTicket Support (www.eticketsupport.com)
- DeskPRO (www.deskpro.com)
- Trouble Ticket Express (www.troubleticketexpress.com)
- TicketXPert (www.ticketxpert.net)

What's the downside? Too many web-based business owners use support ticket systems as a substitute for other customer service channels, such as e-mail and phone. It's annoying to need to contact an online store and be forced to submit a ticket rather than talk to a human being. If you decide to use this kind of system, make sure that the customer has other options for reaching you. Also provide the customer with a realistic expectation as to when they will receive a response—and then make sure that happens on time.

Effective customer service leads to more repeat business and referrals to your website—which is a sure sign of success. When you have developed a loyal base of customers who are buying from you again and again and telling their friends and colleagues about you, then you have a great web-based business on your hands, my friend. Congratulations!

The Least You Need to Know

- Provide outstanding customer service. You'll attract more repeat customers and better word-of-mouth that way.

- Put your refund, product return, and other customer service policies in writing. And post them clearly on your website and in your other customer communications.

- Don't be defensive when a customer complains or requests a refund. Deal with such issues professionally.

- Explore ways to make your customer service management more efficient. However, never dehumanize it.

Appendix A

Glossary of Online Business Terms

above the fold   In online marketing, this refers to the marketing message that someone can readily see without having to scroll down or click to another page. Messages *above the fold* tend to get the most attention from website visitors and e-mail users.

Adobe Acrobat   This is the software program, created by Adobe, that produces PDF files. These files have become the online standard for sharing documents. Most e-books are published in PDF format.

AdWords   A program offered by Google to run your ads on their search results pages and participating websites.

affiliate   This is a person or company who agrees to promote your website products for a fee or commission. Although some specialize in advertising the affiliate products they represent on search engines and other online venues, most affiliates own a website, e-mail newsletter, blog, or other online property from which they can tout your website offerings.

affiliate link   This is a hyperlink that contains a special tracking code specific to each affiliate. When a buyer clicks on this link, your affiliate management system credits the appropriate affiliate with the sale. An affiliate link usually takes the form of a weird-looking website URL, such as www.forcopywritersonly.com/454rf, or a snippet of HTML code that the affiliate cuts and pastes into the HTML code of his website, blog, or e-mail newsletter.

affiliate program   (Also known as associate, partner, and reseller programs.) A program where you place links or advertising on your website and get paid a commission for clicks and sales. You can either be an affiliate or run an affiliate program for your own products.

analytics   Reports of how well your website, e-mails, and online ads are doing in terms of clickthroughs, web page visits, sales, and other factors.

application service provider (ASP)   This is a company that offers a software application through their website rather than selling it in a box. The advantage is, customers don't have to install anything. Salesforce.com is a good example of an ASP.

article directory   An online directory that makes articles on a broad range of topics available to publishers and website owners who need them for their websites, e-mail newsletters, blogs, and other publications. It's essentially a matchmaking service, helping publishers find the articles they need and authors get their articles published.

autoresponder   An e-mail, or series of e-mails, that is scheduled to be sent automatically whenever a website visitor takes some specific action, such as signing up for a e-mail newsletter or purchasing a product.

banner   An advertisement on a website. It's the Internet's version of a billboard ad. It can either be static or animated.

beta site   This is a temporary upload of a website for testing purposes and is often not publicly accessible. Your web designer may create a beta version of your site for you to look at before it goes live.

bookkeeping   The process of keeping accurate records of your business revenues and expenses, plus all information related to taxes charged and payable. In many jurisdictions, the law requires that you maintain an accurate set of books, but even if it doesn't, good bookkeeping enables you to manage your cash flow, stay on top of expenses, and otherwise keep your business financially healthy.

brick-and-mortar   A traditional business that is not web-based in any way.

cascading style sheet (CSS)   A special series of codes embedded within the HTML code of a website or e-mail that describe how the text should be formatted. It has become the standard in web design because it gives designers more control over how things look and makes it easier to update the content.

clickthrough   A measurement of the number of people who are clicking on a particular link on a web page or within an e-mail. It's often expressed as a percentage. For example, if 500 people received your e-mail containing a link to a special promotion, and the clickthrough rate is 6 percent, then 30 people clicked.

content management system (CMS)   A system that allows you to easily update the content of pages on your website, and add new pages. No knowledge of HTML or FTP is required.

conversion rate   A measurement of the number of visitors to a page who sign up for something or make a purchase, compared to the total amount of visitors. For example, if a web page on your website received 1,000 visitors last week, and 27 placed an order, then the conversion rate of that page is 2.7 percent.

cross-selling   A sales-boosting technique where you offer customers complimentary products to the items they have just ordered or are about to order.

discussion board   Also known as a *forum*. It's an online meeting place where people can post comments and respond to others. Often discussion boards are created for a special interest group, like work-at-home moms.

domain name   A website address, silly.

domain name extension   Those letters after the "dot" in a domain name address. Common extensions are .com, .net, and .org. But there are many others, including those that are specific to countries.

domain name registrar   A company that has been given permission by the Internet Corporation for Assigned Names and Numbers (ICANN) to register top level domains such as .com, .net, and .org. Some websites that sell domain names are only brokers, not registrars. You can view the official list of registrars at www.ICANN.org.

double opt-in   The practice of requesting a confirmation from a subscriber that he or she has indeed signed-up for your e-mail newsletter or other e-mails. This helps protect website owners from spam complaints.

drop shipping   An arrangement made with the manufacturer or distributor of a product to ship the orders your website generates directly to your customers. The advantage is that you don't have to deal with shipping and handling yourself.

e-book   A book that has been published in electronic format so that it can be down-loaded from a website.

e-mail marketing services provider   This is a company that broadcasts your e-mail message to your opt-in list on your behalf. Although the e-mail is sent from their computer servers to your prospects and customers, the message appears to come directly from you. These providers will often store your subscriber database and pro-vide you with myriad other related services as well.

e-mail newsletter   A newsletter that is published primarily in e-mail format. (How-ever, it could also be published as a web page.)

e-mail rendering   This refers to how an e-mail looks in your subscriber's e-mail ser-vice. Because not all services interpret the underlying code exactly the same way, your e-mail may look different depending on which type of e-mail account your subscriber has. That's why it's important to test your e-mail newsletter's appearance in the popu-lar e-mail services that your target audience uses.

e-zine   Another word for e-mail newsletter. Some people use the slang expression, 'zine. As in, "Have you seen my latest 'zine?"

file extension   The sequence of letters following a file name that indicates what type of file it is.

Flash   A multimedia technology that allows sound and animation to play on a web page.

FTP   File Transfer Protocol. The most common way that websites are uploaded to web servers so that they can be displayed on the Internet.

GIF   Graphics Interchange Format. A compressed image format used for pictures and other graphics on websites. It's one of the two most popular web image formats, the other being JPEG.

hit   A web page visit.

HTML   Hypertext Markup Language. The computer code used to create most web-sites.

hyperlink   A hot link on a website or within an e-mail. Clicking on it takes you somewhere or downloads something.

inbound link   Also known as backward link. A link on another website or blog that points to your website. If your site has a lot of inbound links, search engines like Google will rank you higher.

index page   The page on your website, usually the front page, that has the */index* extension. It's the first page that displays when someone types your website address into their web browser.

IP address   A unique 32-digit number that is the address of a computer or device connected to the Internet. Websites also have a unique IP address.

Joint Photographic Expert Group (JPEG)   A compressed image format technique often used for pictures on websites. It's one of the two most popular web image formats, the other being GIF.

keywords   Words used by web searchers to find information on the Internet. For many reasons, it's important that you know which keywords potential clients are using to find websites like yours.

landed cost   This is the cost of shipping an order to a customer plus all applicable customs duties and fees.

link popularity   A measure of a website's importance, at least from the perspective of the search engines, based on how many other sites link to it.

list broker   This is a company that represents magazine publishers, trade show organizers, popular online merchants, and others who have mailing lists available. You just tell the broker what type of list you're looking for and he or she will let you know what's available.

media release company   A service that maintains a large database of media contacts and distributes your press release on your behalf. You can usually select which types of publications and broadcasts to target. Although there are some free services available, the best media release companies charge $250 to $1,500 per release.

merchant account   A special account with a financial institution that allows you to accept credit card payments online.

offer   The proposition you are communicating to potential customers in your advertisement or other promotion.

one sheet   This is a description of your presentation topic that you send to event planners and others who book speakers. It's usually just one or two pages long.

online advertisement   Any advertisement that appears on the Internet or within an e-mail message. The most popular formats are search engine ads, banners, and text-based ads. However, online video and Internet radio advertisements are becoming increasingly popular as well.

opt-in   In e-mail marketing, opt-in refers to when a website visitor has provided you with permission to send him or her your newsletter or other form of e-mail communications. In the United States as well as many other jurisdictions, getting an opt-in from a website visitor before you send him or her marketing e-mails is not just industry best practice, it's the law.

order fulfillment   The process of delivering the merchandise to the customer. It involves activities such as inventory, packaging, filling out the appropriate forms, shipping, and tracking. An order is fulfilled once the customer has received the merchandise he or she has purchased.

PageRank   A measure of a website's popularity or importance as determined by Google.

payment gateway   A company that transmits the transaction information from your website shopping cart to your merchant account for processing.

QuickTime   A popular software from Apple that allows users to play computer sound files such as music and audio books. Similar software is Windows Media Player and RealPlayer.

RealPlayer   A popular software from REAL that allows users to play computer sound files such as music and audio books. Similar software is Windows Media Player and QuickTime.

reciprocal link   When two websites provide links to each other. This is usually an attempt to get better search engine rankings; however, most search engines place little value on links of this kind.

resource box   A small block of text, usually placed at the end of a magazine or newsletter article, that contains information about the author. In a resource box, you are usually able to include a short promotional blurb about your website, along with a link to your website.

sales page   A website page whose primary purpose is to describe the product, service, or offer and motivate the reader to take some specific action—such as clicking to place an order.

search engine advertising   Placing advertisements for your website in the search results of search engines. The most popular program of this kind is Google AdWords.

search engine marketing   A combination of search engine optimization and search engine advertising.

search engine optimization (SEO)   The process of optimizing the structure and text on your website so that it gets ranked higher in organic search engine results.

shopping cart   The software or online service that generates the checkout screens on your website. To work, it needs to be integrated with your payment gateway and merchant account.

site map   A schematic or flow chart on a web page showing how your website is organized and the pages available. This is important in search engine optimization as it helps spiders accurately crawl your site.

spiders   (Also known as search engine spiders.) These are computer programs that visit your site and gather data as to what your website is all about. Search engines use this information to categorize and rank your site.

sticky   An Internet marketing term that refers to the quality of content on your website. If the content is sticky, visitors tend to stay longer and buy more.

streaming media   This allows you to play media directly from a web page without having to download it. Variations include streaming audio and streaming video.

thumbnail   In addition to being an anatomical feature located on your hand, a thumbnail is also a small version of a picture that includes a link to its larger original version. Thumbnails are useful on websites because they have smaller file sizes and therefore download faster.

tracking code   This is a few lines, or snippet, of HTML code that you need to place within the web pages you want your website analytics program to track. When someone visits a page that contains that code, information about where that person came from, and his or her activities on your site, is compiled and reports are created.

traffic   This refers to the people who are visiting your website.

traffic sources   These are the places, online and offline, where potential customers find out about your website.

unique visitor   Someone who has visited your website for the first time. Many website analytics programs provide this information.

up-selling   This is an attempt to sell the customer a premium or upgraded version of the product they are interested in purchasing.

viral marketing   An attempt to create a buzz about a product, service, or other offer so that lots of people are sharing that information online. "Our webinar went viral and, as a result, we got a lot of registrants."

Web 2.0   A term that refers to special websites that are focused on building communities where people can share information and interact in some way. For example, on YouTube, people can share their favorite videos. On LinkedIn, business professionals can meet and connect with other professionals. As a web-based business owner, you can take advantage of social media websites to attract more website visitors and customers.

web host   The company that hosts your website in its servers and makes your website available on the Internet.

webinar   An online presentation—often live, although it can be pre-recorded—that includes slides and narration. It's the Internet's version of a PowerPoint show.

Whois   A directory of domain name registrations where you can look up the name and contact information of a domain name owner, administrator, and technical contact, plus access other key information.

wholesaler   A company that acts as a manufacturer's representative. They may operate as a regional warehouse shipping goods to retailers and online stores in the area. Or they can be a small operation of just a few staff members or even just one person. The role of the wholesaler is to work with retailers in a particular area on behalf of the manufacturer who may be located across the country or even overseas.

Windows Media Player   A popular software from Microsoft that allows users to play computer sound files such as music and audio books. Similar software is QuickTime and RealPlayer.

WYSIWYG   Pronounced "wiz-e-wig," an acronym for "what you see is what you get." Most website design programs provide users with a WYSIWYG feature so you can see how a website is looking as you build it.

Free (and Almost Free) Online Tools and Resources

The Internet is packed with low-cost/no-cost tools for web-based business owners that can save you a lot of time and money. Check out the following list. There are probably at least a few sites here that you can take advantage of.

Keep in mind that just because a website is listed here doesn't necessarily mean I endorse it. As with any online tool or service, read the fine print. Find out what, if any, charges apply. And never install a software program without first having it scanned with a good virus/spyware checker.

Accounting, Invoicing, Time Tracking, and Contracts

Cashboard (www.getcashboard.com) Free time tracking, invoicing, estimates, and online payments provided for up to two active projects. Further projects require a nominal fee.

ContractPal (www.contractpal.com) An affordable method of creating paperless contracts and forms that can be completed, signed, and processed online.

Easy Time Tracking (www.easytimetracking.net) Free version includes time and expense tracking, billable hours, and invoice management.

FreshBooks (www.freshbooks.com) An affordable and easy-to-use basic online invoicing and time-tracking system.

LessAccounting (www.lessaccounting.com) A simple and affordable web-based accounting system geared toward small businesses and freelancers.

LiteAccounting (www.liteaccounting.com) An online application that simplifies invoicing and tracking payments. Free plan available.

Mint (www.mint.com) Free software that downloads, categorizes, and graphs finances automatically. (U.S. only)

myHours (www.myhours.com) A free web-based time management, timesheet, and time-tracking solution.

TraxTime (www.traxtime.com) A low-cost method of tracking time spent on various projects.

QuickBooks Simple Start Free Edition (www.quickbooks.intuit.com) Free accounting software for businesses with simple finances.

Calendar/Task Management

Business IT Online (www.businessitonline.com) Offers small business software solutions including calendar, cashflow, contact, and document management.

ClickBook (www.clickbook.net) A free web-based booking and scheduling system.

Google Calendar (http://calendar.google.com) A free online calendar that allows viewing and updating in real time—by all users.

Remember the Milk (www.rememberthemilk.com) An affordable task management system accessible by mobile devices such as iPhone, Blackberry, and Windows Mobile.

When is Good (www.whenisgood.net) A free online method of coordinating others' schedules with your next meeting or event.

Customer Relationship Management (CRM) and Customer Service

Bizroof CRM (www.bizroof.com) A free hosted CRM application that tracks customer data and provides cash flow analysis and sales force automation.

Free CRM (www.freecrm.com) The free edition is a web-based software solution for customer relationship management, including lead tracking and sales and contact management.

Mojo Helpdesk (www.mojohelpdesk.com) A simple ticket tracking service that tracks customer requests and obtains satisfaction ratings.

Simple Sales Tracking (www.simplesalestracking.com) A web-based sales tool for the tracking, analysis, and forecasting of sales.

Survey Monkey (www.surveymonkey.com) Ideal for obtaining employee and customer feedback; basic free package includes 10 questions and up to 100 responses per survey.

Document Management and Storage

Docstoc (www.docstoc.com) A free online service where users can locate and share professional documents.

Google Docs (http://docs.google.com) A free tool to create and share online spreadsheets, documents, presentations, and forms. Ideal for work collaboration.

SendThisFile (www.sendthisfile.com) Basic plan allows free sending and receiving of large files.

ThinkFree (www.thinkfree.com) Free service includes web-based storage and sharing of uploaded documents, spreadsheets, presentations, and forms.

Writeboard (www.writeboard.com) Creates sharable, web-based text documents. Allows saving of edits and collaboration with other users.

File Conversion

Free File Converter (www.freefileconvert.com) Free conversion from a wide variety of files to different formats, including text, audio, and graphics.

Primo PDF (www.primopdf.com) Free conversion to PDF from over 300 file types, including Microsoft Word, Excel, and PowerPoint.

Switch (www.nch.com.au) Free audio file conversion software with the ability to convert a variety of audio files to .wav, MP3, .wma, or other formats.

Zamzar (www.zamzar.com) Free online file conversion including documents, images, music, and video.

Graphics and Images

Dreamstime (www.dreamstime.com) Free and low-cost stock photography.

Flickr (www.flickr.com) A photo stock service offering free use of unique photos under the Creative Commons license.

Microsoft Office Clip Art (www.office.microsoft.com) Standard, free Microsoft clip art.

Legal Advice

FreeAdvice (www.freeadvice.com) A large database of legal topics and questions responded to by lawyers. Includes an interactive forum.

The Law (www.thelaw.com) A forum primarily for U.S.–based businesses and individuals where lawyers offer free advice. Not a substitute for a true client/attorney relationship.

Marketing/Advertising

Google AdWords (www.adwords.google.com) Pay-per-click advertising via the Google network.

Google Alerts (www.google.com/alerts) Free e-mail updates of the latest Google results based on your choice of topic. Useful for staying current on competitors and target market activity.

Google Analytics (www.google.com/analytics) Free tool to track and analyze website traffic, including comprehensive charts, graphs, and statistics.

MailChimp (www.mailchimp.com) Free e-mail marketing campaign manager includes up to 100 subscribers. Low fees apply based on additional recipients.

Mobile Devices

GooSync (www.goosync.com) Free basic package provides over-the-air mobile device synchronization (cell phone, BlackBerry, etc.) with Google Calendar.

Jott (www.jott.com) Voice-to-text notes allow the free voice recording of a 15-second message from any mobile device or landline phone and converts it to online text.

SyncWizard (www.syncwizard.com) Free service synchronizes your contacts, calendars, and bookmarks with your portable devices.

Office Applications

OpenOffice Suite (www.openoffice.org) Leading free software for word processing, spreadsheets, presentations, graphics, and databases.

Zoho (www.zoho.com) A full suite of online applications free for personal use and offering free and upgraded versions for businesses.

Payment Processing

Google Checkout (http://checkout.google.com/sell) There are no monthly, setup, or gateway services fees for a merchant account, and sales are charged a low fee per transaction.

PayPal (www.paypal.com) A free merchant account allows you to accept payments on your website for a nominal fee per transaction.

Phone, Voice Mail, Conference Calls, Meetings

280Slides (www.280slides.com) Free online presentation software.

Free Conference Call (www.freeconferencecall.com) Provides 24/7 free conference calling including downloadable recording. Normal long distance rates apply.

Simple Voice Box (www.simplevoicebox.com) Standard free program includes a complete voice mail solution including a phone number, ability to record a greeting, voice mail retrieval by phone or online, and a daily e-mail summary of all incoming calls.

Skype (www.skype.com) A global, online free phone service when used with other Skype members, which includes audio, video, and conference calls. Landline and mobile calls are also available at a nominal rate.

Presentations

SlideBoom (www.slideboom.com) Free service for sharing live PowerPoint presentations online.

SlideLive (www.slidelive.com) Free online service for sharing live PowerPoint presentations.

SlideRocket (www.sliderocket.com) Includes tools and templates to create and share PowerPoint presentations online.

Project Management and Collaboration

ClientSpot (www.myclientspot.com) Web-based project collaboration ideal for freelancers and virtual assistants.

OpenProj (www.openproj.org) A free, open-source desktop solution for managing group projects.

Scriblink (www.scriblink.com) A free online whiteboard that users can share in real time—includes chat features.

WorkflowPerfect (www.workflowperfect.com) Free web-based collaboration tool for small to mid-size teams.

Search Engine Optimization (SEO)

SEO Chat (www.seochat.com) Multiple free tools to assist in configuring websites for search engine optimization.

Security

Ad-Aware Free (www.lavasoft.com) Free anti-spyware software for personal home use.

AVG Anti-Virus Free Edition (www.free.avg.com) Provides basic free protection against viruses and spyware.

Spybot—Search & Destroy (www.spybot.com) A free tool that detects and removes computer spyware.

Technical Support

Tech Support Guy (www.techguy.org) A free interactive forum where members can ask computer- and software-related questions and receive qualified answers from technical experts.

Translation

Babel Fish (http://babelfish.yahoo.com) A free online translation service where text can instantly be converted from one language to another.

FreeTranslation (www.freetranslation.com) An online service offering the free translation of text and web pages in a variety of languages.

Website Design and Management Tools

Bravenet (www.bravenet.com) A popular website offering many free web tools and widgets in addition to free and low-cost hosting.

VersoChat (www.versochat.com) Lite version is a free tool that allows online, live chat with website visitors.

Wix (www.wix.com) Free, user-friendly flash website design software.

Index